PHYSICAL EDUCATION
A view toward the future

PHYSICAL EDUCATION
A view toward the future

Edited by

RAYMOND WELSH, Ph.D.

Department of Health and
Physical Education, Hunter College,
City University of New York,
New York, New York

THE C. V. MOSBY COMPANY

Saint Louis 1977

Library of Congress Cataloging in Publication Data

Main entry under title:

Physical education.

    1. Physical education as a profession—Addresses,
essays, lectures. 2. Forecasting—Addresses, essays,
lectures. I. Welsh, Raymond.
GV342.P45   613.7'023   76-27354
ISBN 0-8016-5379-7

VH/VH/VH 9 8 7 6 5 4 3 2 1

To
Kathy, Maureen, and Ray
and
to the future of physical education

NOTES
ABOUT THE AUTHORS

SUSAN AREND, Ed.D., Assistant Professor, Department of Health and Physical Education, Hunter College, City University of New York, New York, New York

> Nine years of professional service • Author of several articles • Participant in various regional and national conferences • *Special interests:* movement analysis, perceptual learning, relationship between perception and action

CHARLES B. CORBIN, Ph.D., Professor and Chairman, Department of Health, Physical Education and Recreation, Kansas State University, Manhattan, Kansas

> Sixteen years of professional service • Author and co-author of four texts and over thirty research and professional articles • Recipient of numerous honors and awards • *Special interests:* motor development, elementary school physical education, psychology of sport

JOSEPH R. HIGGINS, Ed.D., Associate Professor and Co-Director of Program in Motor Learning, Department of Physical Education, Teachers' College, Columbia University, New York, New York

> Nineteen years of professional service • Author of numerous articles • Speaker at many regional, national, and international conferences • Recipient of several research grants • *Special interests:* human movement analysis, organization and structure of movement, development in motor skills

HAL A. LAWSON, Ph.D., Assistant Professor, School of Physical and Health Education, University of Washington, Seattle, Washington

> Ten years of professional service • Author of several articles and presentations, including *Physical Education and Sport: Alternatives for the Future,* Quest **21**:19, 1974 • *Special interests:* policy studies, program planning

47714 ⨍ 10

CAROLE A. OGLESBY, Ph.D., Associate Professor, College of Health, Physical Education, Recreation and Dance, Temple University, Philadelphia, Pennsylvania

Fifteen years of professional service • Author of numerous articles • Well-known speaker at national and international conferences, particularly on the topic of women and sport • Former president, American Association of Intercollegiate Athletics for Women • Member of the Executive Committee, United States Collegiate Sports Council • *Special interests:* masculinity-femininity concepts in sport, self-development and sport, authority and decision making in sport

DEAN A. PEASE, Ph.D., Associate Professor, Department of Health and Physical Education, University of North Florida, Jacksonville, Florida

Thirteen years of professional service • Author of numerous articles and textbook chapters; has written two previous articles dealing with the future of physical education • Recognized authority on competency based teacher education programs • *Special interests:* competency based teacher education programs, teaching behavior

ROBERT N. SINGER, Ph.D., Professor and Director of Motor Learning Research Laboratory, Division of Human Performance (College of Education), Florida State University, Tallahassee, Florida

Author, co-author, or editor of nine texts; author of over forty articles; contributor to seven other published texts; editor (with Raymond Weiss) of *Completed Research in Health, Physical Education and Recreation* • Member of editorial board of *Research Quarterly* and *Journal of Motor Behavior* • Numerous presentations at national and international conferences • *Special interests:* instructional design, motor learning and skill acquisition, sport psychology

GINNY L. STUDER, Ph.D., Assistant Professor, Undergraduate Physical Education Unit, State University College at Brockport/SUNY, Brockport, New York

Eleven years of professional service • Author of numerous articles • Co-publisher and co-editor of *The Moment,* a national publication sharing ideas regarding experiences in movement; co-editor of *Briefings,* a National Association for Physical Education of College Women— National College Physical Education Association for Men publication • *Special interests:* Understanding the structure of movement, analysis and interpretation of movement, the movement experience

Notes about the authors

CELESTE ULRICH, Ph.D., Professor, School of Health, Physical Education and Recreation, University of North Carolina at Greensboro, Greensboro, North Carolina

Thirty-one years of professional service . Author and co-author of several texts; author of numerous research and professional articles . Has given over 400 speeches to various interest groups throughout the United States . Recipient of numerous awards and honors and holder of many high professional offices . Former president of the National Association for Physical Education of College Women; current president of the American Alliance for Health, Physical Education, and Recreation . *Special interests:* significance and meaning of physical education

RAYMOND WELSH, Ph.D., Associate Professor, Department of Health and Physical Education, Hunter College, City University of New York, New York, New York

Fifteen years of professional service . Author of several articles, two of which dealt with the theme of the future of physical education . Participant in numerous local, regional, and national conferences . Former Peace Corps volunteer . *Special interests:* trend analysis, futuristics, sport and society

EARLE F. ZEIGLER, Ph.D., Professor and Dean of the Faculty of Physical Education, University of Western Ontario, London, Ontario, Canada

Thirty-six years of professional service . Author of twelve texts and over 250 articles that have appeared in a wide variety of journals in Canada, the United States, and other countries . Recipient of numerous awards and honors, including an Honorary Doctor of Laws degree from the University of Windsor . Holds membership as well as high office in numerous professional organizations . Former editor of the *Canadian Journal of Health, Physical Education and Recreation* . *Special interests:* philosophy, history, management theory and practice as it relates to physical education and sport

PREFACE

Goethe once said, "I find the great thing in this world is not so much where we stand, as in what direction we are moving." This simple yet profound statement made by one of mankind's great thinkers takes on renewed significance for modern-day man as he attempts to come to grips with his age, an age marked by unprecedented change and uncertainty about tomorrow. For clearly the times are such that it is becoming increasingly difficult to know where we are in the present and even more difficult to determine the direction in which we are moving.

Although change has always been a companion of man, its relative pace for countless generations enabled man to ignore its significance. This is no longer the case. Change has accelerated to such an alarming degree and has become so disruptive during recent decades that it constitutes a major force that must be considered by individuals, groups, and institutions as they attempt to chart some desirable course into the future. Thus we find that the nature of the change facing mankind today represents an unprecedented new social force that urges man to renew his commitment to plan for the future while simultaneously impeding his capacity to do so. It is precisely in this context that *Physical Education: A View Toward the Future*—a text about the future of physical education—was conceived.

Specifically, it was felt that owing to changes now occurring both within and outside the profession of physical education and assuming the likelihood of continued change in the future, this attempt by selected physical educators to systematically assess the likely impact of change on the profession's future is timely as well as useful. It was felt that such an effort would (1) help to clarify the current state of the profession, (2) help to restructure images regarding the possibilities of the profession's future, (3) help to stimulate the formation of plans and contingencies that might ensure the profession's continued viability in the years ahead, and (4) help to stimulate discussion and in general sensitize physical educators regarding the positive and negative possibilities of tomorrow.

At best, writing about the future of anything is a difficult task, and this is no less true of attempts to write about the future of physical education.

Nevertheless, the potential usefulness of such an effort was sufficient to persuade ten physical education scholars with varying areas of expertise to prepare original manuscripts about the future of the profession. Fortunately, the contributors, in addition to their wide range of expertise, also represent a reasonable balance with respect to sex, age, and years of professional involvement. This was thought to be important in gaining the broadest possible view into the future.

In general, the contributing authors consider the time frame for the future as the last quarter of the twentieth century. The manuscripts reflect a futuristic view of the profession, and to a reasonable extent, they describe forecasts of possible, probable, or desirable future developments. It was suggested that the authors use some method or combination of methods of systematic forecasting (for example, intuitive, exploratory, or normative approaches) to arrive at their forecasts. A heuristic or working model for the text was also proposed to guide the authors in preparing their manuscripts. The need to propose a guiding model, diagrammed below, stemmed from my desire to ensure sufficient scope and depth relative to the many facets of the profession. I also believed that by following such a model, the potential usefulness of the text for major students and professional physical educators would be enhanced.

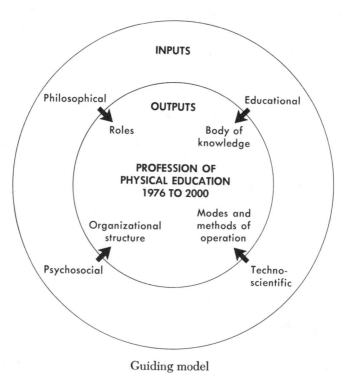

Guiding model

Preface

The model is based on input-output theory, a basic construct used by those who desire to assess future possibilities. In short, the input-output model assumes that every effect or phenomenon has antecedent causes. For the purpose of this text it implied that the authors were to identify inputs (changes of various types, both those occurring now and those likely to occur in the future) and estimate their output (effects) with respect to such aspects as the profession's role(s), body of knowledge, organizational structure, and modes and methods of operation.

While the subject matter of the text is unique, the format of the text is rather traditional. Each of the six chapters is preceded by introductory comments. Although they are not identified as such, the text has within it three natural subdivisions. The first consists of two introductory essays (Chapter 1) that deal with the nature of change facing mankind today, the development of futuristics, and the perspectives, constructs, and methods used by futurists. The second subdivision (Chapters 2 to 5) consists of nine essays devoted to forecasting the future of physical education from four different perspectives, the philosophical, psychosocial, educational, and technoscientific. The third subdivision consists of a brief concluding essay (Chapter 6) that serves as a postscript to the entire text.

Hopefully, *Physical Education: A View Toward the Future* will be a valuable contribution to the professional literature. You the reader will have to make that determination. If nothing else, the effort will be worthwhile if the text merely serves to motivate physical educators to think more seriously about the future of the profession, for most assuredly, as Bob Dylan sings, "The times they are a'changin'."

Raymond Welsh

CONTENTS

Contents

PHYSICAL EDUCATION
A view toward the future

CHAPTER ONE

INSIGHTS INTO THE FUTURE

One of the most distressing aspects of contemporary life concerns change and its disruptive characteristics. People have always sought knowledge about the future in order to plan adequately in the present. This is still the case today, but owing to the nature of change occurring in contemporary society, our capacity to "preview" the future and hence plan in the present has been seriously undermined. Despite the difficulties posed by contemporary change, through the new science of futuristics we appear to be regaining the capacity to obtain anticipatory information about the future that can guide us in the present. The two introductory essays in this chapter elaborate on these and other points. In addition, the information contained within this chapter serves to provide a contextual framework for the entire text. Also implied is that the techniques of futuristics can be used by physical educators as they attempt to chart their own course into the future.

Futuristics: an emerging science

Raymond Welsh

Throughout recorded history, man's assumption of a future together with his desire to control his destiny has served as one of the principal life forces contributing to the survival and progress of the human race.

FUTURE IN THE PAST

The importance of the future in human affairs is attested to by the preoccupation primitive people had regarding birth, death, and afterlife. The decision to form extended families or tribes, to till the soil, and to designate shamans and fortune-tellers also suggests primitive people's belief in a future. The assumption of a future has also been underscored during later periods by the fact of human inventiveness, the formation of city-states, the development of cultural forms and religious beliefs, and the predilection to fight wars, stake out territory, explore frontiers, and establish complex institutions. Thus from the dawn of time consciousness itself, man has been inexorably caught up in a concern for the future—his entire psychic life has been and continues to be permeated with a hope and expectation of things to come.

In philosophical terms, the future has also been thought to hold the answer to the riddle of human existence. The reality of death, the one certainty in man's experience, perhaps combined with a sense of time, has impelled thoughtful men to probe the future, to seek answers, to find meaning, to become whole. This conscious effort to explore the future, whether motivated by philosophical considerations or the equally basic concern for survival, has represented a significant step forward for *Homo sapiens*. Fred Polak calls it "man's first great leap toward freedom" (1972, p. 286).

Thus since the dawn of history, future-conscious men have populated the earth. Their attempts at foresight and purposefulness and their willingness to consider the consequences of present action in the light of future possibilities have had a significant impact on the progress of the human race. It may be said that when men first began to think of tomorrow, they began to create their tomorrows and thus became the forerunners of today's modern futurists.

FUTURE IN THE PRESENT

While the future has always played a role in human affairs, the future to us today has taken on new importance. In earlier periods the time span of important change was considerably longer than an individual life; therefore the urgency about matters of the future was far less acute than we find it today. In the past the assumption that the future would be much like the present was essentially proved to be valid. For those born in the twentieth century, the acceleration of important change has compressed changes into a drastically shortened time span, and the earlier assumption of gradual change is no longer valid. In comparing the relative nature of change facing humankind today, Alvin Toffler has commented:

> The final qualitative difference between this and all previous lifetimes is the one most easily overlooked. For we have not merely extended the scope and scale of change, we have radically altered its pace. We have in our time released a totally new social force—a stream of change so accelerated that it influences our sense of time, revolutionizes the tempo of daily life, and affects the way we feel about the world around us. We no longer "feel" life as men did in the past. And this is the ultimate difference, the distinction that separates the truly contemporary man from all others.*

In a later work, Toffler has elaborated further on the nature of change by citing specific changes facing us today and suggesting their possible disruptive potential:

*From Toffler, A. 1970. Future shock, New York, Random House, Inc., p. 17.

2

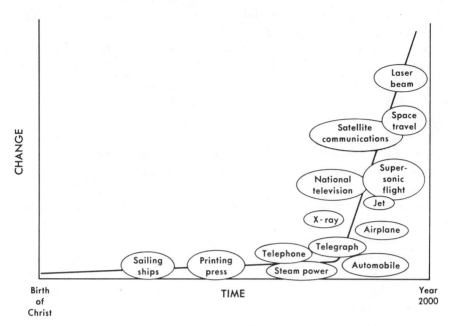

Fig. 1. Accelerated change curve.

Never before has any culture subjected itself to so intense and prolonged a bombardment of technological, social and info-psychological change. This change is accelerating and we witness everywhere in the high-technological societies evidence that the old-industrial-era structures can no longer carry out their functions. . . . The acceleration of change—in technology, in family structure, marriage and divorce patterns, in urbanization, ethnic and subcultural conflict and international relations—means, by definition, the swift arrival of a future that is radically different from the present.*

Fig. 1 illustrates Toffler's thesis that contemporary change is unique by tracing developments in general technology since the birth of Christ. Clearly, change that once occurred over centuries is now compressed into decades. Note also the exponential or self-generating characteristic of change. In short, change feeds and produces change.

Perhaps the self-generating or exponential aspect of change is best exemplified by the introduction of the automobile. Within a few decades it produced a host of new industries and contributed to changes in migration, courtship, and living patterns. These changes in turn gave birth to other significant changes, many of which social scientists still have not fully identified. More recently, the introduction of television has had a remarkable

---

*From Toffler, A., editor. 1974. Learning for tomorrow: the role of the future in education, New York, Random House, Inc., p. 4.

impact. The computer, a relative infant of technology, has already produced profound changes in human affairs, and according to some experts it will have an even greater impact in the future than all the other technological inventions of the past combined.

An additional characteristic of change today is obsolescence. Never before in the history of the human race have knowledge and cultural artifacts had such a short life. "What today is merely a fantasy in a scientist's mind will be a commonplace tomorrow and an antique the day after" (*The Futurist*, 1967, p. 28). The often-heard comment that "today's facts are tomorrow's misinformation" is becoming increasingly true. Another favorite comment highlighting the increasing rate of obsolescence states, "If it works, it's obsolete." Obviously there is some exaggeration in these statements, but when we realize that the first-generation computer, black-and-white television, medical technology, and social services of 10 years ago are curios of the past by today's standards, these views are closer to describing reality than may at first be apparent.

Given the nature of change facing us today, there is little wonder that our orientation concerning the future is drastically different than it was in earlier periods of human history. For clearly, the future will be far different from the present. "Rapid and violent today, change seems likely to be breakneck and convulsive tomorrow. Few [futurists] see any likelihood that there will be any slackening off in the pace of change during the rest of the 20th century. On the contrary, signs point to a truly cataclysmic metamorphosis of human society" (*The Futurist*, 1967, p. 28).

Since a people's shared or collective image of the future tends to shape their behavior in the present, inaccurate images about the future—images that are out of phase with the changing reality—can be dangerously misleading. The challenge to us as contemporary men and women is therefore that we restructure our images of the future in light of a rapidly changing world in order that our present behavior can be consistent with the demands of the future.

Unlike our forebears, whose tomorrows hardly differed from their todays, we are faced with a great deal of uncertainty regarding the future; hence the future has taken on new importance. Instinctively beings who seek foreknowledge and who are cognizant of the radical prospects of tomorrow's world, we have begun to reorder our thinking regarding the future. We have also begun to develop a new sense of time in general and to alter our perspective regarding the relationship between events and time, We still view time with its flow of events as unilinear; i.e., past comes before present and future follows present. However, there has been a noticeable shift in our time consciousness from one that tended to be anchored

4

in the present, with a vague or unfocused sense of future, to one that is more clearly future focused. In addition, this time reorientation places a new emphasis on past time by recognizing that past events also impinge on the present and future. To paraphrase Daniel Bell, time is not an "overarching leap" from present to future; it begins in the past, encompasses the present, and flows toward the future (1967, p. 639).

Armed with these new perspectives, we increasingly tend to view past, present, and future as rushing toward each other and as interacting in ways not imagined by our forebears. Today it is believed that each in its own way has an effect; some effects are recognizable, others are hidden from view, but all will shape our tomorrows. From this perspective the future is no longer viewed as a remote time period toward which we are moving but about which we have no certain knowledge. Perhaps surprisingly, *today the future is being viewed increasingly as a time period that is affecting our present* by influencing our decisions and our destiny. This "time reversal," or influence that the future is thought to be having on the present, is not based on some abstract notion of an unknowable future. Interestingly enough it has evolved from what futurists like to call "previsions" of tomorrow's world. For unlike previous periods, the hazy outlines of the fast-approaching future are discernible. For example, overpopulation, famine, depletion of fossil fuels, pollution of air and water, deterioration of living space, Third World aspirations, and proliferation of nuclear armaments are previsions of the future that clearly influence our judgments and decisions in the present. Similarly, there are also positive previsions of tomorrow's world. In concert these previsions, whether negative or positive, form the basis from which we restructure our images or assumptions about the future. Previsions of the future thus guide our actions in the present by serving as an early warning system of a tentative tomorrow.

Thus far it has been suggested that the future has always played an important role in human affairs. For people living in earlier periods, the collective images of the future tended to be accurate because the future essentially replicated the past. Since shared images of the future served to guide behavior in the present, human behavior in the more tranquil past tended to be consistent with the demands of the future. This is not the case for us today. Owing to the explosive and accelerating change in all facets of our lives, there is evidence that our shared images of the future, and hence our present behavior, are out of phase with the emerging future. In short, we are finding it increasingly difficult to construct accurate images of the future that can guide us in the present. Sensing this, and desiring to prosper in the future, we have thus begun to reorder our thinking regarding the possibilities of tomorrow's world. Specifically, we have drastically altered our

5

view of the future. We have also rediscovered the flow of time and developed a new appreciation for the connections between events that occur in time. And with this rediscovery, we have begun to realize again that *the future is partly knowable, and more important, it is to some extent controllable.* It is this latter awareness, combined with negative thoughts about prospects for the future, that has prompted contemporary man to systematically probe and study the future.

THE EMERGENCE OF FUTURISTICS

As we move into the last quarter of the twentieth century, radical change will continue to affect us, our institutions, and the whole of our culture much as it has done in the recent past. Accepting the inevitability of such change, it is imperative that people devise new means of developing accurate images of the future. Clearly, our future prosperity, even our survival, demand it. To this end, the fledgling "science" of futuristics (also referred to as futurology or future studies) seems to hold great potential. The term "futurology" was first introduced 30 years ago by Ossip Flechtheim to describe the systematic study of the future. Although perhaps it is not a science in the exact sense, futuristics qualifies as a "protodiscipline" or "emerging science" (Gordon, 1972, p. 165). Since modern futuristics is an organized system of inquiry regarding the domain of the future and since much of what makes up our technological and social reality is partially planned or at least routinized, scientific study of the future is possible. In support of the scientific basis of futuristics, Flechtheim states: "While the world society of today is not yet subject to the universal . . . control of any system, it is rationalized and stereotyped in sufficient areas, to permit scientific prognosis that need not merely be guesswork or intuition" (1972, p. 272). The principal rationale undergirding futuristics stems from the conditions outlined earlier in this chapter. Specifically, swift technological and social change that led to societal disruption motivated scholars to seek systematic ways of forecasting possible developments in human society. Thus in the language of futuristics we find that futurists seek previsions of the future during periods of great change to enhance the human capacity to adapt and adjust. In short, futuristics seeks to guide us toward our most desirable future by providing anticipatory information about the possibilities of tomorrow's world. In support of the potential represented by futuristics, Olaf Helmer states, "The future is no longer viewed as unique, unforeseeable, and inevitable; there are, instead, a multitude of possible futures, with associated probabilities that can be estimated and, to some extent, manipulated" (1967, p. 8).

The history of futuristics has yet to be recorded. Military strategists of World War II, together with a few private technological and economic agencies (e.g., The Rand Corporation and Systems Development Corporation) of the late 1940s and early 1950s were the first groups to engage in scientific prognoses. Using three general types of systematic forecasting (intuitive, exploratory, and normative) these groups served as prototypes for an entirely new intellectual institution, the so-called think tank (Jungk, 1971, p. 12).

Jungk offers basic explanations of these forecasting methods. *Intuitive forecasting* attempts to combine knowledge or expertise of a particular area with imagination and insight. The end products of this approach are informed intuitive judgments on probable, possible, or desirable future developments. *Exploratory forecasting* begins with an examination of current knowledge and trends and takes into account recent scientific, technological, economic, and social innovations as well as those likely to occur in the near future. After juxtaposing and extrapolating based on the interaction of the data, exploratory forecasts suggest "which trends should be reinforced and which should be curbed." *Normative forecasting* starts with a future objective, usually based on some idealized view of what life should be like in the future, and works back in a form of reverse planning, identifying the steps or stages needed to arrive at the selected or idealized future (Jungk, 1971, pp. 9-17).

During the last decade there has been a significant increase in the number of institutions, agencies, and individuals who are devoting all or part of their energies to the scientific study of the future. Such study has truly become a worldwide phenomenon. Some of the more famous "future research" organizations that have appeared in recent years include the "Futuribles" organization in France, the "World Future Society" and "Commission For the Year 2000" in the United States, "Mankind 2000" in England, "Gesellschaft für Zukunftsforschung" in East Germany, "Futurology Association" in Japan, and the "Club of Rome" in Italy. During the last 10 years several international future research congresses have been held and others are planned. During this same period numerous periodicals devoted exclusively to futuristics have appeared; *The Futurist*, published by the World Future Society, is the most notable. In addition, the popular literature dealing with the subject of the future has grown enormously (Bestuzhev-Lada, 1971, p. 26).

The sudden and rather explosive interest in futuristics is not without its darker side. It has begun to take on the elements of a fad, and its popularity also suggests that it has begun to arouse more expectations than it can fulfill (Bell, 1967, p. 641). Since futuristics was equated with fortune-telling and the like not too many years ago, these trends could truncate what otherwise seems to be a promising new development. Clearly futuristics is not a panacea. Although it possesses the potential to help mold a more positive world, futuristics will always remain a inexact science capable of large error due to the multitude of unknowable variables that will certainly encumber us as we move into the future. The best that can be hoped is that futuristics will shed some light on our tomorrows by pointing out possible, probable, or more important, desirable possibilities. In short, futuristics seems capable of providing guidance to today's decision makers and policymakers, whether they work in the political, social, educational, or technological spheres, by pointing out both short- and long-term potential consequences of current plans and pending decisions. In addition, futuristics seems capable of lighting the road into the future by focusing our attention on matters whose cumulative effects have not yet reached a critical mass and therefore fall outside the boundaries of normal perception. As such it can serve as an important early warning system for planners of all types.

Earlier it was pointed out that change is a constant reality of the human condition. Therefore it is logical to expect that the emerging science of futuristics itself will exhibit specific changes as the years pass. Since its beginnings approximately 30 years ago, futuristics has already undergone substantial change. In its early years its concerns tended to be somewhat narrow, e.g., with forecasts relative to specific military, political, or technological problems facing an army, government, or corporation. Today, its concerns tend to be more global and humanistic, and the forecasts deal with the near, intermediate, and distant futures. The methods used for conducting futures research also have changed considerably. From essentially straight-line extrapolation with respect to trends and decisions into the future, futurists have added a host of new and more sophisticated techniques. These newer techniques are a consequence of progress in a variety of areas, including cybernetics, mathematics, statistics, sociology, and psychology. However, advances in computer technology, perhaps more than any other single factor, have enabled the futurists to preview the future in ways unheard of a decade ago. We can anticipate further developments in futuristics as the year pass. New tools of inquiry will no doubt be fashioned. More and more factors and processes that affect us and our future will fall under its purview. We might also anticipate that the projected growth of futuristics will be accompanied by a concomitant tendency for more and more individuals and groups to become sensitized about the future, an important precondition for our prosperity in these changing times. These individuals and groups may well borrow the tools of inquiry fashioned by the futurists to help mold their own individual and collective futures.

There is evidence to suggest that individuals and groups have already begun to borrow from the futurists to mold their own collective and individually desired futures.

The collective aspects of choice of futures is reflected in the growing concern of our local societies . . . to long range social programs. We begin to agree, for example, that investment in prenatal care, child welfare, and pre-school education, which may not pay off for twenty or thirty years, are realistic societal strategies.[*]

We also see local and regional groups forming "future assemblies" to explore possible, probable, or preferable futures.

The Hawaii 2000 conference, for example, was an experiment in "anticipatory democracy" in which hundreds of citizens, ranging in background from truck drivers and housewives to students, professors and specialists in various fields, came together under sponsorship of the governor of the state to consider such questions as the appropriate urban/rural balance for the state in the next thirty years, or the desired mix of tourism and other industries, or the future of race relations in the islands.[†]

These alternative future conferences are not isolated events but appear to represent a trend. Participants involve themselves in action-learning experiences by focusing their collective imaginations, social skills, and decision-making abilities on the future. Today's communal groups may also be viewed as prototypes of future assemblies in which groups of individuals attempt to create their own living and working environments or preferable futures.

On the individual level we see evidence of the impact of futuristics, for people today seem more aware of at least the negative possibilities of tomorrow. The meteoric rise in concern about the environment together with the willingness of individuals to take personal initiative with respect to ensuring more healthful living conditions underscore this fact. The growth of interest in human needs, particularly among young people, represents in no small measure a commitment to the future that was not as strong in years past. The idea and importance given to a "future-focused role image" as a motive and means of achieving a preferable future in a personal sense is also an indication of the role that futuristics has begun to play.

CONCLUDING STATEMENT

It has been said that "the proof of improvidence lies in falling under the empire of necessity." de Jouvenel has suggested that "the means of avoiding this lies in acquainting oneself with emerging situations while they can be molded, before they have become imperatively compelling" (1972, p. 283).

---

[*]From McHale, J. 1969. The future of the future, New York, George Braziller, Inc., p. 9. Reprinted with the permission of the publisher. Copyright © 1969 by John McHale.
[†]From Werdell, P. 1974. Futurism and the reform of higher education. In Toffler, A., editor: Learning for tomorrow: the role of the future in education, New York, Random House, Inc., pp. 309-310.

Clearly these statements are addressed to contemporary men and women who because of the nature of change today have had to rely increasingly on the exigencies of the moment in governing their affairs. Such a situation, if allowed to continue, will surely have a negative impact on society's future. To ensure our future prosperity and that of our institutions and culture, we must of necessity invest in new ways to anticipate the course of history. For it is only through an improved anticipatory capacity that we will be able to establish the necessary plans and contingencies to meet the challenges of tomorrow's world. It is in this context that the emerging science of futuristics, with its systematic methods of scanning tomorrow's horizons, can play a vital role.

REFERENCES

Bell, D. 1967. The year 2000: trajectory of an idea, Daedalus **96**:639.

Bestuzhev-Lada, I. V. 1971. A Soviet scientist looks at futurology, UNESCO Courier **24**:22.

de Jouvenel, B. 1972. On the nature of the future. In Toffler, A., editor: The futurists, New York, Random House, Inc.

Flechtheim, O. 1972. Futurology: the new science of probability. In Toffler, A., editor: The futurists, New York, Random House, Inc.

The Futurist. 1967. Compulsory education for adults? A future forecast, The Futurist **1**:28.

Gordon, T. J. 1972. The current methods of future research. In Toffler, A., editor: The futurists, New York, Random House, Inc.

Helmer, O. 1967. New attitudes toward future, The Futurist **1**:8.

Jungk, R. 1971. Breakthrough to tomorrow, UNESCO Courier **24**:9.

McHale, J. 1969. The future of the future, New York, George Braziller, Inc.

Polak, F. L. 1972. Crossing the frontiers of the unknown. In Toffler, A., editor: The futurists, New York, Random House, Inc.

Toffler, A. 1970. Future shock, New York, Random House, Inc.

Toffler, A., editor. 1974. Learning for tomorrow: the role of the future in education, New York, Random House, Inc.

Werdell, P. 1974. Futurism and the reform of higher education. In Toffler, A., editor: Learning for tomorrow: the role of the future in education, New York, Random House, Inc.

Futuristics: perspectives, constructs, and methods

Raymond Welsh

Futuristics, an emerging science developed during the last 30 years, deals with the scientific study of the future. The development of futuristics coincides with an age of unprecedented change and the prospects for a radically different future for humankind. As in past eras, when events reach the point of potential disruption people seem to be equipped to invent precisely those institutions, technologies, and social innovations that are needed to minimize, neutralize, or ameliorate this negative potential. Today, as an unprecedented array of social, technoscientific, and geopolitical changes explodes around the world, we have in futuristics created a tool that has the potential to minimize or control the negative elements of these changes.

PERSPECTIVES

Historically, people have always been concerned about their individual and collective futures. The assumption of a future, together with hopes for and expectations of what is to come, have served as an important motivating force that has contributed to the survival and progress of the human race. This concern about the future is still operant in our era; however, the degree of concern we feel differs greatly from the experience of earlier generations. Today the time span in which important changes occur is drastically altered, and we have been compelled to take a more serious posture with respect to the possibilities of the future. This was not the case in earlier periods of human history, when change occurred slowly and the future essentially replicated the past. As Bertrand de Jouvenel suggests, the "map of the present" for the relatively static societies of the past provided people of those periods with valid information about the future, whereas in today's changing societies the map of the present becomes increasingly more obsolete with respect to providing information about the future—its validity is inversely proportional to the rate of change actually occurring in the society (1972, p. 283). Thus one of the principal perspectives of today's futurists is that past assumptions about the future are no longer viable because of the sudden increase in the rate of change. In short, futurists believe that tomorrow's world will be largely different from today's and that it is therefore necessary to engage in serious study about its possibilities.

Because of their feeling of concern about the future, people have engaged to some extent in its "creation." Harold Shane states, "The future is in large measure a product of man-made change" (1974, p. 182). From the earliest times, people have been involved through their inventiveness with creating the future. This seemingly natural human inclination to attempt to master our destiny sets us apart from all other beings. In recent years this natural tendency has evolved into a more conscious and deliberate commitment to future creation. Today, perhaps due to the cumulative aspect of knowledge, we stand at the threshold of tomorrow armed with an enhanced capacity as well as an urgent need to engage and create the future in ways that transcend past constraints and expectations.

From the perspective of futurists, the future is not fixed or predetermined in any final sense. It can be molded, influenced, and shaped by "what man himself deems necessary, allowable and ultimately desirable, in human terms" (McHale, 1969, p. 15).

11

Physical education: a view toward the future

The fatalistic view of the future as unforeseeable but unique and hence inevitable has been abandoned. We see instead a growing awareness that there is a whole spectrum of possible futures, with varying degrees of probability, and that through proper planning we may exert considerable influence over these probabilities.*

Futurists thus tend to see the future as an open array of alternative possibilities; each has its own mathematical probability of occurring, and choice among them is possible. Before intelligent choice regarding tomorrow's world can be exercised and the necessary planning begun, the futurist, together with the decision makers (the real architects of the future), must engage in a series of hierarchical processes to identify possible, probable, or preferable futures. Among the more important of these processes are data collection, a survey of alternatives, and an analysis of preferences (Helmer, 1972, p. 154).

Data collection. Facts or data about any subject area are the basis for intelligent decisions. For the futurist or for anyone who hopes to choose or influence the future, gathering data about the future is an important first step. However, data collection presents a problem, in that only events of the past can produce facts. In other words, perfect knowledge about the future is impossible. Nevertheless, using data from the past and "present," futurists and their decision-making counterparts can, through "summary processes of the mind" (deductive and inductive reasoning), makes *estimates* concerning the possibilities of tomorrow's world. This process of projecting current data into the future has become known as *forecasting* and represents one of the central activities of futurists. Since much of what constitutes our social reality is planned or systematized, forecasts or data about the future can be quite accurate (de Jouvenel, 1972, p. 272).

Survey of alternatives. A second important step in making choices regarding a future is a survey of alternatives regarding tomorrow's world. Based on forecasts about the possibilities of tomorrow, the futurist or decision maker must survey the alternatives suggested by the "data," identifying the possible futures among which choices can be made.

Analysis of preferences. After identifying and studying the array of alternative futures suggested by the data, futurists or decision makers then must narrow down the number of choices and eventually choose the most preferable future. Consideration of primary, secondary, and possible tertiary effects that might result from each decision would be part of the decision-making process. Obviously, value judgments must be made, for in the

*From Helmer, O. 1972. Prospects of technological progress. In Toffler, A., editor: The futurists, New York, Random House, Inc., p. 154.

final analysis, value judgments represent the sine qua non for choosing or influencing the future.

• • •

While data collection, survey of alternatives, and analysis of preferences are the interrelated intellectual and ideational tasks that form the basis of choosing or influencing the future, they themselves are only part of the total process of future creation. To complete the circle and make the selected future become real, the futurist or decision maker must design, implement, and monitor a step-by-step program of action that would lead to the desired future. Thus *program design and implementation* is a final and necessary step toward creating a desirable future. The fact that this is the logical final step in creating the future strongly suggests the futurist's fundamental belief in the need and importance of planning.*

CONSTRUCTS

As a new tool for studying the future, futuristics is based primarily on the principle of cause and effect. Scientists refer to this principle as scientific determinism, and it is based on a belief that everything in the universe occurs according to natural laws and not by chance. For the futurist the cause-and-effect model and its modern analog, the input-output model, express the assumption that every event or phenomenon has antecedent causes. In the language of futuristics this means that future events will be largely the consequences of present and past events. This belief has prompted François Le Lionnais to state, "The future of the past is in the future; the future of the present is in the past; the future of the future is in the present" (1971, p. 6). Thus in practical terms, decisions made today, together with past decisions will produce effects in the future. In this sense our todays and yesterdays shape our tomorrows. It is for this reason that futurists gather data from the present and past in order to make estimates about the future.

Formerly it was difficult to identify the link between cause and effect, but in recent decades the methods developed by futurists as well as advances in computer technology have helped to minimize this problem.

---

*While this discussion is an accurate description of some general perspectives and processes regarding futuristics, it must be pointed out that "creating" the future represents merely the ideal or goal toward which futurists strive. Future creation is an enormously complex task; its realization is limited by the incomplete nature of the data available about the future. In addition, surprises, or the totally unforeseeable, combined with the idiosyncracies of human nature, make it extremely unlikely that a future could be created in any exact sense.

Today the links are more readily identifiable; in fact, through summary processes of the mind, effects can be inferred long before they actually occur in time. It is precisely this a priori process, or ability to "foresee" the future in a tentative sense, that enables futuristics to provide such valuable assistance.

A modern corollary of the cause-and-effect model, and one that is also used by today's futurists, is the systems model. Somewhat similar to the cause-and-effect model, the systems model operates on the assumption that everything in the universe is arranged in systems; the elements comprising a system are in symbiotic partnership and interact with one another by means of a network of feedback loops. Thus that which affects one element of a system will by definition also affect other elements within the same system. Since there is increasing evidence that governments and businesses together with a host of other institutions are deliberately organizing themselves in accordance with the principle of systems, the systems model seems to be a valid construct for studying the future. In short, the greater the amount of planning or systematizing, the easier it becomes to gather the data necessary to make valid forecasts or estimates about future events.

METHODS

Because theirs is a new area of inquiry, futurists have had to develop a host of new methods for conducting research. The need to develop new research strategies stems from the impossibility of obtaining detailed, measurable, and hence verifiable data about events that have not yet taken place. Thus the futurist must rely on interpretation, generalization, and speculation to a greater degree than would be the case in the more established sciences. This does not imply that the practitioner of futures research lacks a data bank of facts with which to work. Indeed, past events as well as the laws that govern the relationships between events are a considerable reservoir of factual material. It is precisely the facts gleaned from the past and projected into the future, combined with considerable investment in interpretation, generalization, and speculation, that enable the futurist to make forecasts or estimates about future events. *The forecast thus represents the product of futures research and serves as the information base for intelligent policy decisions regarding the future.* For example, if the leaders of a particular country wanted an estimate regarding the country's population in 1985, they would have the following data on which to base their forecast: the nation's current population, its current birth and death rates, and its immigration quotas. This data, which could be reduced to numerical series and considered together with the exponential dynamics of population growth and the country's dollar investment in birth control measures, could yield a forecast that would be reasonably accurate for most purposes. However, owing to other unconsidered factors such as the population's attitude regarding family planning and economic conditions, it is possible that the forecast could exhibit a great degree of error. From this example it is evident that forecasts are probability statements about the future; their degree of accuracy is dependent on the completeness and relevance on the data on which they are based. It is also apparent that forecasting requires sophisticated intellectual activity. In addition, the example of population forecasting also suggests that the farther into the future a forecast is projected, the greater the probability of error, since larger time intervals lead to the likelihood of the confounding effect of totally unforeseeable factors. In short, forecasts regarding the near future tend to be more accurate than those made with respect to the intermediate or distant future.

Forecasting

"Forecasting" is the term for the intellectual activity that leads to a forecast. During the brief history of futuristics (approximately 30 years), dozens of forecasting methods that have been developed are enabling futurists to improve the accuracy as well as the scope of their forecasts. As a result, forecasts that have been developed systematically are being attended to seriously by international bodies, governments, businesses, and educational systems as well as by a host of other groups whose survival or future prosperity depend on accurate estimates of future events. There are three general types of forecasting methods: intuitive forecasting, exploratory forecasting, and normative forecasting. *Intuitive* forecasting, perhaps the least scientific of the three, is an attempt to combine knowledge or expertise of a particular area with imagination and insight. The end product of this general method takes the form of informed intuitive judgments or forecasts about probable, possible, or desirable future developments in the area under study. *Exploratory* forecasting is perhaps the most scientific of the three general methods. It begins with a rigorous analysis of current knowledge and trends in a particular problem area and takes into account recent technoscientific, economic, and social innovations and those that are likely to occur in the future. The futurist then juxtaposes and extrapolates on the interactive elements of the data to make forecasts. Obviously the computer is an indispensable tool used by exploratory forecasters to handle the quantity and complexity of the data used to make their forecasts. *Normative* forecasting is used extensively by those who would literally like to create the future. By operating from some preconceived image of an ideal future, normative forecasters make forecasts regarding the steps or stages that must be traversed in order to arrive at the desired or idealized future.

15

With the growth of humanistic thought, normative forecasting seems to be gaining in popularity (Jungk, 1971, pp. 12-15).

While there are dozens of specific methods of forecasting (or conducting futures research) that could be classified under the three general types of forecasting just outlined, it will be most helpful to describe the most representative methods of intuitive, exploratory, and normative forecasting used by today's futurists.

Intuitive forecasting. Representative of intuitive forecasting are the "brainstorming," "Delphi," and "fictional" methods. The brainstorming method involves the face-to-face discussions of interdisciplinary teams gathered for the purpose of generating consensus forecasts regarding future developments in specific fields. The focus of the discussion may be either general or specific (e.g., world health problems or health problems of urban Americans). Since the experts are in face-to-face discussion, brainstorming encourages the participants to be freely influenced by the ideas of their colleagues. A weakness of the brainstorming method involves the interplay between overly persuasive panel members and the tendency of individuals to "bandwagon" (Jungk, 1971, p. 12).

The Delphi method of intuitive forecasting is similar to the brainstorming method but does not suffer from its weakness. The Delphi method also involves gathering interdisciplinary teams for the purpose of generating forecasts with respect to some field or problem, but the face-to-face encounter allowed in brainstorming is replaced in the Delphi method by debate and the exchange of ideas accomplished through an intermediary. Thus the synthesizing of opinion or consensus leading to a forecast proceeds without bandwagoning or the possibility of undue influence exerted by a particularly strong personality. The actual forecasts resulting from the Delphi technique are arrived at after a series of "rounds" (usually three) wherein questions are asked and responses are collated and fed back by the investigator. In each succeeding round the expert is required to reassess his position with respect to the views expressed by the other participants. In this way the spread of opinions regarding a future development is narrowed to the point at which a consensus forecast can be made. Generally considered to yield more accurate forecasts than face-to-face encounters, the Delphi method also has an advantage in that panelists can participate via the telephone or a computer network, even though they are separated by vast distances (Gordon, 1972, pp. 170-171).

The fictional method of intuitive forecasting is interesting if not very accurate. Almost exclusively dependent on the expertise and insights of a single individual, it has nevertheless produced some surprising successes. Jules Verne and H. G. Wells, while they did not consider themselves futurists in the modern sense, managed to accurately predict underwater and space travel. Arthur Clarke, a modern science fiction writer, has had comparable success in predicting breakthroughs in space technology. Thus while perhaps they are tangential to the core of systematic methods for studying the future, fictional methods as represented by science fiction can through individual genius, shed some light on the possibilities of tomorrow's world.

"Scenario" is another fictional technique for forecasting. Characterized by Daniel Bell (1964) as the writing of "alternative futures," this narrative description of the future course of events serves as a "guide to policy makers in sketching their own responses to the possible worlds that may emerge in the next decade" (1964, p. 866). The scenario technique as employed by Herman Kahn and other modern futurists goes beyond the forecast and attempts to explain the underlying assumptions on which the alternative futures are based. Operationally, the scenario technique holds certain variables constant, using "as if," "standard world," or "surprise free world" models; in this way assumptions can be simplified and an interesting if not always accurate account of future possibilities can be written (Kahn and Wiener, 1968, p. 705).

The intuitive forecasting methods outlined above, although widely practiced and capable of yielding accurate forecasts, suffer because individual and collective insight plays the dominant role. In other words, the accuracy of the forecast is almost totally dependent on the individual or collective genius of the forecasters. In addition, intuitive forecasts usually can not be judged a priori relative to the mathematical probability of their coming true because probability estimates do not often accompany the forecast. Nevertheless, it has been found in experiments conducted to evaluate selected intuitive methods that they do serve to narrow opinion toward a true answer (Gordon, 1972, pp. 167-171).

Exploratory forecasting. Representative of exploratory forecasting are the "trend extrapolation," "cross-impact," and "simulation" methods. In its simplest form the trend extrapolation technique is an attempt to assess the trajectory that current trends are likely to take into the future. Implied in the trend forecast is the belief that conditions that give rise to the trend under consideration will not change within the range of the forecast. Therefore trend forecasts that deal with the near future tend to be more accurate than those that attempt to account for the intermediate or distant future; their reliability is inversely proportional to the time span of the forecast. In addition, high-inertia trends—those most resistant to change, such as the diffusion of the computer, energy utilization, and population growth—are easier to forecast using trend extrapolation methods than such low-inertia trends such as dress styles, recreational interests, and public attitudes to-

17

ward social legislation. Trend extrapolation forecasts commonly yield a quantitative statement about some future event, the likely date of its occurrence, and a probability estimate within a defined margin of error regarding the accuracy of the forecast. In recent years the trend extrapolation method has been enhanced by techniques devised to simultaneously consider relevant factors, particularly with respect to their strength and durability, that give impulse to the trend, as well as the trend itself. Curve fitting, factor analysis, and multiple correlations techniques have been used for this purpose (Schon, 1968, pp. 759-770).

Perhaps the most sophisticated method of forecasting in general and exploratory forecasting is the contextual mapping or cross-impact technique. This method permits the futurist to move beyond the isolated trend forecast by clustering related forecasts that appear to have mutual interactive characteristics in order to assess the mutually reinforcing or mutually inhibiting aspects of one forecasted trend on another. As an extension of the systems model outlined earlier, the cross-impact technique is based on the belief that since "most events and developments are in some way connected with other events and developments," they therefore have the potential to influence each other (Gordon, 1972, p. 180).

The cross-impact method groups or clusters several independently developed forecasts along with their mathematical probability of occurrence within a matrix, or cell. These forecasts are selected and grouped because they appear to have some interrelationships. Then a determination is made with respect to the positive or negative impact that each forecast has on the other, using the paradigm, "If forecast A occurs, then the probability of forecast B occurring is either increased or decreased." After all the forecasts have been analyzed in this way and the strengths of the interactions have been estimated, the original forecasts and the probability of their occurrence are readjusted. The importance of the cross-impact method to the science of futuristics is great, for it facilitates an integration of forecasts made in such areas as science, technology, politics, economics, and education by expanding the data base. The cross-impact approach can be immensely helpful to decision makers, for it provides a method of evaluating alternative policy decisions a priori by pointing out the sometimes hidden consequences of pending decisions (Gordon, 1972, pp. 180-184).

The simulation method is yet another exploratory forecasting technique widely used by today's futurists. In actuality the simulation method involves a host of complex methodologies in which simulated environments or systems are constructed for the purpose of working through tentative decisions to determine possible outcomes. Simulated mechanical, mathematical, metaphorical, and game models of a variety of technological and social

18

systems have been developed. These have enabled futurists to make reasonably accurate forecasts. Of course the closer the simulated model is to the reality, the more reliable the forecast. Since more is known about the products and processes of technology, it is easier to construct technological systems and models than systems and models designed to approximate social structures. As advances in the social sciences are made and we gain a better understanding of the dynamics of human behavior, simulation methods regarding social systems will no doubt tend to yield more accurate forecasts (Piganiol, 1971, pp. 29-31).

Gaming as representative of the simulation method deserves special comment because it attempts to take people's responses to an event or decision into account by using people who are assigned roles in accordance with a game model. As these people play out their roles, they exhibit some of the possible reactions people might have concerning an actual decision or event. Since human reactions are the most difficult to calculate, gaming strategies are becoming a valuable tool for improving the accuracy of forecasting, particularly where the human element plays a major role.

Normative forecasting. The last of the three general types of forecasting is normative forecasting. Perhaps in response to the increasing criticism that science and scientists are too mechanistic or value neutral when it comes to human affairs, futurists have been turning increasingly to normative forecasting techniques. Most normative forecasting methods involve two essential steps. The first is the identification or description of some idea or desired future toward which people can strive. The second step involves identification of the steps or stages that must be traversed in order to achieve the desired future. Of course value judgments are the vital element in all normative methods and serve to make the normative approach to futures research the most humanistic. The primacy of values in normative forecasting is best summed up by Fred Polak:

> In setting himself purposefully to control and alter the course of events man has been forced to deal with the concepts of value, means and ends, ideals and ideologies, as he has attempted to blueprint his own future. . . . Awareness of ideal values is the first step in conscious creation of images of the future and therefore in the conscious creation of culture. For a value is by definition that which guides toward a "valued" future.*

One of the principal criticisms directed at futuristics concerns the forecast itself. Specifically, it has been argued that once a forecast is enunciated,

*From Polak, F. L. 1972. Crossing the frontiers of the unknown. In Toffler, A., editor: The futurists, New York, Random House, Inc., pp. 288-289. (Originally published in *Image of the Future* by A. W. Sijthoff International Publishing Co.; abridged edition by American Elsevier Publishing Co., Inc., 1973.)

it carries within it the seeds either of its own accuracy or failure, since those hearing it will either be inclined to act either for or against its realization. Since futuristics is a "science of action" rather than an "objective science," this criticism has never been contested and in fact serves to strengthen the normative techniques (along with others) of forecasting. The "decisional method" and "relevance tree method," two of the principal techniques of normative forecasting, are based on the assumption that men will act to ensure the realization of the forecast. America's project to land a man on the lunar surface and return him safely to earth by the end of the 1960s was a normative forecast made in 1961 by President John F. Kennedy that proved to be dramatically accurate. This historic example of normative forecasting serves to illustrate the dynamics of both the decisional and relevance tree methods of forecasting (Jungk, 1971, p. 14).

Both the decisional and relevance tree methods begin with a normative decision or forecast regarding some future event. In the example just cited, this was the safe landing of a man on the moon and his return to earth by some specific time in the future. Once the forecast is established, reverse planning is used to identify all contingencies and establish priorities. Alternative approaches are also assessed and decisions are made regarding the best possible course between tomorrow and today.

CONCLUDING STATEMENT

We have highlighted some of the baseline perspectives, constructs, and methods used by today's futurists. Although the field of futuristics is infinitely more complex than has been revealed in this discussion, an effort has been made to provide some basic insights into this new and exciting branch of knowledge. For in futuristics we are not only witnessing an extraordinary, unprecedented thrust toward the scientific appraisal of human destiny, we are also simultaneously gaining new tools for the positive intervention in the creation of the future. Although it would be foolish to overestimate the potential of this new science to alter the course of history, it would be even more foolish to underutilize it or ignore the opportunities it offers.

REFERENCES

Bell, D. 1964. Twelve modes of prediction: a preliminary sorting approach in the social sciences, Daedalus 93:845.
de Jouvenel, B. 1972. On the nature of the future. In Toffler, A., editor: The futurists, New York, Random House, Inc.
Gordon, T. J. 1972. The current methods of futures research. In Toffler, A., editor: The futurists, New York, Random House, Inc.
Helmer, O. 1972. Prospects of technological progress. In Toffler, A., editor: The futurists, New York, Random House, Inc.
Jungk, R. 1971. Breakthrough to tomorrow, UNESCO Courier 24:9.

Insights into the future

Kahn, H., and Wiener, A. J. 1967. The next thirty-three years: a framework for speculation, Daedalus 96:705.

Le Lionnais, F. 1971. What future for futurology, UNESCO Courier 24:4.

McHale, J. 1969. The future of the future, New York, George Braziller, Inc.

Piganiol, P. 1971. Pondering the imponderable, UNESCO Courier 24:29.

Polak, F. L. 1972. Crossing the frontiers of the unknown. In Toffler, A., editor: The futurists, New York, Random House, Inc.

Schon, D. A. 1967. Forecasting and technological forecasting, Daedalus 96:759.

Shane, H., and Shane, J. G. 1974. Educating the youngsters for tomorrow. In Toffler, A., editor: Learning for tomorrow: The role of the future in education, New York, Random House, Inc.

CHAPTER TWO

PHILOSOPHICAL FORECASTS

Rejecting the discontinuity of time between past, present, and future, Ginny L. Studer believes that we gain guidance for the future from the traditions of the past and present. Using a combination of intuitive and normative forecasting models, she believes that by studying our heritage of human identity and knowledge, physical educators and hence physical education might find the energy as well as the creative channels for the construction of a more meaningful profession in the future. Beginning with an essentially humanistic view of people and profession, Studer further believes that through a synthesis and coalescence of the dichotomies and fragmentations that currently mark the profession, new ways of knowing and serving will emerge in the future.

Earle F. Zeigler, author of the second essay in this chapter, uses a combination of intuitive, exploratory, and normative forecasting techniques to provide some philosophical perspectives on the future of physical education and sport. Zeigler has organized his discussion around responses to such questions as, Where have we been? Where are we now? Where ought we to be? How are we to get there? and What should we avoid along the way? Zeigler offers some concrete ideas, suggestions, and recommendations regarding the future of the profession. In addition, he argues in favor of the philosophical stance of "positive meliorism" so that the profession's potential may be more fully realized in the years ahead.

Synthesis and coalescence

Ginny L. Studer

Futurist literature is replete with descriptions of genetic engineering, cyborgs, time travel by deep freezing, chemical injections of knowledge, roadless vehicles, and space colonies. It is often easy to allow the imagination to play with probable and perhaps necessary gadgets when contemplating futures. A somewhat more difficult task, usually reserved for philosophers, poets, painters, and composers, is to identify the enduring human qualities and, through disciplined conjecture about preferable tomorrows, clarify the delicate equilibrium between our dreams and our realities. As Arthur Clarke has said, "We are living at a time when history is holding its breath, and the present is detaching itself from the past like an iceberg that has broken away from its icy moorings to sail across the boundless ocean" (1953, p. 7).

If, as many futurists claim, an understanding of the traditions of the past cannot adequately prepare us for the future, then we must be ready to accept the visions and created realities of contemporary soothsayers and crystal gazers. Since most of us do not recognize such powers, we may adopt an uninvolved posture, paying little heed to all the mind-boggling phantom futures projected onto reality. If, on the other hand, we decide that we already have had enough of Ardrey's "universal human slave inherently obedient to other people's reason" (1961, p. 344), then individual and collective involvement is necessary to explore the traditions and transitions of human destiny.

A wealth of materials for the creation of many futures lies in the arts and literature of the past and present. As McHale has said, "We need more, and more diverse, alternative futures, not fewer" (1969, p. 10). Perhaps we therefore ought to become involved in a multiplication of traditions instead of their abolition. Traditions alone do not constitute a creative force for the future. However, their study may provide refreshing energy capable of repudiating dead forms while providing creative channels for living ones, without the danger of manufacturing self-fulfilling prophecies.

From the many traditions available that might give guidance for future alternatives, it seems particularly prudent at this time in history to continue studying the heritages associated with human identity and knowledge. So long as we posit human futures, we must at least be curious about the transitions and relationships between who is and who will be, and what is known and what will be known. As Brown has said:

> Tuning in to the interior self is an ancient yet ever new concept . . . old in the sense that it is everyman's dream to know and understand his inner being, and new in the sense that current changes in social awareness are breaking down the taboos against explorations of the inner self. The new freedom to know the self is lucidly expressed in the thousands of new encounter groups, the new "awareness raising" groups, in the new seeking for religious inspiration, in the changing curricula of universities.[*]

It is possible that the key to coping with "future shock" lies in understanding who we are, each one of us and all of us, as feeling, thinking, believing, intuiting, moving beings. The contemporary renewal of humanistic concerns in the literature of educational philosophy and social criticism has

---

[*]From Brown, B. B. 1974. New mind, new body: bio-feedback: new directions for the mind, New York, Bantam Books, Inc., pp. 5-6.

23

its foundation in the liberal arts. Recent philosophical and scientific research also reflects a synthesis of knowledge regarding human identity through a harmonizing of Eastern and Western traditions:

> The need to bring about a unification of Eastern and Western culture is of fundamental moment for all of us. Politically, we have suffered during the last decades three mighty wars which have set Asians and Westerners against one another. Culturally, we experience the partiality of Western materialism and rationality, and the partiality of the tendency seen in the East to withdraw from matter, action and concrete thinking. Personally we know that the "East within ourselves," full of the morning light of wisdom and intuition, will emerge in human fullness only when united with the light of practical reason and with steadiness of activity. So the union of East and West is, in these and other ways, an urgent task for both development and human evolution.*

The task of blending the logic and mystery of past understandings of human identity with our present intuitions may provide the guidelines for the educational process of the future.

The liberal arts study of human movement can contribute to understandings of identity. Although relatively unexplored, there is a tradition in the arts, literature, and philosophy that portrays man in motion. By exploring this inheritance we may gain new insights into past and present human identities as well as contribute to the synthesis of knowledge necessary to define preferable futures.

The increasing recognition of sport, dance, exercise, and play as avenues that foster positive human growth provides physical educators with unlimited opportunities to be imaginative regarding new directions and alternative futures. Uncertain of our physical education heritage, we often have sought pragmatic solutions to problems. We have tended to press for recognition only of our present particular interests, values, or needs, leaving the future in the hands of societal crises and educational pressures. Our professional posture has been defensive, protective, and rarely secure.

With the increased interest in futurism, scholars and practitioners together may surmise, construct, and convey without the stigma of mere intellectual adventurism. Our aspirations for new futures require creativity, energy, and bold leadership as we reexamine both the body of knowledge and the processes of physical education.

A RESTRUCTURING OF KNOWLEDGE

> It is the superb paradox of our time that in a single century we have proceeded from the first iron-clad warship to the first hydrogen bomb, and from the first telegraphic communication to the beginnings of the conquest of space; yet in the understanding of our own natures, we have proceeded almost no-

*From Carter-Haar, B. E., and Miller, S. 1975. The meeting of East and West: a conversation with Haridas Chaudhuri, Synthesis 1:20.

where. It is an ignorance that transcends national or racial boundaries, and leaps happily over iron curtains as if they did not exist. Were a brotherhood of man to be formed today, then its only possible common bond would be ignorance of what man is.°

One of the great traditions in philosophy has been a study of human identity. In all its simplicity, the fact that the question is still asked may provide the wisdom for the answer. We seek to know ourselves personally and collectively. Throughout the growth of knowledge we have spent much time in analyzing what is known about humankind. Categories of knowledge have been developed for the study of body and soul; reason and emotion; id, ego, and superego; matter and spirit; distinctions between and similarities to other animals, individuals and groups; freedom and authority; and the many other sciences of human nature. What is needed is synthesis.

> We have a two-fold obligation: first, to study man as a whole, without rejecting anything that he has learned throughout his history unless we can prove scientifically that it is harmful. This we can achieve not by coordinating existing sciences—man does not consist of externally coordinated parts, since he forms a whole—but by Anthropics, the Science of Man. Second, in the absence of any proof that we can produce a better man by changing the relationship between the body, the senses, the mind and the soul, we should work toward a complete man with a harmonious development of all his elements, a total man whom I cannot name anything but human man.†

A total conceptual revision of the definition of knowledge is necessary to avoid our contemporary preoccupation with its microscopic dissection. As we unite many of the dichotomies with which we presently describe our complex natures, we may come to understand a simple relationship between the mystical and the analytical. New knowledge may evolve from the union of thinking and feeling and from rational and nonrational ways of knowing. We may be more capable of asking real questions of human existence rather than those questions limited by academic disciplines. Disciplines, as we know them, may be resources for answering questions but not the stimulus. Answers to the questions may no longer be limited by what tools are available for study; rather, we may study what we are honestly curious about and what we really need to know.

Whereas in the past, scientific research has been commended for its value-free orientation, future research may make value commitments toward futures preferable in human terms. We may be capable of blending the independent heroes of existential literature with the dependency con-

---

°From Ardrey, R. 1961. African genesis, New York; Atheneum Publishers, p. 158. Copyright © 1961 by Literat S. A. Reprinted by permission of Atheneum Publishers.
†From Doxiadis, C. A. 1967. The coming era of ecumenopolis, Saturday Review, March 18, p. 12.

cepts of contemporary anthropology, biology, and psychology because we understand them both intimately. Ways of expressing what we experience to be the relationship between self and world may evolve as scientists and artists become one, metaphorically creating their own constructs. Diversity and simplicity together may guide searches for knowledge, altering the trend toward specialization to one of unity and actualization.

If the knowledge structures of human identity undergo such revision, the study of human nature will be more closely allied with what we experience it to be; as our capacity for experience changes, so will our identities, providing us with continuous new sources of knowledge about ourselves. Facts will be transformed and viewed as processes, trends, and patterns. Personal and interpersonal experientially based knowledge will allow us to think outside the given categories, to redefine the problems, and to utilize our indivisable imaginations in the study of alternatives.

> The tragedy of the world is that those who are imaginative have but slight experience, and those who are experienced have feeble imaginations. Fools act on imagination without knowledge; pedants act on knowledge without imagination. The task of the university is to weld together imagination and experience.[*]

At the present time, most universities are organized on the basis of segmented and formal disciplines: history, botany, psychology, English, etc. If the future does provide new ways of knowing together with syntheses of existing knowledge concerning human identity, then the organization of universities must also change to reflect the new, open structures for knowledge. Whether it is an adjunct or an established discipline in the university setting, physical education must also change its orientation to provide for the use of knowledge about human movement in understanding the problems of the twenty-first century.

> We should have learned by now that the key to education for the future is a sense of individual responsibility in each student for choosing, with guidance when necessary, the type of education which will benefit him or her the most. We have the right, even the obligation, to know what motivates each person to learn and to document this motivation, but we have the duty to find ways to respond to this unique motivation.[†]

As we collectively attempt to synthesize knowledge of movement in relation to the traditional questions of human identity, our task will be infinitely less difficult than it would be in many other areas of study. Analytical and experiential descriptions, mystical accounts, technological explanations,

---

[*]From Whitehead, A. N. 1929. The aims of education, New York, The New American Library of World Literature, Inc., p. 94.
[†]From Commission on Non-Traditional Study (Samuel Gould, chairman). 1974. Diversity by design, San Francisco, Jossey-Bass, Inc., Publishers, p. 39.

poetic analogies, and interpretive representations of movement are already integrated into what appears to be every phase of human endeavor and as a result into almost all academic disciplines. As involvement in the liberal arts study of movement increases, we must avoid the prevalent tendency to categorize knowledge into distinct and mutually exclusive wholes. Rather, we might begin to identify process-oriented, experientially based constructs in order that many individual types of synthesis can grow and be created. If instead we continue to divide and subdivide, physical education may become a miniuniversity within the total educational environment. Much of our organizational structure has already predetermined this course. There are sport sociology, the philosophical perspective on the study of physical activity, anthropology of play, dance history, games of English-speaking people, physiology of exercise, aesthetics of movement, sport psychology, and social psychology of game behavior, in addition to team activities, racket sports, rhythmics, and dance. As synthesis of the study of movement occurs, many new avenues for inquiry may develop that not only bridge the gap between traditional arts and sciences but lead to a humanizing study of the nature of our identity. We will gain freedom of inquiry, and we will overcome the fragmentation that has divorced body from mind, from senses, from intellect, from emotion, from reality, from art, from abstraction, from fact, from the joy of moving.

When movement is viewed as an integral human phenomenon, it can be studied in all of the dimensions in which we experience it. The study of movement can then be ordered by process referents in which the contents of moving are viewed as momentary and interrelated. It is possible that several different process models of referents will develop as we synthesize knowledge of movement with human identity, for there are particular and universal essences in both.

In the transitions from fragmentation to integration and from a commitment to analysis to synthesis, many alternatives may appear and provide guidance. It is conceivable that one step in the change might reflect the interdisciplinary approach now popularized in universities at large; that is, we may integrate the subdisciplines of physiology of exercise, sport sociology, and history of dance with various movement activities for the purpose of studying such topics as age characteristics reflected in movement, the concept of excellent performance, women in sport, and theories of play. The significance of such an integration lies in recognizing it as one of the many possible beginning phases in the transition to a synthesis that focuses in a positive way on the whole person in the whole world.

The literature of futuristics offers other viable alternatives for structuring our present understandings of physical education without abandoning its traditions. One alternative focuses on a convergence of new attitudes toward time, resulting in a redefinition of the concepts of work, play, and leisure. As technology becomes more and more involved in productive (product-oriented) work and human maintenance and survival needs are satisfied earlier and more easily, activities that help to fulfill human beings may become our appropriate work.

> I believe that man can abolish toil and abolish it well before the end of this century, that he can develop, instead, work. I see man working in four areas: first self development; . . . second, the human care of human beings; third, the whole area of human relationships. It takes a lifetime to get to know somebody, and if you don't like to call it work, I don't care. It's still something to do, and that's what worries a lot of people: what will man do next? Fourth, politics—the creation of a good community.*

If the concept of work is redefined to include all types of engagements in the reconstruction of self-world relationships, then what are the implications for synthesizing play and work? Certainly, if such a reconceptualization occurs, there will be a dramatic reversal in the trend that continues to raise the age level for admission to society by increasing the length of formal education. All ages will be involved in work-play, providing for continuous syntheses of knowledge about human identity in all our endeavors. The traditions in physical education that relate to a study of the whole person moving and interacting with others throughout life can contribute immensely to such a synthesis of attitude and knowledge. While most research and scholarship in physical education still reflects the use of analytical tools, synthesis is also occurring.

The importance of continuous study of the literature within and outside the contemporary boundaries of physical education cannot be overstated if we are to avoid tunnel vision within the field and separation from the mainstream of the future. The challenge for physical education, relative to restructuring the body of knowledge for the future, lies in synthesizing the significance of experiences in movement with the ongoing processes directed toward achieving an understanding of human identity. Meeting this challenge requires a type of renaissance within each of us as we gain new perspectives and expand the orientations of what it is we do best in research and scholarship.

PROFESSIONAL REORGANIZATION

In the tradition of philosophy, many physical educators have become involved in concept and linguistic analysis in an attempt to define the param-

---

*From Theobald, R., et al. 1967. Dialogue on poverty, Indianapolis, The Bobbs-Merrill Co., Inc., p. 115.

eters of physical education. The value of such attempts has often been questioned due to lack of agreement on mutually exclusive categories. Perhaps in the future we will recognize that the value of these definitive efforts lies not in the final clear and precise products of definition but in the process of identifying the many ways in which the concepts of physical education overlap and relate to each other. Synthesizing and restructuring the body of knowledge about human movement provides for and is dependent on coalescence of professional organization.

At present, our professional organization reflects the principles of separatism, specialization, and hierarchy. As a result the field is fraught with dichotomies, fragmentation, and duplication. We have sport sociologists and dance historians, kinesiologists and philosophers, men and women, amateurs and professionals, coaches and teachers, performance teachers and theory teachers, humanistic psychologists of sport and behavioristic psychologists of sport, researchers and scholars, and so on.

At the present time some attempts have been made to review those principles that have segmented us. Differences of degree rather than kind do not necessitate categories of distinction and elitism, but rather may provide the basis for a blend of similarities. The future may extend the process beyond the merger of men's and women's groups to a total reexamination of professional organization. Present distinctions may be extinguished by the acceptance of a common goal. One possible goal may be human service, which is what all individuals and groups may be involved in with reference to vocation-life studies. Such a coalescence of professional organization may be generated by the synthesis of the body of knowledge of human identity.

MODES AND METHODS OF OPERATION

Posttechnological education has thus far contributed to two often exasperating trends that characterize our times: one is to mechanize human beings, the other is to humanize machines. Perhaps the ultimate goal is the same; man machine = machine man:

> It is somewhat terrifying to realize that the bulk of biological and psychological scientific effort has been devoted to learning how to control man's emotion and behavior, yet the reins of control are rarely, if ever, offered to the individual being controlled. The majority of academic, governmental, and industrial societies embrace varying types of behavior control and cybernetics, and delight in the prospect of automatized man.*

Contemporary interest in humanism and behavioral goals and modification represent conflicts with which we now struggle in the process of chang-

---

*From Brown, B. B. 1974. New mind, new body biofeedback: new directions for the mind, New York, Harper & Row, Publishers, p. 3.

ing the concept of technological education to meet future concerns and life styles. Whereas in the past we have often been concerned with education for the future as preparation for living, future concepts of education may provide for the signification of the process of living. Before, we were concerned with the identification of appropriate sequences, progressions, and transferable values for particular age groups; future education may allow us to accept and value more time for contemplation, relaxation, creative thought, love, friendship, solitude, and the beauties of nature, the arts, and the humanities:

> What we must look for from the universities is the development of an education that turns out individuals of the highest intellect and broadest outlook, able to understand man and machine, and live creatively with both. Such an education could not be expected in a four year curriculum or even a six or eight year one. It would start as early as the beginning of school or sooner and involve continuing education of one type or another throughout a person's lifetime.[*]

It is perhaps not so ironic that this country, one of the wealthiest, most powerful, and most productive, whose society is among the most time conscious and time saving, has in the past placed one of the lowest values on cultural traditions. Why do we save time? Future technology may well free us to pursue individual and collective realization in the truest tradition of liberal education.

As the process that enhances our capacity to be at home in the universe, education can occur without the closed time structures of school terms, grade levels, credit hours, and the multitude of commencements. Such a reconceptualization of education may become overwhelmingly simple in the day-to-day affairs of increasing our understanding of who we are and where we are in the life process of humankind. Education and life may become more synonymous, providing the basis for eliminating the often false distinctions between education and vocation. As a result professional education may suffer a decline, since "jobs" may be at best only incidental. Human service may provide guidelines for educational processes rather than productivity.

Implications for the redesign of the modes and methods of operation of physical education are multiphasic. At the present time many physical educators appear to be interested in expanding the indefinite boundaries of the field to encompass more of the popularized sport world. Diversity seems to be a goal demonstrated in the development of research specializations and career alternatives such as sport administration, sport communications, and

---

[*]From Seaborg, G. T. 1967. The cybernetic age: an optimist's view, Saturday Review, March 4, p. 48.

athletic training. Diversity may be viewed as an expansion of a somewhat neglected domain rightfully belonging to physical education or perhaps as a defense mechanism working to preserve at least a portion of traditional professional physical education at a time when there is little need for a continuous proliferation of gym teachers. However, if life and education are synthesized into a human service framework, the modus operandi of physical education will continue to be fundamentally consistent with our educational tradition. Consequently, it may be necessary to redesign much of the business and technology recently incorporated in the field of physical education in order to reflect principles of process rather than product orientation.

Changes in our concepts of time and the emphasis on process rather than on products may serve to revitalize research and scholarly efforts in physical education. If immediate results and products are no longer the primary focus, we may envision more long-range research projects. Isolated facts and bits and pieces of information will be valuable, not in themselves but as they are synthesized into patterns, processes, and completed pictures. As we continue our study of an expanded concept of physical education, imagination and creativity may guide our curiosity about the nature and potential of movement as one source for understanding human identity. Instead of a complete devotion to explaining what has been and is accomplished in movement, an increased curiosity may develop in what can be and ought to be accomplished. Rather than studying, proving, and teaching that one way of throwing a ball is more efficient than another, we may begin to research new ways to propel round objects through space based on our understanding of human effectiveness. If the process of synthesis receives as much attention as the development of analytical tools, we may be able to avoid some of the duplication and repetition that exists in the literature today and instead be stimulated by new and changing questions, concepts, and ideas.

Research directed toward understanding human body potential is certainly significant in our search for greater clarity regarding human identity. Again it would seem that synthesis is imperative. The heritages of Western art, literature, science, and philosophy, the Eastern forms of Tai Chi, Yoga, Zen, and Aikido, the traditions of physical education, and the relatively recent developments in human body potential all contribute to a more complete understanding of the human body in relation to identity. New questions and new designs for research can grow out of such a synthesis without fear of duplication or omission.

Research that merges fact with feeling, what is with what ought to be, and the known with dreams and hopes may allow us to erase many of the artificial lines that separate intellectualism, emotionalism, and knowledge; together they give new strength and provide for a total coalescence of knowledge and experience. Many emotions are associated with experience in movement. In a single moment there is simultaneity of reality, feeling, wishes, thoughts, memories, and fantasies. Studying the totality of the moment deliberately and openly, as a regular and integrated aspect of our scholarship, may give new strength to our understanding of the significance of movement experiences.

> It will be crucially important that each person master the skill of feeling what others feel. This skill, more than new laws or new politics, will soon become crucial to the survival of the race. Such empathy is possible only if one is deeply aware of his own feelings. The future will very likely judge nothing less appropriate than detached, fragmented, unfeeling men. . . .°

Do contemporary experiences in a broad range of movements continue to demonstrate that human nature is about the same as it was a couple of thousand years ago? That the ability to love is as much a part of our nature as the ability to hate? Research in physical education that emphasizes synthesis can answer these and many other questions that lead to knowledge of who we are and where we are in process.

At the present time student choice, freedom, and individualized instructional patterns dominate the practices of humanistic physical education. Action research that demonstrates the long-range importance of the individual in groups is imperative. While it is apparent that students must become less passive than they have been, we cannot allow future education to surrender to self-indulgence. Both our heritage and our views of the future reveal that humans are not and cannot be totally individual. Instead we might turn some of our research interests toward solving some of the problems of human relations, inventing new ways of making collective decisions, and discovering what can be learned about organization and group dynamics through self-organization of groups. Sport, dance, exercise, and play provide a variety of laboratories for such research.

It is time to immunize research in physical education against the publish-or-perish syndrome. In the future, isolated products of research may no longer be valued, and publication may be viewed as only one narrow channel of communication among the variety developed through technology and kinesics. Rather than immediate communication, it appears that the value of future research in physical education will depend to a much greater extent on the synthesis of what is already known with the development of new hypotheses that unite understandings of human identity.

A curriculum designed to enhance our understanding of individual and collective identities consists minimally of human needs, interests, and problems, and their relationship to existence. Such a curriculum will require di-

°From Leonard, G. B. 1969. Education and ecstasy, New York, Delacorte Press, p. 127.

versified learning environments as the process of education becomes more synonymous with life and culture. Homes, parks, hospitals, museums, community centers, clinics, social organizations, and churches as well as schools provide opportunities to learn in and about movement in relation to identity. There are no limits to the expansion of student access to learning opportunities. Evidence of the initial stages of expansion is apparent. At the present time physical education programs in various parts of the country include diverse flexible time patterns and spatial arrangements in curricular experiences. There are altered patterns of residence, weekend retreats, summer workshops, resident conferences, mini– and maxi–school terms, and credit for life and recreational experiences. Each option appears to provide students with new ways of synthesizing knowledge and experience. Physical educators also seem to have taken the first steps in overcoming the pejorative attitude toward technology, which has sometimes in the past jeopardized communication with students and interferred with the development of human movement potential. As a profession we appear to be making most of our progress toward the education described by the futurists in the areas of curriculum and program planning. What curriculum planners appear to need is more substantial content, which is dependent on our ability to restructure the body of knowledge and redesign research based on the principle of synthesis.

Content does not need to consist of facts in relation to other facts. In an educational process synonymous with living, content can and does exist in the form of questions. It is perhaps a function of educational reformation to renew efforts to reward good questions instead of just good answers:

> Try to love the questions themselves like locked rooms and like books that are written in a very foreign tongue. Do not now seek the answers, which cannot be given you because you would not be able to live them. And the point is, to live everything. Live the questions now.*

Emphasizing the process rather than the products of physical education does not exclude the necessity for learning particular knowledges, skills and techniques of research. The process of learning these can in fact cultivate freedom, individuality, self-expression, and creativity, allowing for ecstatic moments that transcend the mastery of particulars. Accordingly, mastery becomes part of the process of creative change instead of an end in itself.

At the present time there is not a sufficiently complete picture of the body of knowledge in physical education for us to know whether or when mastery of particular knowledges and skills is appropriate at specific developmental stages. As a result, multiage groups, mature adult programs, and

*From Rilke, R. M. 1934. Letters to a young poet, New York, W. W. Norton & Co., Inc., p. 35.

cross-age helping/teaching/learning have been very successful. While we believe that one of the things we need to teach young children is creative leisure, we also recognize the need for courses in which the unique, untampered-with perceptions of children are relearned by adults. Childlike awareness and its implications for moving, playing, learning, and knowing have become increasingly valued and valuable in humanistic education.

> Why not then continue to look like a child upon it all as upon something unfamiliar, from out of the depth of one's own world, out of the expanse of one's own solitude, which is itself work and status and vocation.*

In the expansion of the educational process, imaginative approaches to teaching physical education will be important because they will contribute to the integration of the formal with the personal, the factual with the emotional, and the past with the present and future. Contemporary research in teaching effectiveness seems determined to identify and isolate positive competencies for physical education teacher behavior. A synthesis of the tradition of good teachers, projected to future needs for an expanded educational process, may indicate that good teachers will be no different than they ever were. Characteristic of good teachers is a contagious love of learning and a belief in the futures of those they teach. While teaching in the future will require diversity in behavior and understanding, future good teachers will continue to believe in and facilitate the tenent that understanding human identity individually and collectively is an underlying necessity if education is to be effective.

THE PROFESSION'S ROLE

The literature of future-directed educational philosophy indicates diversity in professional roles. It is important to remember that more choice and more freedom require more wisdom if they are to add up to more humanity. The role of professional physical education in the future requires that we become more than regenerative passengers in the synthesized educational process. Neither can we afford to live egocentrically on a plateau of social interest in our subject matter. Instead, we must keep growing quietly, seriously, and collectively. We must work at overcoming present professional problems in order to contribtue to an educational process that will foster individual creative expression while helping to form visions of a future guided by informed values and ethical principles.

At present some of the finest minds in the profession are not being directed toward the greatest future dilemmas of physical education. Instead

---

*From Rilke, R. M. 1934. Letters to a young poet, New York, W. W. Norton & Co., Inc., p. 46.

they are immobilized by academic and professional hurdles, obstacles, and barriers. The recent emphasis on professional accountability has promoted a proliferation of technological systems of physical education administration. Characteristic of these systems, principles of scientific management have been incorporated with the intent to maximize production. Such administrative organizations have lowered morale, weakened the commitment to goals, and accelerated alienation from top administrators. Professionals who have arrogated power to themselves, whether for personal, altruistic, or efficiency purposes, must be guided to the realization that what they are doing is dangerous and alien to our traditions and to the future coalescence of the profession. It has often been assumed that working together through the use of group process skills is inappropriate and dysfunctional because it requires more time and therefore delay in response to crises. On the other hand, future educational processes do not appear to have the temporal structures of the present, and certainly the process of synthesizing knowledge in the field is dependent on professional coalescence.

Denouncing present evils, however, is a relatively easy task. Much more difficult is the task of developing a comprehensive prescription for curing our ills. As Norman Cousins has said, "People who fear the worst tend to invite it. Heads that are down can't scan the horizon for new openings. Bursts of energy do not spring from a spirit of defeat. Ultimately, hopelessness leads to helplessness (1974, p. 4).

Overcoming our often defensive posture is an important step in the restoration of confidence, and confidence is essential if we are to meet present and future challenges. Professional confidence, however, cannot be sought as a goal in its own right; rather it seems to be a byproduct of active commitment of talents and energies to some cause or goal outside itself:

> The case for hope has never rested on provable facts or rational assessment. Hope by its very nature is independent of the apparatus of logic. What gives hope its power is not the accumulation of demonstrable fact, but the release of human energies generated by the longing for something better. The capacity for hope is the most significant fact in life. It gives human beings a sense of destination and the energy to get started. It enlarges sensitivities. It gives values to feelings as well as to facts.*

Involving professionals in accord with their concepts of self contributes to confidence and hope. Working together to reconstitute ourselves will at the same time generate the professional unity we need to enter the future as responsible partners and educators. A professional role that demonstrates trust in all people—students, faculty, and administrators, a commitment to

---

*From Cousins, N. 1974. Hope and practical realities, Saturday Review, December 14, p. 5.

openness, and perhaps above all patience will be ready for a future characterized by change and flexibility, participation and dialogue, creativity and imagination, and synthesis and coalescence.

REFERENCES

Ardrey, R. 1961. African genesis, New York, Atheneum Publishers.

Brown, B. B. 1974. New mind, new body: bio-feedback: new directions for the mind, New York, Bantam Books, Inc.

Carter-Haar, B., and Miller, S. 1975. The meeting of East and West: a conversation with Haridas Chaudhuri, Synthesis 1:2.

Clarke, A. C. 1953. Childhood's end, New York, Harcourt, Brace & World, Inc.

Commission on Non-Traditional Study (Samuel Gould, chairman). 1974. Diversity by design, San Francisco, Jossey-Bass, Inc., Publishers.

Cousins, N. 1974. Hope and practical realities, Saturday Review, December 14.

Doxiadis, C. A. 1967. The coming era of ecumenopolis, Saturday Review, March 18.

Leonard, G. B. 1969. Education and ecstasy, New York, Delacorte Press.

McHale, J. 1969. The future of the future, New York, George Braziller, Inc.

Rilke, R. M. 1934. Letters to a young poet, New York, W. W. Norton & Co., Inc.

Seaborg, G. T. 1967. The cybernetic age: an optimist's view, Saturday Review, March 4.

Theobold, R., et al. 1967. Dialogue on poverty, Indianapolis, The Bobbs-Merrill Co., Inc.

Whitehead, A. N. 1929. The aims of education, New York, The New American Library of World Literature, Inc.

Philosophical perspective on the future of physical education and sport

Earle F. Zeigler

Forecasting the future has been great fun for a variety of amateurs, semiprofessionals, and professionals in recent years. Although people have always been curious about the future, recent efforts are much more scientific than they were previously. Industry and government were evidently the first to become seriously involved in forecasting. It may also be stated that the field of education has not been noted for its work in intuitive, exploratory, or normative forecasting. Professionals in physical education (and sport?) undoubtedly have done less in this area than colleagues laboring in related or allied fields. Thus an effort to gain some philosophical perspective on the future of physical education and sport would seem to be most worthwhile, despite the many inherent difficulties in undertaking such a task.

No serious citizen of our North American society could be blamed for being pessimistic about the future, and yet we must be mindful of the adage that most people enjoy those who are optimistic and who laugh at least periodically, whereas people who chronically "cry and sing the blues" never win popularity contests. I have espoused "positive meliorism" as the best approach to life in these highly complex and deeply troubled times. (You may recall that "meliorism" implies that society has an "innate tendency" to improve, and that people should strive consciously to bring about steadily improving societal conditions.)

The meliorism I am recommending is a philosophical stance that is difficult to justify, although each of us should be sufficiently reflective to work out a rational response to those who insist that we must plan, work, and sacrifice for the future. Heilbroner asks the provocative question, "What has posterity ever done for me?" With this query he sets the stage for the declaration that "no argument based on reason will lead me to care for posterity or to lift a finger on its behalf" (1975, p. 14). Fortunately for his, your, and my grandchildren, he subsequently presents the existentially oriented reminder that "it is one thing to appraise matters of life and death by the principles of rational self-interest and quite another *to take responsibility for our choice*" (1975, p. 14). Heilbroner himself does not appear ready to declare a religious commitment to replace the rational argument he finds it impossible to develop, but he is amazed by and respectful of "the furious power of the biogenetic force we see expressed in every living organism" (1975, p. 15). Thus he hopes for the emergence of a "survivalistic ethic" that will help us to develop the commitment necessary to aid people everywhere to make the material sacrifices requisite for posterity's survival.

Of course, there are many who say that survival under *any* conditions might not be worth the price we will be required to pay. I am one of those who is greatly concerned about individual freedoms in this kaleidoscopic world. Freedom is used here to describe the "condition of being able to choose and carry out purposes" (Muller, 1961, p. xiii). It certainly seems logical to provide as much individual freedom as possible in an evolving democratic society. However, many individual freedoms appear to be challenged, and there is evidence of social decline and lowering of morale. Hoffer states, "It is easier to turn free men into slaves than slaves into free men; easier to lose the readiness to work than to acquire it; easier to lose courage than to regain it" (1974, p. 116). Brubacher stressed that individual freedom must be constantly maintained in his analysis "Higher Education and The Pursuit of Excellence." Emphasizing that United States' citizens have inherited a magnificent tradition and national purpose, he stressed that most people seem to take the presence of individual freedom too matter of factly. Writing at a time when the Cold War with Russia was quite "warm," he urged his readers to get "not just fired up, but incandescent about freedom," adding that "freedom can only be won by being constantly rewon" (1971, p. 17). It is obvious that the concept of individual freedom will be put to the test time and again in the years ahead.

Reich's *The Greening of America* (1970), addressed to our present condition, offered Conscious III as a way of approaching societal renewal melioristically; Reich predicted that a type of freedom in life-style might become available relatively soon in American life. Although his devastating description of the United States' innumerable internal and external problems seemed all too accurate, his explanation of the way in which a new consciousness could "save the future for democracy" was regarded by many as far too simplistic. Granting the utopian idealism of his unbounded faith in the rebirth of human values through the efforts of the "new generation," the fact that the large majority of these so-called revolutionaries has become involved in the majority life-style has weakened his case considerably.

Much more realistic and pragmatic as this philosophical position is applied to problem solving is "the real greening of America" as prophesied by John Fischer. Referring to the "ingrained orneriness of human beings," he postulates that the Good Society may be the "impossible dream." However, Fischer—much more modestly than Reich—anticipates that through the efforts of what he calls "social inventors" the possibility of creating the Almost Good Society still exists (1975, p. 2). Stating that he had had no idea of the *enormity* of governmental failure at all levels, Fischer wrote of his invitation to serve on President Lyndon Johnson's National Advisory Commission on Rural Poverty in the mid-1960s. In 1968, when the work of the commission was completed, he was particularly struck by three of the consequences. The first was the great migration of people into the cities, with the result that some 84% of the population was crowded into 212 metropolitan centers. Second, it was agreed that there was a far-reaching loss of confidence in American institutions, with a resultant alienation of a great many people. However, it is the third consequence that Fischer feels holds the greatest hope for the "real greening" of America. The most noteworthy and significant result of the failure of government to serve the people adequately was that "new institutions started to rise on the ground where the old ones had crumbled"; determined, hopeful men and women were working diligently and effectually in a wide variety of ways to bring about social reconstruction (1975, pp. 5-8).

This discussion is designed to place the theme of this essay in *social* perspective as an introductory statement to a *philosophical* perspective on the immediate future of the profession of physical education and sport. In keeping with the objectives of this book, which involved an input-output guiding model, I felt that my "philosophical inputs" could not be limited to an *intuitive* forecasting technique, an *exploratory* forecasting technique, or a *normative* forecasting technique alone. It has been much more appropriate and profitable to employ elements or aspects of all three techniques while at the same time making certain that the "inputs" quite clearly provided information and ideas that pertain directly to the profession's role, body of knowledge, organization, and modes and methods of operation in the last quarter of the twentieth century. Thus I anticipate that the ideas, suggestions, and recommendations of this essay can be used with profit, and I fervently hope that they will not be regarded as utopian in the sense that there is no possibility of moving from our present position to an improved future.

The format for this presentation therefore coincides some of my previous work in philosophical analysis. The approach, after an overview of the past, involves the use of elements of each of the forecasting techniques that are typically employed (i.e., intuitive, exploratory, and normative). Thus the remainder of this essay is an attempt to respond to five quite broadly based questions: (1) Where have we been? (2) Where are we now? (3) Where ought we to be? (4) How are we going to get there? and (5) What should we avoid along the way?

WHERE HAVE WE BEEN?
Views of human nature

At present even the *rate* of change seems to be accelerating, a fact that is obviously the source of much widespread concern. This "future shock" has produced waves of nostalgia as people seek the dubious security of a return to "the good old days." For example, an essay published in *Time* magazine in 1975 tries to determine which were "The Best of Times—1821? 1961? Today?" Fortunately, the answer offered by the essayist, Thomas Griffith, was not definitive in the sense that the reader was urged to actively seek a return to the past. While granting that "the question does involve large-scale subjectivity," Griffith concludes that "the matter with our times is not so much a question of impossibilities but of complexities that can be faced if only public trust and will are restored" (1975, p. 51). This is actually nothing more or less than the stance of positive meliorism.

A variety of historical approaches can be used to answer the question about our past, but it is undoubtedly best to take a general view of the whole and its principal parts. As we examine several historical views of the nature of man, keep in mind the obvious implications of these "images" or definitions of human nature for education and more specifically for physical education and sport.

For years I have been intrigued by educational philosopher Van Cleve Morris' fivefold definition of human beings (1966) which describes us roughly on a historical time scale as follows:

1. *Rational animals.* In this definition of classical Greek thought people were split into body and mind, thereby requiring the educator to offer a balanced curriculum.
2. *Spiritual beings.* Aquinas offered the image of people of three dimen-

sions (mind, body, and soul) and a hierarchy of values in which "animal nature" assumed the lowest position.

3. *Receptacles of knowledge.* People as "knowing creatures" were obligated to absorb as much knowledge as possible in order to improve their lives on earth; inasmuch as the body was thought to develop "naturally," physical education could provide a change of pace for students.

4. *Minds that can be trained by exercise.* This is a redefinition of the platonic-aristotelean concept of people as minds and bodies; here both aspects of the organic unity were to be exercised (with the result that often only "lip service" was given to bodily exercise in a feeble effort to preserve some balance in the curriculum).

5. *Problem-solving organisms.* People are regarded as animals in the process of evolution whose capabilities have come from a developing ability to solve problems whose minds and bodies are simply considered to be "instrumental extensions" of one another. Within such a pattern physical education's task could be to teach people to move efficiently and purposefully (with meaning) within the context of human socialization in an evolving world (Zeigler, 1975a, p. 405).*

In the 1960s, Berelson and Steiner, in their book *Human Behavior* (1964), presented ordered generalizations based on the findings of 1056 selected studies. From the standpoint of the behavioral sciences rather than from Morris' more philosophically oriented definitions, they traced six images of humankind throughout recorded history. The first of these, the *philosophical image* (pp. 662-667), viewed people of the ancient world as distinguishing virtues through the employment of their reason. This was followed by what they called the *Christian image*, in which the concept of original sin and possible redemption through the transfiguring love of God became available to those who controlled their sinful impulses. The third delineation was the *political image* of humankind in the Renaissance, when through the introduction of power and will people managed to take greater control of their social environment, liberating in the process sufficient energy to bring about numerous political changes that resulted in the creation of national ideals that coexisted with somewhat earlier religious ideals. During the eighteenth and nineteenth centuries a fourth image emerged. This *economic image* provided an underlying rationale for eco-

---

*It is interesting to note in passing that Professor Morris has moved steadily to a position that seems to combine both pragmatism *and* existentialism, having added an existential-phenomenological dimension to the "problem-solving organism" just postulated above. For a discussion of this subject, see Morris, 1966.

40

nomic development with regard to the possession of property and things together with improved monetary standards. Efforts were made to equate the concept of "individual good" with that of "common good," while at the same time the third basic political division, class, was more sharply delineated.

The early twentieth century saw the development of a fifth, or *psychoanalytic image*, which introduced another form of love, that of ego and self, as human instinctual impulses were delineated more carefully than ever before. An effort was made to understand the role of childhood experiences in human life and the ways in which unconscious controls often ruled human actions because of the often incomplete gratification of certain human drives related to libido and sex. Finally, because of the rapid development of the behavioral sciences, Berelson and Steiner postulated the *behavioral science image*. This view of humankind characterized people as creatures continually and continuously adapting reality to their own ends. In this way people seek to make life more pleasant and congenial—to the greatest possible extent *their own* reality.

Persistent historical problems in physical education and sport

Although I am interested in the classical, so-called antiquarian approach to historical writing about physical education and sport, I am struck by the insight shown by Professor John S. Brubacher (of Yale and Michigan) in his persistent-problems approach as applied to educational history. Adapting this approach to physical education and sport allowed me to consider the same five social forces used by Brubacher (1966)—the influence of values, politics, nationalism, economics, and religion—but in the process to relate these "influences" to physical education and sport (Zeigler, 1968). Subsequently, I introduced what will undoubtedly be a *sixth* social force or influence—that of ecology (Zeigler, 1975b). Similar treatment has been given to other persistent or perennial problems related more directly to education and in this case to physical education and sport. They are how to regard or employ certain problems that may be identified as "professional concerns," including (1) professional preparation, (2) the curriculum, (3) methods of instruction, (4) the role of administration, (5) the concept of the "healthy body," (6) the use of leisure, (7) physical education and recreation for women, (8) the place of dance in physical education and recreation, (9) amateur, semi-professional, and professional athletics, and (10) the concept of "progress," a topic that is crucial to society, its entire educational system, and physical education and sport (whether as part of educational institutions or simply as a cultural force in the society).

Twentieth-century objectives

Ford Hess (1959) has assessed the United States' objectives regarding physical education in the light of historical events. He identifies what he labels the "health or hygienic objective" as most important between 1900 and 1919. The 1920s were a decade when a "socio-educational objective" became the dominating goal, and the 1930s saw a trend toward increased emphasis on what Hess called a "socio-recreational objective" as most important in physical education. Obviously, in the context of the all-out conflict of World War II, "physical fitness" almost inevitably became the main objective of physical education in the period between 1939 and 1945. Immediately after the war, despite continuing international tension and other wars, there was a deemphasis on physical fitness per se, and the trend seemed to be in the direction of what might be called "total fitness" in the decade from 1950 to 1960.

WHERE ARE WE NOW?

Before we attempt to gain some perspective on the future, it seems basic to make an attempt to understand just where we are at the present time. An effort will be made to achieve this understanding in several different ways while examining current social trends and the status of education within the culture. Then the present situation in physical education and sport will be assessed briefly.

The clash between ecology and economics

Citizens of the United States will quite soon need to decide between continuous-growth and no-growth economic policies. In the eyes of B. G. Murray, an ecologist, it does not appear to be an either-or matter (1972, p. 38). Obviously, the majority of citizens have not the slightest inkling about the need for such a decision; they are not aware that scholars are recommending a no-growth policy. Is this not the land of capitalism and democracy, where a steadily increasing gross national product is one of the best indicators of economic prosperity? One wonders whether this is a case in which the optimists are saying, "Full speed ahead, if we ever hope to reduce poverty in the United States," with the pessimists responding that "population and economic growth must become steady-state by the next century (if that won't be too late)."

Murray examines the concepts of growth, movement of materials, and competition in his comparison of these conflicting models. The ecologists's rule with regard to growth implies that a system will eventually collapse unless it stops growing at some point and *recycles*. Second, Murray is concerned with the biogeochemical cycles operative within nature, "the movement within ecosystems of minerals, water, oxygen, carbon dioxide, and nutrients essential for life" (1972, p. 38). Here the serious difficulty created by people is that both food requirements and the demands of vast technological progress are simply not recycled in such a way as to sustain even a steady-state situation indefinitely. In other words, the "movement of materials" as explained by Murray is all in one direction, i.e., for the temporary service of the earth's populations, which are expanding exponentially!

The other fundamental rule of ecology relates to competition. It is simply that sooner or later competition excludes some of the competing agencies (or species). In practice, this means that if two organisms are competing for an exhaustible resource (and what organism is not in a closed system?), one of the competitors will be dispensed with by its rival "either by being forced out of the ecosystem or by being forced to use some other resource" (1972, p. 64). Thus we must ask how humankind can proceed with a basic contradiction between the economic theory explaining that "competition is supposed to maintain diversity and stability systems," and an opposing theory based on the ecological model just described, which has been tested in both natural and laboratory situations.

Obviously, other notes of gloom and doom could be sounded at this point, but most of us have heard or read so much about local, regional, national, and international problems that we are subconsciously beginning to reject such negative information. In one way the results of this rejection could be highly unfortunate, especially if the grim tidings have not alerted us and created the motivation to act with regard to the deteriorating situation. Once again we are faced with the efficacy of the concept of positive meliorism. Norman Cousins has sounded just the right note with ample volume and clarity, arguing that perhaps "the most important factor in the complex equation of the future is the way the human mind responds to crisis" (1974, pp. 6-7). Citing Toynbee's famous "challenge-and-response" theory, Cousins stresses that it is now up to the world culture, and the individual nations and societies within it, to respond positively, intelligently, and strongly to the challenges besetting us in the last quarter of the twentieth century. He concludes by declaring that "the biggest task of humanity in the next fifty years will be to prove the experts wrong" (1974, p. 7).

The status of education

Shifting our focus from our society in general to education at any or all levels in particular, the reports being received are anything but encouraging. Something seems to have happened to the schools and universities and typically to the learning process that is being encouraged within them. The schools accept bright-eyed youngsters at the age of 6 years (or sooner). These children are almost invariably eager and ready to learn, and then this desire is quite thoroughly blunted within a few short years. The youngsters are indoctrinated into what is called, for lack of a better term, "the modern way." This usually involves excessive drill, speed, competition, dull lectures, tests, quizzes, memorization, final grades, various types of overt and covert discipline, and subsequently the "work hard to get ahead" approach, which should enable them to make money when they emerge from the formal educational system as young adults. This will enable them sooner or later (and usually sooner because of easy credit arrangements) to buy all of the "good" things that presumably characterize "good living." All of this has supposedly helped to produce one of the highest standards of living in the world. The plan seems to be for all to get an education so that they can make more money than otherwise, thereby achieving the presumably high standard and the ability to "keep up" with friends and business associates. Of course, many of the modern conveniences are most satisfying and rewarding because technological advancements have freed both men and women to take advantage of various opportunities to improve the quality of their lives. However, the deficiencies of the educational system—often based on deficient curriculum content and poor teaching methodolgy—point out the overall inadequacy of modern education. All of us have become quite familiar with Toffler's concept of "future shock," but few of us seem prepared to examine in any depth the educational values and norms by which we function daily. Witness the plight of universities on this continent:

> The modern university has never been more necessary and central to our national life than it is today, (yet) we must also say in the next breath that no other major institution in this country is now so open to disbalance and in so precarious a state of health.*

What is being recommended here is that our universities should be more democratic, more concerned with social problems, more alert to students' justified demands, and more critical of their own performance.

Of significance to this discussion is Toffler's prognostication about "education in the future sense" (1970, pp. 353-378). He states that "one of our most critical subsystems—education—is dangerously malfunctioning." "Our schools face backwards toward a dying system, rather than forward to the emerging new society" (1970, pp. 353-354). The people preparing for tomorrow's world, those "who must live in super-industrial societies . . . will

*From Gould, S. B. 1969. Excerpts from 3 lectures by Chancellor of State University on "The Academic Condition," The New York Times, September 23, p. 30.

need new skills in three crucial areas: learning, relating, and choosing" (1970, p. 367).

The status of physical education and sport

As might be expected, the field of physical education and sport has not escaped from the serious malaise that has permeated the very fabric of society and education today. We in this field have one of the most blurred images in the entire educational system. This image probably originated because of the many conflicting educational philosophies in each of the state and provincial educational systems extant on the North American continent. This image with its fuzzy boundaries continues today for essentially the same reason and, of course, because of a considerable amount of individual and collective confusion within the field. To understand the origins of this dilemma, we must therefore look at both our heritage and our present philosophical foundations.

For the first time in the history of the profession, some scholars in the field have become aware of the need to turn to philosophy, sociology, and anthropology as well as to history, as always, for assistance in historical and descriptive analysis. Although such an approach until most recently has been largely oriented toward the Western world, there is a great need to apply the techniques of normative and critical philosophizing to physical education and sport. Such an endeavor is long overdue when we consider our "bewildered public" trying to understand what we mean by a conglomerate term such as health, physical education, recreation, and athletics, not to mention safety education, dance, driver education, physical fitness, movement education, physical activity, exercise studies, human kinetics, leisure studies, kinanthropology, human motor performance, applied life sciences, park administration, and sport, to list some of the commonly encountered terms.

Unfortunately, the field of athletics or sport, seems to be as poorly prepared as any (in the United States as opposed to Canada) in the educational system to help young people prepare for the future. This is largely attributable to overemphasis on such aspects as competition (as opposed to cooperation), winning at any cost, and extreme commercialism. In our pluralistic, highly differentiated society we appear to be so torn by internecine warfare that we would undoubtedly find it almost impossible to even determine where ancient Athens was situated geographically, much less to reach some agreement about the relevance of the Greek ideal to physical education and sport today. Not until very recently, and then only because of federal legislation and serious financial problems, have the men in the profession wanted anything much to do with the women.

Conversely, and for good reason, the women have not been overly impressed with the image of the male physical educator and *coach*. Excesses and poor educational practices abound in interscholastic and intercollegiate athletics, and many physical educators are justifiably upset at the thought of a confrontation with the "athletics establishment" on their campuses. Educational administrators are generally of little or no help in this struggle and conveniently manage to look the other way or to speak platitudes to avoid displeasing the press, the public, alumni, or legislators. When a group of physical education administrators recently was asked about this perennial problem, the blithe and typically naive response was, "Oh, we don't have any problems with athletics on our campus; we are completely *separate* from them!" Is it any wonder that students at all educational levels indicate serious misgivings about both athletics and physical education? They certainly do not look to us for creative educational innovation. Somehow we must provide opportunities for young people to commit themselves to values and people in their sport and physical activities. We should be helping children and young people to actualize themselves much more effectively. The traditional distinction between the concepts of work and play should be combatted. Quite obviously, regular exercise has life-preserving qualities, but through the elimination of artificiality in curriculum content and teaching method the psychological order of learning should assume increasing importance.

WHERE OUGHT WE TO BE?

Until quite recently many people in the United States were wont to say, "We have the highest standard of living in the world." If a Canadian heard that remark, he would be apt to point out that the American had not looked to the north lately. Further, someone else would add that the Scandinavian countries might have surpassed both the United States and Canada. Then along came the wag who remarked, not altogether facetiously, "That's true; the United States has the highest standard of *low* living in the world!"

Obviously, we are immediately thrust into a debate as to what is meant by "high" and "low" and how these criteria are determined. Any attempt to respond to this problem with complete accuracy would be doomed to failure. However, statements such as this should cause all of us to take stock as we conjure up the "spirit and tone" of life on this continent between now and the year 2000. Where ought we to be?

We will need to think very seriously about the character and traits for which Americans and Canadians will educate in the years immediately ahead. Kateb (1965) considers the problem of increased leisure and abun-

46

dance very carefully. He sees no fixed pattern of future perfection such as that often foreseen by others. While engaged in such speculation, he explains that he is entering the realm of philosophical anthropology. Kateb suggests a progression of possibilities or definitions regarding the good life. There are in fact six such views of the good life, as follows: (1) laissez faire, (2) the greatest amount of pleasure, (3) play, (4) craft, (5) political action, and (6) the life of the mind. Kateb's final conclusion, one that could have been predicted from a university scholar, is that the life of the mind offers the greatest potential in the world as we know it—or may know it in the future (1965, pp. 454-473).

Whatever conclusion you may reach regarding the good life or how you will seek to improve the quality of life for yourself, your family, and your students in the future, it should now be apparent that much planning will be needed shortly and that we *must* prepare youth to adapt to change itself, an art that will not be acquired with the same facility that these words are spoken. Many people discuss the future quite readily, but when an attempt is made to get people to do some concentrated and complex planning for the future, the validity of the now-archaic homily that "words are cheap" is evident.

Sport and physical activity within the good life

Admittedly Kateb's recommendations concerning the six possible approaches to the good life each have some merit, but in a democratic nation it should be possible to strive for a very high quality of life through the correct blending of these various possibilities for each individual in such a way as to correspond most closely to the hierarchy of values that individuals determine for themselves. If change and novelty mean that in the final analysis there are no immutable and unchangeable values in the fabric of the universe, it behooves us all to keep open minds to avoid rigidity, stultification, and decay.

Thus the individual in our society should be allowed the greatest amount of freedom consistent with the encroachment on freedom that inevitably occurs within the context of an evolving democracy; this is the degree of laissez faire that can be allotted to any one individual at this time. Second, it should be kept in mind that there are different types of pleasure ranging from the sensual to the more refined and abiding types, and in this regard the "greatest amount of pleasure" will probably result from active and creative participation in the various facets of activity that life has to offer. In addition, the concept of a unified organism implies that human beings have the inherent capacity to explore successfully physical interests as well as social, aesthetic, creative, communicative, and learning interests.

Third, the idea that play represents one approach to the good life is momentarily appealing, but then we are faced with determining what is meant by "play." Some 20 years ago I used the phrase, "Let play be for children, and let recreation be for adults." By that I was implying that recreation was a form of "mature play" in which intelligent adults engaged. Now a more analytical approach to the problem has shown that the term "play" has approximately 70 different meanings and indeed deserves serious analysis because of the confusion created by the many ways in which we use the term. For example, we speak of the "play" of kittens, and we also use the word "play" to describe the contest that takes place each fall between the Chicago Bears and the Detroit Lions. On the one hand, we could say that all of us should seek to preserve some of the spirit of kitten's play in our lives. On the other hand, it becomes immediately apparent that life insurance rates would rise un-believably if we sought to play games with our families and friends in the same spirit evident in professional football games.

Fourth, it was argued by Kateb that "craft" also constituted an approach to the good life. We might assume that craft is "art" or "skill" and also that a person might engage in such a craft as a money-making occupation. Re-maining with the fundamental nature of the definition, it can be argued that craft belongs in each person's life for the life enrichment and satis-faction that it brings.

Fifth, the idea of "political action" has been presented, and this con-cept is perhaps the only one of the six offered by Kateb that bears no relationship to sport and physical activity. However, it seems clear that political action belongs in the life of each citizen in a democratic state. Enlightened, responsible political action is the duty of every mature person in a democracy, and if this is not the case there is every possibility that this type of political organization, as opposed to a monarchy or oli-garchy, will not survive beyond the twentieth century.

The sixth and last approach, and that which Kateb has asserted is the best, was what he termed "the life of the mind." Kateb felt that this ap-proach offered the greatest potential in the world at present and in the future. He concluded with the thought that "the man possessed of the higher faculties in their perfection is the model for utopia and already exists outside it . . ." (1965, p. 472). Once again it appears that such an approach to life, i.e., the pursuit of the so-called life of the mind, should be part and parcel of the life of each person in our society. It is always amusing to witness the attitude taken by many intellectuals in university circles as they go about their daily lives as "disembodied spirits" in pursuit of the "life of the mind." Such reasoning seemingly implies that the findings of psychology and closely related disciplines concerning people as unified organisms were never corroborated. Of course, it is possible to make a good case for the position that the life of the mind in many ways can be improved if such activity takes place within a healthy, physically fit body (to give such a state of well-being its minimum amount of credit).

Therefore men and women in the future should combine all six of the approaches to the good life recommended by Kateb into one all-encompassing approach. Further, I feel that at least five of these six approaches are directly or indirectly related to the role that sport and physical activity can take within a society *generally* as well as *specifically* in the lives of individuals. However, the discussion thus far does not really do full justice to the vital importance of "human movement with purpose in sport, dance, play, and exercise." Learning in the context of the educational experience is usually directed toward mastering various subject areas; it is not designed to encompass *all* of the changes that take place in individuals based on their total life experience. Somehow the "human motor performance" or "movement experience" aspect of education has been slighted. Huxley has designated this as the "education of the non-verbal humanities . . . (the education of the) psycho-physical instrument of an evolving amphibian" (1964, p. 31). If our kinesthetic sense were prepared more efficiently through the educational process, the effects of such experience would inevitably influence subsequent behavior. Thinking (and we do think with our whole body) has generally been characterized as symbolic experience, the assumption being that the formation of habits results from direct experience. An interesting finding, for example, is that thinking is facilitated when there is a general increase in muscle tone. In addition, as thought becomes more concentrated, general muscle tension becomes even greater.

The education of "ecological man"

The field of physical education and sport must become fully aware as soon as possible of the environmental crisis confronting humankind in the last quarter of the twentieth century. The influence of ecology has now become so vital that I have decided to designate it as a sixth "persistent historical problem." Very simply put, we have achieved a certain mastery over the world because of our scientific achievements and subsequent technological advances. Through our mastery of much of the earth's flora and fauna, we are told by Mergen that we are "at the top of the food chain" (1970, p. 36). Because of the exponential (geometric) growth of human populations, increasing "pressures will be placed on our lands to provide shelter, food, recreation, and waste disposal areas. This will cause a greater pollution of the atmosphere, the rivers, the lakes, the land, and the oceans" (Mergen, 1970, p. 36).

Even though the difficulty of moving from a scientific "is" to a philosophical "ought" has been recognized in the realms of science and ethics, there are obviously many scientific findings (now classified as environmental science) that should be made generally available to the public as well as to those enrolled in schools or universities. Simply making the facts available of course, will not guarantee that people will develop strong and positive attitudes on the subject, but education must play a vital role in the development of an ecological awareness. This can take place if sound educational planning occurs at all levels—from early childhood education through tuition-free courses that are now being made available to older citizens by many universities.

Granted that this educational duty should fall to the professional teachers at *all* educational levels who are specialists in *all* of the subject areas taught in the curriculum, our primary concern here is with those who teach or coach in physical education and sport (and possibly in some combined effort with the allied professions). Physical educators and sport coaches quite naturally have a *general* educational responsibility to all class participants, inasmuch as they are directly concerned with people's relationships to themselves and others as well as to other living organisms and also the physical environment and the remainder of the biological environment. But what are the *specific* implications for the physical educator and coach? This person is confronted daily with the fact that for a variety of reasons modern, urbanized, technologically advanced life in North America has created a population with a very low level of *physical* fitness and a resultant decrease in overall *total* fitness. What has developed, therefore, is a ridiculous situation in which people on this continent are to a large extent overfed and poorly exercised, whereas a multitude of people on many other continents on earth are underfed and often quite strenuously exercised. All of this produces a world situation that could spell disaster to us all before we enter the twenty-first century.

The important thing to remember is that the profession of physical education and sport is *uniquely* responsible for the exercise program that will enable each individual "to be a rugged animal fit to withstand the excessive wear and tear that life's informal and formal activities may demand" (Zeigler, 1964, p. 55). In addition, it is this same physical educator who usually becomes involved with the health education courses in which nutritional practices and habits are discussed. These two factors, exercise and nutrition, relate directly to two fundamental aspects of the ecological crisis, pollution and nutrition. Without becoming involved in the moral issue of birth control, physical educators and coaches should do all in their power to curtail pollution. When the air we breathe and the water we drink become increasingly impure, how then can fitness be maintained? All of us are confronted with the problem of helping to feed others, both at home and abroad, and at the same time discovering how to inform and motivate young people to eat correctly so that relatively lean bodies capable of vigorous exercise will result. Regardless of philosophical bent or inclination, these elements must be included in every program of physical education and sport.

Physical education and sport objectives for the future

As physical education professionals look to the future, keeping in mind what would seem to be the field's unique responsibility because of the environmental crisis that is now upon us, what aims and objectives should be stressed? In the past I have concerned myself with the analysis of various philosophical positions and stances, and from these I have subsequently drawn implications for education in general and physical education and sport in particular. Such structural analysis, even when fortified by the results of scientific investigations, has often left the resultant analyses open to the criticism that I had committed the so-called naturalistic fallacy (i.e., deriving an "ought" from an "is"). Nevertheless, there are still philosophers who believe that the most fundamental goal of philosophy is to help us "assimilate the impact of science on human affairs" (Kaplan, 1961, p. 16). Following his concern with whether the individual is to be the "master of the machine," Kaplan states that "the business of philosophy is to provide a system of ideas that will make an integrated whole of our beliefs about the nature of the world and the values we seek in the world in fulfillment of our human nature" (1961, p. 16).

Thus I have seen that the pendulum has swung in one direction just about as far as it is going to go and that there is a definite trend in the direction of employing philosophy to assist people in the determination of life goals. The time is ripe for the promulgation of a set of aims and objectives for physical education and sport that will conform to the pressing needs of the next 25 years.

In the next 25 years it will be absolutely necessary to affirm the priority of people in athletics and physical activity of all types. As the late Arthur Steinhaus stated so well, "Sport was made for man, not man for sport." As important as so-called *physical* fitness is, it will be very important to promote the concept of *total* fitness. Sport and physical education can provide excellent problem-solving experiences to children and young people; hence students should have the opportunity to select a wide variety

51

of useful activities, many of which can help to develop Deweyan social intelligence. The activities that are offered should bring natural impulses into play in physical education. Such classes and intramural sports and physical recreation are more important to the large majority of students than interscholastic or intercollegiate athletics and deserve priority if conflict arises over budgetary allotment, staff availability for instruction and guidance, and use of facilities. However, provided that these needs and interests have been met, full support should be given to team (as well as to individual and dual) experiences at as high a competitive level as possible in keeping with the overall educational aim. Such an aim will be achieved only under the finest type of educational leadership.

In order to create the ideal situation in the future, I am inclined to add certain elements of an *existentialist* philosophy of education, while granting the difficulty of drawing implications from an approach as highly individualistic as existentialism. Here the concept of "universal man" should be highly regarded as an educational aim, and the absolute necessity of the opportunity of individuals to choose for themselves should be kept in mind, just as soon as awakening awareness makes such individual freedom possible. Such choice should be based on knowledge, skills, and attitudes as determined by self-evaluation. Somehow the child who is "authentically eccentric" should be made to "feel at home" in the physical activities program. The young person is playing and taking part in sport and physical activity for actualization of self, hence the great importance of the athlete personally selecting the values that are being sought in the activity. Because the opportunity for creativity is so important, physical skills such as modern dance should have prominence in the program.

I have been impressed further with the *reconstructionistic* tenet that social self-realization in a world culture is fundamental in a world living as dangerously as ours seems to be at present. Such a philosophical stance would concur with the position that there can be no such thing as a fixed or universal curriculum in physical education and sport. Curriculums should be developed through shared planning and should include wholesome physical recreational skills as well as relaxation techniques to combat life's many tensions. Mental hygiene and sex education are also integral aspects of a total program. The importance of self-expression should be recognized, and this does not of necessity conflict with the individualism of an existential orientation; there should be considerable emphasis on democratic methods to aid groups in realizing goals established through consensus.

HOW ARE WE GOING TO GET THERE?

It is not possible to discuss each of the many strategies that have been suggested in an effort to reverse the trends that are bringing about such a rapid deterioration of the quality of life on earth. Theodore Taylor explained recently that most people are ignoring "the possibility for large-scale extension into space of human technology and habitats" (1974, p. 56). Moving in a different direction, the renowned violinist, Yehudi Menuhin, explains his belief that art "inherently" holds great hope for humanity (1974, pp. 82-83). Or we might consider Jean Houston's recent offer to "put the first man on earth" through what she calls a "psychenaut" program, which:

> would be an exploration of inner space. It would map the mind and tap its unrealized capacities. It would acquaint the psychenauts with the phenomenal contents of their own beings—their mind-body systems—and teach them to employ and to enjoy the multiplicity of human qualities that seem almost unattainable on first encounter. Through intensive training, psychenauts would have new control over their creative energies, their health, their experience of time and space, heat and cold, pain and pleasure.*

Let us now return to the primary task, that of recommending certain steps that must be taken if we hope to develop the type of physical education and sport experience just described. This will undoubtedly be a most difficult task because the profession of physical education is definitely suffering from what Walter Kaufmann has recently identified as "Decidophobia," or the fear of making autonomous decisions without the aid of "crutches" such as religions, political ideologies, philosophical positions, microscopic deviational maneuvers, and other "band-aids of life" (1973, pp. 1-35). The question is how the field can bring itself to display "accountability," "relevance," and "involvement" so that it will not be out of step with the younger generation. If it is reasonable to assume that this can be done—and our social scientists should help us now to determine what the prevailing opinions and attitudes are—it would then be incumbent on our professional associations to cooperate in directing their efforts toward this goal. The tasks are (1) defining the issues, (2) placing them in some order of prioriy, and (3) taking professional action to bring the field to the point where it is "in step" with the changing times.

The ten "stances" that have got to go!

Stance No. 1: the shotgun approach to professional preparation. The profession has had difficulty in projecting a clear and unified image of itself. Does the profession seek to perpetuate the idea that physical education includes health, physical education, recreation, and athletics, not to mention safety education, driver education, dance, physical fitness, movement education, and park administration? Or can we agree that our task in formal and informal education is to teach people to move efficiently and with pur-

*From Houston, J. 1975. Putting the first man on earth, *Saturday Review*, February 22, pp. 28-29.

pose in sport, dance, exercise, and expressive activities within the context of human interaction (Zeigler, 1973, pp. 48-49).

Stance No. 2: the athletics über alles approach in education. The perennial struggle between physical education–oriented and athletics–oriented people in both public and private educational systems is continuing unabated with a great many people condemning excesses that appear almost daily in programs for children and young men especially. Now women are demanding their "rights," and we are beginning to witness excesses there, too. Simply divorcing physical education from athletics to the greatest possible extent does not appear to be the answer. Are most of us going to allow poor educational practices in competitive sport to multiply almost unchallenged because materialistic influences and general inertia seem almost insuperable? Does the profession dare to speak out on this problem in a statesmanlike, forcible manner, or are our tenured (continuing contract) positions really not impregnable?

Stance No. 3: the women are all right in their place approach. Ever since Mabel Lee served as the first woman president of the American Association of Health, Physical Education, and Recreation (AAHPER) in 1931 and 1932 there has been no apparent need for a women's lib movement within the ranks of AAHPER. This condition of "equal opportunity" has been present at the district and state levels within AAHPER as well, even though its operation on an arbitrary basis often leaves something to be desired where the "spontaneity" of elections is concerned. Yet the United States Department of Health, Education, and Welfare (HEW) has gathered ample evidence that professional women in universities, for example, have often been paid and promoted as though they were second-class citizens. From another standpoint, many women in physical education at the university level are fearful of the enforced amalgamations of men's and women's departments in which they are outnumbered by men, or in which the top administrative officer would probably be a man. Physical education at all educational levels is undoubtedly weaker where men's and women's units are separate. Furthermore, *separate* national associations at the university level simply perpetuate this problem.

Stance No. 4: the body-of-knowledge approach and its implications. For some reason that has not yet been explained, there seems to be a battle between those who feel that the field's mission is to prepare physical education teachers and sport coaches primarily for the secondary level and those who are saying "How can we have a true profession (discipline?) unless we prepare scholars and researchers in sufficient quantity to give us a body of knowledge on which to base our efforts?" This conflict produces those who appear to choke on the term "physical education" and go about promoting the concept of, say, "human kinetics" at the university level, while disavowing responsibility for what takes place under the name of "physical education" in the schools. I do not feel that an either-or decision must be made on this issue; as a matter of fact, both approaches are needed, but some members of the profession cannot help but feel that they are being challenged by the newer "disciplinary approach." This has often resulted in an overt downgrading of the concept of scholarship in various ways and a concerted effort to keep undergraduates from being "defiled" by scholarly effort. Conversely, it has often resulted in a "let's keep up with the Joneses" attitude because many departments and schools of physical education have been attempting to implement Ph.D. programs without adequate staffs, facilities, and equipment. One real need, however, is vastly improved doctor of education (Ed.D.) programs in which people are taught how to be better teachers, administrators, and coaches.

Stance No. 5: the password is "treadmill" approach. As if there were not enough problems, we are now faced with a struggle in many universities between faculty members teaching and researching in the bioscience aspects of physical education and sport (primarily in exercise physiology or "exercise science") and faculty members attempting to form undergraduate and graduate options (or streams) in the humanities and social science aspects. Of course, this is not the first time in education in which "haves" have become worried about "have-nots" wanting to get some support for their work. Even though scholars in the humanities and social sciences have traditionally received far less financial support than their colleagues in the natural sciences, the present decline in financial support to universities may make this problem more acute. Physical education and sport, a field that is largely concerned with nonverbal arts and sciences, seems to have unique possibilities in many directions. For this reason it is very shortsighted for those in fairly well-established research units to seek to thwart even limited development in the humanities and social science aspects of the field. In the final analysis, such efforts could well be self-defeating and could lower the overall status of physical education and sport in the educational hierarchy.

Stance No. 6: the name that was good enough for my father approach. The late, great C. H. McCloy of the State University of Iowa once said that the name "physical education" was so firmly established that to change it would be about as difficult as rolling back Niagara Falls. However, there has been a recent attempt to change the term "physical education," and now there seems to be a concerted effort on the part of at least two segments of the profession to discard the term presently in use. I have no particular vested interest in preserving the present term, and in fact for a number of years I have recommended the term "physical education and sport" as adequate while the profession makes up its collective mind. It does seem unwise for institutions to rush ahead with a wide variety of terms denoting either disciplinary approach, a professional approach, or some combination of both until national professional associations are fully prepared to take a firm stand on the matter. For example, a title such as "applied life studies" doesn't really offer an adequate definition of function.

Stance No. 7: the let Joe and Mary do it approach. The tendency to prefer or assume that someone else will take responsibility is a difficulty typically faced in a democratic society in which it is so necessary to involve a large proportion of responsible citizens to bring about desired political change. If more citizens do not become more actively involved, many of the world's democratic states might well revert to some form of oligarchy or dictatorship. It seems to be equally as difficult to involve so-called *professional* physical educators and coaches actively in the development of their professional associations to higher levels of achievement. The typical attitude seems to be "let Joe and Mary do it," and this attitude is doubly damaging to the profession because of the uphill struggle in which physical education has been engaged because of the perennially lower status of physical activity and sport in the hierarchy of educational values. There are so many fundamental changes needed that it will take true missionary zeal to correct the present deficiencies. One example of a needed change is the prevailing lack of emphasis on physical education and sport at the elementary school level. Everyone knows that programs should be greatly improved, but how many professionals are actively doing anything to achieve the improvement?

Stance No. 8: the Mickey and Minnie Mouse curriculum approach. For decades physical education undergraduate and graduate programs have been the targets of innumerable criticisms because of their presumed lack of intellectual content. It has usually not been difficult to gain admittance to our programs and not much more difficult to complete them with reasonable success. The reasons for this are well known, but the time has long since passed for some steps to rectify the problem. The resolution of this problem is not simple, but it must be worked on sincerely and resolutely. First, all undergraduates must have an improved level of general education in the humanities and the social and natural sciences. Second, there should be a "disciplinary core" developed as an "irreducible minimum" of course experiences for all, and this should be carefully balanced from the standpoint of the humanities and social science aspects and the bioscience aspects of the body of knowledge. Third, there should be an opportunity for options (or streaming) in the upper undergraduate years, to allow students to specialize either in (1) a disciplinary approach that could eventually lead to work as a scholar or researcher, (2) a teacher-coach approach to physical education and sport, or (3) a human motor performance approach with emphasis on the theory and practice of sport or dance. Last, it is necessary to improve the approach for acquiring the needed knowledge, competencies, and skills required of a *professional educator* functioning in the field of physical education and sport.

Stance No. 9: the I must have my pound of flesh approach. For far too long the field of physical education, perhaps as a defense mechanism, has insisted on a physical education requirement at all educational levels. Further, such a requirement has all too often been characterized *either* by some sort of an "essentialist" physical fitness routine *or* a program in sports skill instruction that was inadequate and that failed to motivate young people to want to continue with such activity in later life.

I do not recommend complete elimination of the physical education requirement, but I do suggest (1) better programs introduced at the elementary school level, (2) evaluative techniques used on a regular basis (including adequate self-evaluation devices), and (3) broadening the scope of the program to include knowledge, skills, and competencies in motor performance, movement fundamentals (including body mechanics analysis), aquatics proficiency (including lifesaving), combatives proficiency with emphasis on self-defense, folk, square, ballroom, and modern dance, and sports skill proficiency, primarily in indoor and outdoor physical recreational activity. If the curriculum included such a group of activities and was well taught, it would not be difficult to *require* involvement of the young person *until* a minimum level of proficiency was achieved in each category. Once a minimum level of proficiency is reached in any area, a person should not be forced to continue to participate, and most certainly the program should be elective after the tenth grade.

Stance No. 10: the I'm not really academically respectable approach. Most people in the field have suffered from a built-in inferiority complex for many years. In many instances it has been warranted. The point is that this attitude is not warranted because of the subject matter but rather because of the inadequate body of knowledge on which teaching was typically based, the inadequate teaching methodology being employed, and the low level of professional dedication and zeal demonstrated by the typical physical educator or coach in providing a high level of instruction. Teachers and coaches should *never* worry about the so-called academic respectability of their subject area. The teaching of human motor performance with purpose through such activities as sport, dance, exercise, and play is vitally important now, and its status should not diminish in the foreseeable future.

WHAT SHOULD WE AVOID ALONG THE WAY?

The question of what to avoid on the way to the year 2000 also deserves consideration. It will of course be absolutely necessary to maintain a certain flexibility in philosophical approach. All of us can know people for whom Toffler's concept of "future shock" has become a reality. Life has become so stressful for these individuals that future prospects seem dim and life at present seems almost out of control.

Closely related to the maintenance of flexibility in approach is the assumption of a philosophical stance that I described earlier as positive meliorism, a position that assumes that we should strive consciously to bring about a steady improvement in the quality of our lives. Thus I recommend that we *avoid* what might be called "naive optimism" or "despairing pessimism" in the years ahead. Obviously, there will be many occasions on which it will be quite simple to fall into such an "attractive trap."

Third, the professional in physical education and sport should continue to work for "just the right amount" of freedom in his life generally and in his professional affairs specifically. As pointed out earlier, freedom for the individual is a fundamental characteristic of a democratic state, and it must be remembered that such freedom as may prevail in certain countries today had to be won "inch by inch." There are always those in our midst who seem anxious to take freedoms away, and this is true whether crises exist or not. The concept of individual freedom cannot be stretched to include anarchy; however, the freedom to *teach* what we will in physical education and sport, or conversely the freedom to *learn* what one will in such a process, must be guarded almost fanatically. The rule of the majority must prevail in a democratic society if such a social system and culture is to survive in today's highly competitive world. Therefore we should do all in our power to avoid "tyranny of the majority" in aspects of life where privacy and individual freedom of choice are at stake.

A fourth pitfall in this matter of avoidance along the way is the undue influence of certain negative aspects inherent in the various social forces capable of influencing our society and everything within it. A few examples of these negative aspects should suffice. Consider the phenomenon of nationalism and how an overemphasis in this direction can soon destroy a desirable world posture or even bring about unconscionable isolationism. Another example of a "negative" social force could be the obvious clash between certain economic theories, capitalism, advancing technology, and materialism *and* the environmental crisis that has developed.

Moving back to the realm of education, John Brubacher has inquired why educational practice stands "in such sharp contrast to the ideals which we have inherited from the past" (1961, pp. 7-9). Brubacher stresses that we should avoid "the notion that one can 'get by' without excelling." He explains that we should avoid what has consistently been identified as "a basic anti-intellectualism in American life," and yet he sees that the "cultivation of intelligence (as) an end in itself" is not the answer, either (1961, pp. 7-9). Brubacher seems to be asking for the "golden mean" between the cultivation of the intellect and the cultivation of a high degree of intelligence because it is needed as "an instrument of survival" in the Deweyan sense.

Lastly, while seeking to explain academic apathy, I recommend that teachers avoid imposing a narrow academic approach on students in an effort to promote the pursuit of excellence. In concluding this series of suggestions as to "what to avoid," I want to make several additional recommendations. Over a period of years I have seen decisions concerning admission to undergraduate physical education programs made almost solely on the basis of a narrowly defined academic proficiency, which is evaluated typically on the basis of numerical grades and standardized intelligence test scores. There is nothing so terribly wrong about the use of these tests, but the crux of the problem is that there is so much more to the selection of people who will function as teachers and coaches, scholars and researchers, teachers of teachers, or specialists in the theory and practice of human motor performance in some phase of sport, dance, play, or exercise. Thus, I suggest that we cease to rely so heavily on narrow intelligence and/or achievement test scores and that we reconstitute examinations and develop testing batteries to measure other dimensions of excellence such as "sensitivity and commitment to social responsibility; ability to adapt to new situations; characteristics of temperament and work habit under varying conditions of demand," and other such characteristics and traits such as those recommended in 1970 by the Commission on Tests of the College Entrance Examination Board (*The New York Times,* Nov. 2, 1970).

Finally, let us avoid a narrow outlook in the years ahead. The rate of change will probably increase steadily, and there will be a greater number of life-styles from which people can choose. Thus we will need to be ready to confer with others in a continuing search for common denominators and consensus regarding a recommended curriculum in physical education and sport. At the moment it appears that there is agreement on the following:

1. *Regular* physical education periods should be *required* for all school children through grade ten.

2. It is vitally important for a child to develop positive attitudes toward his own health in particular and toward community hygiene in general.

3. Leisure should be put to good use, and physical educators and

coaches should do all in their power to help young people to develop physical recreational skills for use in later life.

4. Physical vigor is extremely important for citizens of all ages for a number of vital reasons. However, there is no general agreement as to what physical fitness really is. There are national norms but no national standards.

5. Boys and girls should have experience in competitive sport at some stage of their development. However, this statement needs both clarification and qualification before it can be truly meaningful.

6. Programs should be made available for children and young people who need therapeutic exercise for remediable physical defects. However, there is evidently no general agreement as to who should be responsible for such programs or how, when, and where they should be conducted.

7. Character and personality development are highly important. There is a general belief that physical education and sport can contribute to the development of certain fine attributes under sound educational leadership. To date we do not seem to be able to evaluate such development. Further, we are not certain about those attributes that we seek to develop.

CONCLUDING STATEMENT

In this essay I have tried to provide some philosophical perspective on the future of physical education and sport as a profession as we move toward the year 2000. Progress is never a straight-line affair, and we can only hope that the curve will be upward in achieving the general aims and specific objectives outlined by the profession. Even the concept of progress is relative, and its definition depends on whether goals and values are stable or evolving according to the nature of the world in which we live. By now it is obvious that the influence of environmental issues will be very great in the years immediately ahead, unless we decide, consciously or unconsciously, to ignore the warning signals that are flashing about us from so many directions. Planet Earth, whether we like it or not, has now become a "global village," and we must improve communication and cooperation with peoples of all lands. We are our brothers' and sisters' keepers, and to ignore this duty is to court doomsday for us all.

The profession of physical education and sport, through its steadily growing body of knowledge about human motor performance with meaning in sport, dance, play, and exercise, can play a vital part in the formal educational system and in lifelong education and recreation as we move inevitably toward the twenty-first century. We have no choice; we must dedicate ourselves to a philosophical stance of positive meliorism so that the field's potential role may be fulfilled.

REFERENCES

Berelson, B., and Steiner, G. A. 1964. Human behavior: an inventory of scientific findings, New York, Harcourt, Brace & World, Inc.

Brubacher, J. S. 1961. Higher education and the pursuit of excellence, Marshall University Bulletin 3:3.

Brubacher, J. S. 1966. A history of the problems of education, New York, McGraw-Hill Book Co.

Cousins, N. 1974. Prophecy and pessimism, Saturday Review/World, August 24, p. 6.

Fischer, J. 1975. Vital signs, U.S.A., New York, Harper & Row, Publishers.

Gould, S. B. 1969. Excerpts from 3 lectures by Chancellor of State University on "The Academic Condition," The New York Times, September 23, p. 30.

Griffith, T. 1975. The best of times—1821? 1961? today? Time, September 1, p. 50.

Heilbroner, R. L. 1975. What has posterity ever done for me? The New York Times Magazine, January 19, p. 14.

Hess, F. A. 1959. American objectives of physical education from 1900-1957 assessed in the light of certain historical events, Ed.D. dissertation, New York University.

Hoffer, E. 1974. What we have lost, The New York Times Magazine, October 20, p. 108.

Houston, J. 1975. Putting the first man on earth, Saturday Review, February 22, p. 28.

Huxley, A. 1964. Tomorrow and tomorrow and tomorrow, New York, The New American Library of World Literature, Inc.

Kaplan, A. 1961. The new world of philosophy, New York, Random House, Inc.

Kaufman, W. 1973. Without guilt or justice, New York, Peter H. Wyden, Inc., Publisher.

Kateb, G. 1965. Utopia and the good life, Daedalus 94:454.

Mergen, F. 1970. Man and his environment, Yale Alumni Magazine 33:36.

Menuhin, Y. 1974. Art as hope for humanity, Saturday Review/World, December 14, p. 82.

Morris, V. C. 1956. Physical education and the philosophy of education, JOHPER 27:21.

Morris, V. C. 1966. Existentialism in education: what it means, New York, Harper & Row, Publishers.

Muller, H. J. 1961. Freedom in the ancient world, New York, Harper & Row, Publishers.

Murray, B. G., Jr. 1972. What the ecologists can teach the economists, The New York Times Magazine, December 10, p. 38.

The New York Times. 1970. Article on "College Board Reform" describing a report by the Commission on Tests of the College Entrance Examination Board, November 2, p. 33.

Reich, C. A. 1970. The greening of America, New York, Random House, Inc.

Taylor, T. 1974. Strategies for the future, Saturday Review/World, December 14, p. 56.

Toffler, A. 1970. Future shock, New York, Random House, Inc.

Zeigler, E. F. 1964. Philosophical foundations for physical health, and recreation education, Engelwood Cliffs, N.J., Prentice-Hall, Inc.

Zeigler, E. F. 1968. Problems in the history and philosophy of physical education and sport, Englewood Cliffs, N.J., Prentice-Hall, Inc.

Zeigler, E. F. 1973. Physical education has decidophobia: five "stances" that "have got to go!" JOHPER 44:48.

Zeigler, E. F. 1975a. Personalizing physical education and sport philosophy, Champaign, Ill., Stipes Publishing Co.

Zeigler, E. F. 1975b. The education of "ecological man": implications for sport and physical education, Paper presented before the Canadian Association of Sport Science, Ottawa, Ontario, October 3.

CHAPTER THREE

PSYCHOSOCIAL FORECASTS

By applying the Weberian thesis on the effects of "rationalization," Hal A. Lawson argues convincingly that the sociohistorical trend toward "instrumental rationality" has produced certain inversions of means and ends within the institutions of physical education and sport, with the result that they are becoming substantively irrational in contemporary society. Lawson offers both theoretical and factual support for his position and makes several insightful forecasts by assuming the likely continuation of these trends into the future. Turning to normative forecasting, Lawson describes a more acceptable alternative for the future of physical education and sport and introduces a promising planning model that might allow for its realization.

In the second essay on psychosocial forecasts, Carole A. Oglesby foresees the possibility of an alternative future marked by a transformed, self-confident, inner-directed profession that has moved beyond the self-conscious, other-directed mode of today. Her description of this alternative future in which stereotyping based on age, sex, and locale and other dichotomies are replaced by a more holistic image of man and profession lends substance to her forecast. Oglesby follows a normative forecasting model and identifies the steps or stages the profession must traverse to realize this forecasted future.

From futures forecasting to futures creation: a planning model for physical education and sport

Hal A. Lawson

As a policy analyst and program planner in physical education, I want to explore some psychosocial aspects of current and future programs.* Initially I outline some basic assumptions for the purpose of alerting you to

*When futures forecasting and futures creation are combined in the same investigation as I will combine them in this chapter, the thrust is clearly that of policy analysis and program planning rather than that of basic research (MacRae, 1975; Iceton, 1974; Holt and Turner, 1974).

my metatheoretical presuppositions. Next I will assess past and present reality in the context of physical education and sport and then employ normative forecasting to depict more favorable alternatives for physical education and sport. Finally, I will discuss the task of moving from ideal to real, i.e., from forecasting the future to its creation. In this context I will elaborate on a planning model that links futures forecasting to futures creation and that can be employed in policy analysis and program planning in physical education.

ASSUMPTIONS

The first responsibility of a writer engaged in futuristics is identification of the fundamental assumptions that collectively form the basis for his analysis. In the interest of brevity I offer the following assumptions in condensed form.

1. In the tradition of humanism, I accept an anthropocentric view of the individual in the historical process. The individual can and does possess the capacity to act purposefully and rationally. Self-directed behavior on the part of the individual coincides with the motivation that produced the behavior. Thus "active" individuals are in a position to direct and control their own acts (Etzioni, 1968, pp. 22-23).

2. Consequently, changes that occur in a society can be attributed to its members. The relationship between the individual and society should be complementary; i.e., the two should act and interact to form a dynamic social network. This interaction should result in the twin products of individual self-development and societal progress. Nevertheless, I grant that at present modern American institutions have become somewhat reified and that the "active" capacity of the individual has been retarded. The restoration of the proper balance between and among people, their machines, their vast amount of information, their institutions, and their society is presented here as the major challenge of the final part of the twentieth century (Ellul, 1964; Weiner, 1967; Marcuse, 1964).

3. Social knowledge that can be gained from the study of social reality is not without use in confronting contemporary problems. Such knowledge, however, is subject to limited utility in problem solving. Knowledge gained from the study of past-present reality remains rooted in that specific time frame. This knowledge is often situation specific, and it lacks normative judgments about that which ought to be (as opposed to past-present knowledge, which deals with that which *is* or *has been* the case). Questions of "what ought to be in the future" reflect values of individuals and groups. Ideally, decision making should be predicated on an admixture of social knowledge and the conflicting values of individuals (Vickers, 1965; Habermas, 1970).

4. Social institutions such as sport and education (of which physical education is one facet), in concert with the other institutions in a society, are instrumental in the dissemination and maintenance of a single *Weltanschauung* (or ideational world view). This interconnected world view constitutes perhaps the most important factor in molding the very character of a society, in that the dominant *Weltanschauung* constitutes a powerful and effective mechanism for social control. In order for change to occur, therefore, social knowledge and normative human judgments must be brought to bear on the previously dominant world view to reveal its inapplicability and shortcomings. Only then will there be any concerted agreement that change is in order. Next, both knowledge and human values must be melded to form a new ideational network. As J. K. Galbraith (1973) has observed, the emancipation of belief is the precursor of any meaningful and permanent alteration in either society or its institutions (Salamini, 1974; Sallach, 1973).

5. Because of the interplay between knowledge and personal values, critiques of the existing state of affairs in physical education and sport and subsequently the alternatives presented are rarely value neutral (or "value free"). At the same time, it should be emphasized that the revisionist perspective does not include nor does it assume the immediate demise or overthrow of the existing order. Criticism is extended and alternatives are offered to improve that which already exists or that which could exist. Institutions and their programs are malleable; they demand constant monitoring, adjustment, and even replacement in a society that is characterized by change. In essence, freedom itself is predicated on human reasoning. Reasoning in turn presupposes a knowledge of alternatives among which choices are made. This critique and its alternatives are directed toward this ideal.

6. Whereas in the past both individuals and organizations have eschewed dissonances or conflicts, today it is known that individual and collective welfare can be enhanced in the presence of unsettling elements. As one examines studies of individual learning (Festinger, 1957) and studies of intra- and intergroup relations (Lewin, 1947; Coser, 1956), the positive functions of intraindividual and social conflict become apparent. Clearly, the analyses that create dissonance perform a vital function, and professional groups such as physical educators, rather than becoming defensive (Janis, 1971), should embark on a course in which conflict may be profitably utilized.

FUTURES FORECASTING BY EXTRAPOLATION

One of the more logical ways of initiating an analysis devoted both to forecasting the future and to the creation of alternative delivery systems is to inspect the status quo in physical education and sport.* Such an inspection should provide clues to answering at least two important questions: (1) What social processes were instrumental in shaping the form and functions of current programs? (2) What are the immediate and long-term consequences of these programs? The result of this kind of probing might provide the basis for a form of exploratory forecasting, i.e., an extrapolation from current trends. For example, we can gain insights regarding the extent to which the outcomes of these programs are consistent with the ideals we hope to attain. Where dissonance between actual and ideal outcomes can be identified, modifications might be suggested (e.g., new and specific guidelines for professional role performance, a reorganization of the body of knowledge, transformation of the mode of organization and methods of operation, or a reevaluation of the very ideals of the profession) that would facilitate dissonance reduction.

Rationality and the process of rationalization: the characteristic trends of modern American life†

In recent years, social scientists have devoted considerable attention to the study of the insightful and possibly prophetic works of Max Weber. While a detailed examination of Weber's ideas lies outside the scope of this paper,‡ the application of Weberian ideas to an analysis of physical education, sport, and implicitly to other American institutions requires that certain key Weberian concepts be understood. These are rationality and the process of rationalization in addition to the manifest and latent consequences of rationality and rationalization that Weber outlines.

In order to understand Weber's use of the concept of rationality we must turn to his typology of social action. Weber suggested four ideal typical forms of social action: (1) traditional, (2) affective, (3) value rational, and (4) instrumentally rational. Traditional action is determined by custom and habitual beliefs. Since such action is almost second nature, it is analogous to a conditioned reflex that is elicited by a routinized set of conditions or circumstances (Aron, 1970, p. 211). That is, custom and not reasoned judgment exercised in relation to alternative actions determines the individual's action.

---

*Polak (1973) has asserted that any study of the future must begin with a critique of past-present action. In an earlier exploratory paper I provided a critique of past-present programs (Lawson, 1974). My initial attempt, however, lacked the theoretical unity that I hope to provide here.
†I wish to acknowledge my indebtedness to a colleague, A. G. Ingham, for his assistance in preparing this section of the paper, both by clarifying further for me aspects of Max Weber's work and by offering editorial suggestions.
‡For detailed information on Weber's work, see Weber, 1958, 1963, 1968a,b; Wrong, 1970; Coser, 1971.

The second type of social action, affective social action, is an emotional response to a given set of circumstances. It is not governed by specific goals or values but rather is unpredictable in many instances (e.g., a football player punches an opponent after perceiving a provocation).

For Weber, rationality involved the ordering, arranging, and even the choice of goals in relation to a system of higher meanings (Swidler, 1973, p. 36). Furthermore, Weber distinguished rationality in form (formal rationality) from rationality in substance (substantive rationality). Insofar as action is expressed in numerical, calculable terms and is goal oriented, it is formally rational. Yet the substantive rationality of the action can be judged apart from its form. The major criterion utilized in determining substantive rationality is the extent to which the individual is served, i.e., the extent to which personal and social well-being are enhanced by the action. Weber's final two ideal types of social action emerge from the conception of rationality.

Value rationality *(Wertrational)* is rational action in relation to the pursuit of a value. As Aron notes, the actor acts rationally not to achieve the extrinsic result but rather, for example, to "remain faithful to his own idea of honor" (1970, p. 221). Value rationality, then, is characterized by an alternative weighing of the means by which the actor hopes to achieve the prized value. The value itself, however, is not subject to alteration. In fact, total devotion to the attainment of the value, often in the face of deleterious consequences to the individual, may render the effects of value rationality substantively irrational. An example of value rationality is provided by the classical framework for the *agon* (Morford and Clark, in press).

Instrumental rationality *(Zweckrational)*, the fourth type of social action, involves an alternative weighing of both the means for goal attainment *and* the goals themselves. Unlike the unwavering adherence to a value or standard that characterizes value rationality, instrumental rationality is both calculated and conditional. Athletes who consistently readjust both performance goals and their training regimens for goal attainment exemplify instrumental rationality.[*]

Weber studied such diverse areas as religion, law, economics, politics, and music. In each of these spheres he found evidence of the decline of affective, traditional, and value-rational action in favor of instrumentally rational action. Weber labeled this overriding trend in all aspects of society "rationalization":

> By rationalization Weber meant the process by which explicit, abstract, intellectually calculable rules and procedures are increasingly substituted for senti-

---

[*]Rational-purposive (or purposive-rational) action is often substituted in the literature for the term "instrumental rationality" (Marcuse, 1964).

ment, tradition, and rule of thumb in all spheres of activity. Rationalization leads to the displacement of religion by specialized science as the major source of intellectual authority; the substitution of the trained expert for the cultivated man of letters; the ousting of the skilled handworker by machine technology; the replacement of traditional judicial wisdom by abstract, systematic statutory codes. Rationalization demystifies and instrumentalizes life. It means that . . . there are no mysterious incalculable forces that come into play, but rather than one can, in principle, master all things by calculation. This means that the world is disenchanted. Rationalization creates a utilitarian world dominated by what Paul Tillich called "the dance of ends and means."[*]

Rationalization, then, is a process that is ubiquitous. As Cotgrove summarizes the process of rationalization, it is a process of systematizing, routinizing, and formalizing (by means of rules) the spheres of life that were governed formerly by affect, tradition, and value (1975, p. 59).

How do the concepts of rationality and rationalization apply to physical education and sport? In a pioneering effort, Ingham (1975) addressed himself to this question in his analysis of professional sport. He noted that sport, once relatively unstructured and with both folk and elite origins, became institutionalized. Institutionalization led in turn to the regulation, formalization, legitimation, and transmissibility of sport (1975, p. 337), i.e., to its increasing rationalization. Specialization on the part of athletes and the increasing number of specialists who have attempted to regulate and control sport have not only reflected but are also responsible for its increasing rationalization. Rather than relying on practices dictated by tradition, affect, and value, athletes instead became increasingly dependent on experts (e.g., coaches, exercise physiologists, biomechanicians) who specialized in applying their technologies to the goal of improving athletic performance. Thus sport became instrumentally rational to a greater degree than ever before at the expense of traditional, affective, and value-rational action (Ingham, 1975; Morford and Clark, in press).

Instrumental rationality was fueled by and at the same time contributed to changing ideational and material conditions of urban industrial life. What Tillich called "the dance of means and ends" became reflected in the ever-increasing tendency to translate qualitative goals and the means of their attainment into quantitative formulations. As Wrong observed, the "cultivated man of letters" or the generalist was everywhere being replaced by specialists who, by virtue of their training, were best qualified to offer judgments regarding the efficiency and effectiveness of proposed means-ends schema. In the name of efficiency, initial specialization led to further subspecialization in all areas of life, including sport and physical education. As a result, we are "condemned to realize only a share of what

[*]From Wrong, D., editor. 1970. Max Weber, Englewood Cliffs, N.J., Prentice-Hall, Inc., p. 26.

[we] might be, doomed to perform all our lives in a limited function whose prime merit and nobility lies in the acceptance of these very limitations" (Aron, 1970, pp. 293-294).

The domination of specialists in all aspects of life produces ultimately new modes of social organization. Clearly, specialists by definition tend to be expropriated from the means of production; they are allocated a specific task to perform, a task that is only one part of the total product. Thus the productive process in order to be effective must be coordinated and supervised. Bureaucracies emerged in part as a response to this requirement. Organized and maintained by rational principles, a bureaucracy was the ideal instrument for both coordination and supervision of tasks performed by specialists.

By its very presence, then, bureaucratic organization not only represents but also facilitates the substitution of specialists for generalists and dilettantes. Among its advantages are its requirements for role occupancy. Expertise rather than nepotism or patronage is the criterion for selection and advancement. Bureaucracy in this light can be viewed as an agent of democratization. Moreover, as an instrument (means) for achieving quantified performance goals, bureaucracy is an unequaled mode of social organization.

The dangers of bureaucracy emerge in contexts in which a bureaucracy becomes both a means for goal attainment and a goal in itself. That is, bureaucracies can and often do escape human controls because of the very specialization that made them necessary. Judgments in every sector of society come to be made by experts. Themselves caught up in bureaucracy, experts are not in a position to search for or indeed consider the "total picture." Equally problematic is the technical nature of expert information, which further shields experts from the public (Habermas, 1970). Thus while the bureaucratic organization of specialists in all sectors of society has brought with it a rational mechanism for the achievement of goals, it simultaneously has eroded the capacities of individuals in urban industrial societies to reassess and redirect the purposes or goals that bureaucracy should serve. Instead, means such as bureaucracy, i.e., "technique" (Ellul, 1964), are pursued for their own sake. Once means to an end, they become ends in themselves.

This "paradoxical inversion" of ends and means, attributable to rationalization and bureaucratization (Loewith, 1970, p. 114), culminates in institutions reacting back on the individuals for and by whom they were created (Berger and Luckmann, 1967). In sport (and in other institutions) individuals are socialized to accept as a part of their consciousness this portion of the objectivated world—*its* meanings are made *their* meanings, *its* rules become *their* rules. In brief, predefined expectations become the basis for individual actions (Ingham and Loy, 1973). These institutional purposes are taken for granted, thereby allowing technique to become the dominant concern. Although they remain formally rational structures, in their effects on people they are no longer *substantively* rational. As Weber observed, institutions become in fact substantively *irrational* by virtue of their actions on individuals, encapsulating them in an "iron cage." Among the results are "specialists without spirit, sensualists without heart," who nevertheless see their own and society's condition as "progress" (Weber, 1963, p. 182).

Extensions of instrumental rationality and rationalization to physical education and sport: international sport and school physical education programs

Ingham's treatment (1975) of the rationalization of professional sport and its resultant paradoxes stands as the archetype of the Weberian thesis applied to sport. However, if rationalization is all encompassing, as Weber claimed, there should be evidence of its effects in other sectors of physical education and sport. Two additional examples are international sport and school physical education programs.

*International sport.** International sport during the twentieth century has gained a prominent position in the world political game.† The objective of this game has been described by Wheeler:

> The overriding world struggle taking place today is the struggle for the political rationalization of the world community as a whole. For our part, however, rather than meeting this challenge, we are devoting our energies to preventing it from emerging, by maintaining the nation-state system. A more quixotic view of the world we live in is hard to imagine.‡

An historical analysis of the world political game reveals both static and dynamic elements. While the participants, rules, and patterns of interaction have often changed, the objective of the game (i.e., the political rationalization of the world community) has remained constant.

However, as a consequence of World War II, the advent of nuclear weapons, and recent technological and economic developments, the form of the world political game has tended toward greater stabilization. Its partici-

---

*I would like to acknowledge W. R. Morford's editorial suggestions, which contributed to the development of this discussion.

†That relations among larger social systems often assume rationalized game forms has been recognized in a number of quarters. Hence, there are simulation games for foreign policy, military strategy, and the like. For a discussion of the vicarious uses of games and their structural components, see Avedon and Sutton-Smith (1971).

‡From Wheeler, H. 1971. The politics of revolution, San Francisco, Boyd and Fraser Publishing Co., pp. 142-143.

pants, the United States, the Soviet Union, the United Kingdom, France, West Germany, Japan, and China, are all firmly entrenched and readily identifiable.* Although many other nations, notably those of the Third World, also aspire to participant status in this world game, their capabilities are minimal. The economic resources of the world are unevenly distributed, thereby offsetting the parity necessary for bona fide participation in the game.

Apologists for international sport tend to disagree (Brundage, 1953). International sport, they have argued, provides an apolitical avenue for understanding and communication. It is figuratively an olive branch that can counteract the divergent backgrounds of athletes representing the participating nations. This naive view of international sport, however, overlooks the very notion of what constitutes politics.

> Politics deals with organizing and coordinating for the realization of goals and values. It is the science of final causes, par excellence, because politics begins at the ends, so to speak. The desired end result is the formal "cause" of everything that is required to realize it. This is the classical meaning of political science. It consists of principles for directing, integrating, and coordinating a system in its entirety.†

To better illustrate the politics involved in the conduct and use of international sport, it is instructive to emphasize that all social systems produce their own ideologies, or collections of beliefs, in support of the established goals of the system proper. Sport, one of the social institutions of competing nations, serves the common function of pattern maintenance. That is, institutionalized sport is undeniably intertwined with the separate characteristics of each sociocultural system. It is of course the uniqueness of these characteristics that provides the basis for the desired distinctions among nations. By virtue of the functional relationships of the components (teams) to the parent entities, international sporting events provide arenas for competing nations, arenas that at the same time reinforce the concept of the nation state (Coser, 1956). Consequently, international sport can be viewed as a principal agent in the perpetuation of what Wheeler (1971) terms "a myopic world view."

Clearly, then, apologists for international sport are referring to the original *intent* or the original goals of international sport. One such goal is captured in the so-called olive branch function. A second and equally

---

*Indeed, if winning Olympic medals constitutes a valid indicator, then stabilization in international sport has occurred already. Levine's study (1974) points toward the relationships among industrialization, economic wealth, and the ability to win Olympic medals. Moreover, that studies such as this one focus on the medal counts of nations is in itself an indication of the instrumentally rational use of sport.

†From Wheeler, H. 1971. The politics of revolution, San Francisco, Boyd and Fraser Publishing Co., p. 47.

important goal for international sport was to provide the opportunity for *individual* athletes to demonstrate their prowess among an international field of equal competitors. The intent of these goals may have been noble, but they have been sacrificed as international sport has been rendered instrumentally rational. Furthermore, international sport will be used increasingly in the future for ends that are substantively irrational.

Of the two primary goals of international sport, the demise of the olive branch function merits initial consideration. As a vehicle by which nations attempt to influence other polities, international sport has become instrumentally rational. Montagu foresaw the role of the media specialist in connection with this function:

> It is the fact, unfortunately, that around every batch of sportsmen visiting the "West" from the new democracies, cluster pressmen, impresarios, agents, secret service officials, trying to tempt them to desert as a part of the "cold war."[*]

Moreover, the former Olympic swimming champion Don Schollander unwittingly revealed the contradiction between what international sport is intended to accomplish and the climate of suspicion and fear that actually exists. "Sports is an international language, the one area in which communication is possible across national, political, and verbal barriers" (1971, p. 124). But:

> I felt that for us to share our knowledge with the Russians would be cutting our own throats. The Russians were making great strides in swimming—very quickly. The people in the State Department and in the AAU didn't have to swim against the Russians in international competition. I did. I was the one who would suffer if I lost and I decided that I just was not going to cooperate.[†]

Moreover, Lukacs (1962, p. 178) makes reference to the paradoxical nature of current international diplomacy. On the one hand, such public relations are seemingly open and in many ways primitive. Accordingly, the creation of proper public images for international sport teams and athletes as instruments of open diplomacy receives strict attention. In spite of the apparent open nature of diplomacy, however, Lukacs also indicates that increasing amounts of subtlety and secrecy underlie the open methods; international sport is involved with this more subtle level as well.

The nonverbal symbols that characterize international sport reflect the effort to create and maintain a favorable, identifiable image. Flags of competing nations fly overhead during competition. Uniforms of the athletes reflect the colors of the flag of the parent country. The two symbols are

---

[*]From Montagu, T. 1951. East-West sports relations, London, National Peace Council, p. 20.
[†]From Schollander, D., and Savage, D. 1971. Deep water, New York, Crown Publishers, Inc., p. 134. © 1971 by Donald A. Schollander and Michael D. Savage; used by permission of the publisher.

71

united more often than not in ceremonies both before and after the competitions. The identities of athletes thus become merged with that of the nations they represent.

More subtle measures emphasize this nationalist orientation. This country's attempts to secure funds for the Olympics are an example. Citizens are asked to give a fixed amount of money to send "our team, our athletes" to the Olympics. In return, contributors receive a nationally sanctioned tax deduction and, perhaps more important, a badge or emblem that signifies the contributor's standing as a part of "our team." Thus the athlete, wearing the colors of the home country and competing under the home flag, becomes an extension of the contributor (who wears a badge that is similarly colored), and vice versa. Victories and losses in the competition can thus be shared, as noted by Goodhart and Chataway.

> Most people will watch for one reason only: there will be a competitor who, they feel, is representing them. That figure in the striped singlet will be their man—running, jumping or boxing for their country. For a matter of minutes at least, their own estimations of themselves will be bound up with his performance. He will be the embodiment of their nation's strength or weakness. Victory for him will be victory for them; defeat for him, defeat for them.°

There is yet another reason for the increasing demise of the olive branch aspect of international sport as a function of its increasing rationalization. The advent of nuclear weapons has altered the capacity of warfare to resolve conflicts among players of the world political game. The stakes are too great—mass annihilation on all sides negates the possibility of a winner. Consequently, warfare must take less direct forms, e.g., on "neutral" grounds (Korea, Vietnam, the Middle East), often among allies or extensions of nations in the world political game, and most importantly, with restrained intensity as suggested by policies of containment. In addition, this alteration in the conflict-resolving functions of warfare necessitates a search for other means of conflict resolution. International sport, massive foreign aid, and manpower- and resources-exchange programs are among the competitive forms that assume the roles previously associated with direct warfare and diplomacy. Mass communications make international sport and the other substitutes for open war the subjects of ostentatious bidding-selling schemes that bring the primary players of the world political game into direct confrontation.

Conflict resolution has therefore shifted toward symbolic demonstrations of aggression. Duncan (1962) has commented from this perspective on the symbolic hatred that may characterize ludic (play) forms. By virtue of its

°From Goodhart, P., and Chataway, C. 1968. War without weapons, London, W. H. Allen & Co., Ltd., p. 3.

inextricable and reinforcing ties to participating nations, international sport has sanctioned such hatred. As the body count has become an index of military efficiency in "limited" warfare, the medal count in a them vs. us context has attested to the superiority of one system over another in international sport.* Cognizant of this newly created role of international sport, massive effort to mobilize finances and resources have resulted in specialized hierarchical agencies (i.e., bureaucracies) whose function has been to prepare athletes (weaponry) capable of demonstrating superiority and of contributing to the expanded power base of the sponsoring national system.

Less-powerful nations that aspire to visible roles in the world political game can take advantage of the bidding wars among more powerful and visible counterparts by obtaining highly successful coaching personnel. These personnel are obtained through exchange programs or lured by the promise of high-ranking governmental positions (often the case in Third World countries). The military analogy is inescapable, involving both military advisers (coaches) and weaponry (athletes who compete in the behalf of exchanging countries). In both cases, it is not uncommon to find both Russian and American technical personnel and demonstration teams (representing both sport and the military) in countries that wish to achieve greater prominence in international sport for a larger purpose, that of gaining recognition as bona fide participants in the world political game.

Conversely, there is also precedent for major powers in the world political game to deny lesser entities access to international sporting events. As Duncan (1962) stipulated, conditional equality is necessary in all ludic forms.† In the world political game the alterations necessary for achieving minimal equality are in large part responsible for the fundamental conformity among nations. Consequently, aspirants to participating roles in the world political game must make concessions and demand concessions in return. For example, the emergence of the People's Republic of China into the world political game was signaled most effectively by the form that apparently ensured conditional equality—sport. China then demanded that she replace Taiwan on the International Olympic Committee.

*Such media-created statistics were revealed in the ludicrous situation surrounding the 1956 and 1960 Olympic Games. On both occasions, both the Russian and the American media claimed overall victories as determined by independent sets of criteria.
†Montagu has underscored the role of the constitution of international sports federations in performing this task:

> The wording of the constitutions of some international sports federations could be construed as implying that, if the new applicants were accepted into membership, all sports bodies in the membership had thereby implicitly recognized the independent national status of the applicants' countries, and this might weaken the standpoint of the respective sports bodies governments in subsequent diplomatic relations (1951, p. 11).

If the olive branch function of sport has been sacrificed as a function of its instrumentally rational uses, so too has the individuality of athletes been eroded. In the classical tradition, forms of international sport were designed to reward *individual* excellence. Indeed, premodern wars rarely prevented international sport from continuing as scheduled. In the context of cultures that were played (Huizinga, 1968) such gestures were not unexpected. Honor, virtue and other elements of value rationality were built into international sport and were subsequently maintained because of the isolation of the sport from the world political game. In contrast, consider the plight of the modern athlete who denies that the victory is a collective achievement and proclaims such on the victory stand. Consider also the negative sanctions of external regulatory agencies in international sport, sanctions that have culminated in the retraction of individual victories since the days of Jim Thorpe.

On the other side of the coin, athletes have begun to use international sports in an instrumentally rational fashion to protest intranational grievances. Victory ceremonies for international sport thus become further tainted by the use of the media by athletes who voice concerns that have no connection with the contests. Indeed, Scott and Edwards (1969) revealed the practice of "buying off" such protests both in anticipation of them and after they have occurred. Such measures are to be expected in connection with the efforts to create and maintain a favorable image of sport for purposes of international diplomacy.

Furthermore, one of the greatest deterrents to the individuality of athletes in international sport is created by bureaucracy. Both within national boundaries (e.g., the N.C.A.A. and A.A.U.) and across them (e.g., the I.O.C.), bureaucratically organized agencies have arisen to direct and control both international athletes and sporting events. At least one athlete observed the effects of these agencies on individual athletes:

> What I saw in South Africa was a classic example of the exploitation by men in the power structure, of athletes they were supposed to be serving and protecting. These men didn't care a rap for their athletes or for any athletes. They cared about their own power. They cared about making money for their organizations in order to perpetuate that power—and that's all they cared about.[*]

Strikingly evident in this comment is the conclusion that sport bureaucracies are equally susceptible to the ends-means inversion suggested by Weber and that the athlete suffers from such bureaucratic dysfunctions.

The early specialization required of athletes is a final indication of their

---

[*]From Schollander, D., and Savage, D. 1971. Deep water, New York, Crown Publishers, Inc., p. 80. © 1971 by Donald A. Schollander and Michael D. Savage; used by permission of the publisher.

changing role in international sport. As a consequence of rationalization, specialization takes different forms and brings payoffs for athletes that differ from country to country. In fact, the terms "amateur" and "professional" no longer suffice to determine athletic eligibility because of the state-related devices by which professionalization can be blurred (Montagu, 1951, p. 6; Schollander and Savage, 1971, p. 55). Thus in some socialist systems with meritocratic ideologies and negligible class distinctions, emphasis is placed on the early identification and subsequent training of athletic talent. Employment for adult athletes is directly related to athletic performance. For example, successful athletes are commonly employed as physical education teachers or coaches, positions that carry social prestige as well (Riordan, 1974a; Levine, 1974). In this country's highly developed athletic systems, by contrast, the promise of a lucrative venture in professional sport and a paid college education are motivating factors. Likewise in this country successful athletic achievement in international sport brings prestige and economic gain. On finishing his ultimate Olympic achievements, Mark Spitz announced openly his retirement from any forms of swimming and signed for more than 1 million dollars in commercial endorsements. Such actions surprise few people in systems that stress the instrumentally rational uses of visible athletic achievement on behalf of the nation.

To recapitulate, the tendency of nations to use international sport as a tool in the world political game has taken its toll on the original purposes of the former. Consistent with the Weberian thesis on the effects of rationalization, international sport has become dominated by what Ellul (1964) calls "technique."

> Beneath the surface rhetoric, then, the entire function of the games—both for the individual and for the international community—has been reversed. For most of the leading competitors, sport is a whole- or part-time business. Temporarily or permanently, their livelihood and career prospects are bound up with success in it. If deCoubertin were still alive, "paid gladiators" is the phrase he would surely produce. Then again, far from being a meeting place where individuals demonstrate the unreality of nationalism, the games have become a focus for it. Most of those who report the games and nearly all who follow them regard them first and foremost as a test of their own nation's virility.*

It is ironic that effective mass persuasion, according to Bandura (1969), rests on the ability to control the attentional processes of the targets, the form of the communication, and the conditions surrounding the reception of the messages. To reiterate, international sport is communicated by *nationalist* media that in turn are geared to the reinforcement and control of nationalism. Consequently, if international sport does not serve its

---

*From Goodhart, P., and Chataway, C. 1968. War without weapons, London, W. H. Allen & Co., Ltd., p. 18.

original purpose, neither does it serve its designated functions in the world political game. In lieu of influencing supposed neutral entities with the goal of control and hence greater power, international sport only rigidifies the boundaries of respective nations. Thus the obvious conclusion that can be drawn is as the following: International sport, instrumentally rational in its design and use, has become substantively *irrational* in its conduct and in its effects on athletes.

If international sport continues to follow the same course in the future, the following forecasts and conclusions appear to be warranted.

1. The emergence of a new prototype of athlete would appear to be a certainty. What Brundage would consider blatantly professional today will no doubt become the norm for athletes of the future. At least professionalism provides conditional equality between and among athletes.

2. Huizinga (1968) has noted that play forms utilized for the fulfillment of sociopolitical designs represent, in fact, false play. The role of international sport in the world political game represents false play, and it will continue to be plagued by demonstrations, assassinations, kidnappings, and similar outrages that are geared toward sociopolitical goals.

3. International sport will remain the vehicle for visible mini-twitches of the muscular nations involved in the world political game. Accordingly, "setups," or conditions of competition rigged to produce a controlled, predetermined outcome (Schollander and Savage, 1971; Goodhart and Chataway, 1968; Montagu, 1959), will be used increasingly in the quest for a favorable image. Countries will continue to be denied participation because of international or domestic policies. Moreover, threatened and or actual withdrawals from competitions will continue to be prompted by political concerns.

4. The universal adoption of a nation as a sponsoring unit in international sport will remain a major mechanism for defeating voluntary efforts toward the unification of smaller, less powerful nations that in combination could enter the world political game. By helping to obscure similarities and accentuating points of difference, international sport therefore will continue to preclude Pan-Africanism and larger Third World unification movements.

5. A convergence in modes of organization for international sport will continue. Sport bureaucracies, themselves branches of national governments, are being implemented in such Western countries as Canada, West Germany, and Great Britain. The Tunney bill (the Amateur Athletic Act) would have the same effect in the United States. Ironically enough, the structures and functions of international sport in the world political game mask not only this indication of convergence, but also the similarities in social structures, communications, etc. that are the bases for a world com-

munity. International sport will continue in this fashion in the near future.

Physical educators and their school programs. Entire volumes have been devoted to the task of analyzing and documenting the origins and historical development of physical educators and their school programs (Weston, 1962; Van Dalen and Bennett, 1971; Lockhart and Spears, 1972). A detailed examination of these works with reference to the Weberian concepts of rationality and rationalization lies outside the province of this essay. It is necessary, however, to offer some historically interpretive observations about physical educators and physical education programs to illustrate in summary form the applicability of Weber's concepts. Subsequent to those observations, I shall identify the present and future consequences of the process of rationalization as it is embodied in both school programs and in the efforts of physical educators to professionalize.

Instrumental in the installation of formal programs of physical education in the American public schools was a pervasive social reform movement known as progressivism. After its genesis in the late 1860s, progressivism gained widespread acceptance among intellectuals who were troubled by the consequences of urban industrial life. Among those intellectuals who were most attracted to progressivism were those who viewed the schools as the most effective means for equipping people from all ethnic and socioeconomic origins to serve as effective, enfranchised members of society. Schools were viewed by these Progressives as mechanisms for individual development and assimilation. At the same time, it was believed that such individual benefits contributed simultaneously to social change. Thus Progressives viewed the schools as agents of social change while simultaneously serving individual needs and aspirations.

The eminent spokesman for progressivist efforts to reform the schools was John Dewey. Dewey and his contemporaries singled out the strict formalism of classical education as being inappropriate for urban industrial conditions. They argued that educational forms and processes capable of preparing students for urban industrial life were more appropriate. Gross (1963) summarized the four main assumptions that formed the basis for Dewey's view of the schools and their programs: (1) education should be based on the inherent nature of the child, (2) education proceeds from direct experiences rather than books, (3) education should be geared toward preparation for life, and (4) education should democratize culture by virtue of its extension to people from lower socioeconomic classes. It should be emphasized that for Dewey and the Progressives the process and goal of education were identical, namely, the reorganization and reevaluation of personal experiences in order to extract its significance.

The influence of Dewey and the Progressives was ultimately formalized in 1918 in a 32-page, 35-cent pamphlet titled *Cardinal Principles of Secondary Education.* This publication, one of the most significant educational documents in American history, identified the educational goals of health, citizenship, worthy use of leisure time, and ethical or character training, among others. According to Hofstadter, the significance of this document should not be underestimated.

> This statement, *Cardinal Principles of Secondary Education,* was given a kind of official endorsement by the United States Bureau of Education, which printed and distributed an edition of 130,000 copies. It became the occasion of a nation-wide discussion of education policy, and some teacher-training institutions regarded it so highly that they required their pupils to memorize essential portions (thus violating a central canon of the new educational doctrines).°

This document was instrumental in broadening the functions of the school from a traditional formalism to a more comprehensive concept of life-adjustment education, which included vocational training, personal and family life education, and physical education.

After agreeing on basic assumptions and goals, the task that confronted progressivist educators was that of determining the means for implementing their program and accomplishing their goals. While indicating the adverse consequences of traditional approaches, progressivist educators pleaded for a pedagogy based on applied principles derived from the new behavioral and social sciences. Furthermore, they stressed the importance of instructional techniques and materials tailored to the differing needs, interests, and experiences of children. Because children's experiences were central to this pedagogy and because classicism in schools was to be discarded in favor of life adjustment education, school subjects that were added captured both childhood experiences and the projected needs and roles of adults. In brief, progressivist educators called for a pedagogy and a school structure which were in Weber's terms *instrumentally rational.* Classical or formal education, pursued either to achieve humanistic ideals or for its own sake (a form of value rationality), succumbed to the instrumental rationality of life adjustment education.

Physical education rode the crest of this wave of educational reform because proponents of some form of physical education were able to capitalize on the undocumented yet commonly accepted belief that character training and ethical and moral development stemmed from participation in sports and games. To reiterate, at the core of such beliefs as they applied to physical education in particular and to schools in general was the assumption

---

°From Hofstadter, R. 1963. Anti-intellectualism in American life, New York, Alfred A. Knopf, Inc., p. 334.

that citizenship, ethical and moral behaviors, and concomitant values could and should be the goals of formal instruction. It should be noted, however, that these beliefs regarding the outcomes of sports and games were equally influential in fostering sport programming and instruction in nonschool contexts. For example, Berryman and Ingham (1972) noted not only the growth of the public playground but also the initiation of church-sponsored programs during the height of the progressivist era. Spring (1974) pointed to the pivotal position of sports and games in the growth of community recreation programs. Belief in the outcomes of sports and games thus was widespread.

To summarize, the mushrooming of sport programs during the first three decades of the twentieth century was triggered by the social reformist efforts of Progressives. Their efforts affected not only the schools but other institutions as well.* For American youth, sports instruction and programming in schools, churches, and communities were utilized for their presumed ethical and moral and character-building capacities. For adults, on the other hand, sport programs were advocated for their restorative values. Given the demands of the workplace, these programs for adults were intended as a means of revitalization both to improve performance on the job and to provide more personalized benefits. In view of this function of sport programs for adults and as a part of this concept of life adjustment education, an additional function of school physical education programs was to act as a "feeder system" for adult programs. By providing mass instruction in sport skills to school-age youth, it was believed that the goal of mass participation in sport programs for adults, could be realized.

This view of sport programs rested on a unique view of American society, one that was not shared by all Progressive reformers. As Spring (1974) noted, work in the urban industrial milieu was deemed meaningless by advocates of recreation and physical education. Consequently, compensation for work had to be sought during leisure hours. Thus rather than questioning the prevailing economic and social order as many Progressives were inclined to do, advocates of recreation and physical education accepted these aspects of society as given and went about their tasks of compensating for and cushioning the effects of the prevailing order, an action that would

---

*The school, however, was most markedly affected by progressivism (Cremin, 1961). Weston (1962, pp. 73-74) documented the substantial growth of school physical education programs after *Cardinal Principles of Education* first appeared. In 1918 the United States Commissioner of Education organized a national conference devoted to the task of implementing school programs nationwide. The number of states that subsequently enacted legislation for physical education, according to Weston, increased from 17 in 1919 to 1921 to 29 in 1930. For discussions of other possible interest group involvement, see Lewis (1969) and Spring (1974).

in essence serve to maintain existing economic and social conditions. Therefore the actions of advocates of recreation and physical education could be viewed as essentially conservative against a progressivist backdrop of liberalism (Spring, 1974, p. 484).

Certainly historical precedent can be established for the use of sport for utilitarian reasons. Yet the pervasiveness of attempts during the progressivist era to harness sport for its perceived instrumentality constitutes a cardinal example of the process of rationalization. Sport, once relatively unstructured in its elite and folk origins and hence value rational, was rendered instrumentally rational by the Progressives. Once left to the individual's whims and wishes, the formalized installation of sport programs in schools and elsewhere brought with it predictability and calculability.

Although Progressives were successful in broadening the functions of the school by including physical education and other subjects, their efforts were at the same time beset by a number of conceptual difficulties. These conceptual difficulties in turn culminated in contradictory practices and programs. For example, life adjustment education, according to Cremin (1961) became defined in 1918 and 1919 in relation to the historical period that circumscribed it. Thus after an examination of the ideational factors and material conditions of that period, the structure and curriculum of the school were duly constituted. Having determined the end product, i.e., life adjustment education, the preoccupation of Progressives shifted toward rationalized mechanisms for their accomplishment.

A major rationalized mechanism for the attainment of life adjustment education in various subject areas was the provision of specialists. Physical education constituted yet another example of this tendency, and preparation programs for specialists in physical education were established. Commenting on the first programs of professional preparation in physical education, Kroll noted that these programs were structured in relation to existing programs in the schools (1971, pp. 75-77). In other words, occupational role requirements were identified initially, and then a program of professional preparation was designed to mirror those requirements. In the case of physical education, four basic functions for professional preparation programs were identified. The first function, that of acquiring technical skills, included not only performance competencies in activities but also in teaching methods and principles. Second, the administration, supervision, and direction of physical education programs were included. A third function focused on stating objectives and processes for determining them. Finally, the little mention given scientific training, according to Kroll (p. 76), centered on determining the developmental tendencies of children and subsequently pairing children with programs of appropriate activities.

The point to be emphasized here is that if life adjustment education was defined in relation to the period that circumscribed it, and if teachers in subject areas such as physical education were prepared in relation to that same historical period, then a dysfunctional element was built into the revised system of schooling from the beginning. As specialists who both reflected and kindled the process of rationalization, physical educators while acquiring the appropriate background for successful skills technicians were not exposed to a knowledge base that could be used ultimately to stimulate change. Instead, their technical training reduced physical educators themselves to a form of technique, i.e., another rationalized mechanism. Thus if we accept the assumption that ideational factors and material conditions changed after the period of 1918 and 1919 and if we accept the tenets of the Progressives to the effect that schools should both reveal *and* shape the society, then we have in the case of physical education yet another example of ends-means inversion. Clearly, the emphasis on technical competence in professional preparation at the expense of a knowledge base resulted in programs that were directed toward a bygone era. At the same time, despite the label physical *education,* technicians (physical educators) became merely transmitters of technique to others, thereby engaging in technical training. Although a superior class of athletics may have resulted from the effects of what amounted to mass apprentice instruction, physical education programs in form and in process more nearly resembled physical *training* programs by virtue of their dominant concern with optimal techniques of performance.

These patterns have been maintained to the present by at least two mechanisms. First of all, the model for professional preparation, while it has become rationalized to a greater degree, has remained essentially unchanged. Competencies in the most recent form of professional preparation, Performance-Based Teacher Education, have been stated in behavioral or measurable terms to avoid misunderstanding and to aid in evaluation. Yet these competencies are still being derived on the same basis. That is, after inspecting teacher roles, undergraduate programs are structured accordingly, but a knowledge base remains a facet of third-order importance (Houston, 1972).*

---

*Once again an irony emerges. The relegation of a knowledge base to a position of third-order importance precludes the application of available knowledge to the assumptions of both the performance-based approach and to school physical education programs. If that knowledge were to be applied, a number of spurious assumptions would be bared. This should cause both the approach and current integral facets of school programs to be replaced; but we are dealing with the effects of an ends-means inversion here, and consequently shortcomings such as spurious assumptions are rarely identified.

Second, the provision of specialists in all areas of the school (Sarason, 1971) has ushered in modes of bureaucratic organization. Although facets of schools remain nonbureaucratic (Dreeban, 1973), the school as a workplace has been altered drastically as a consequence of increasing bureaucratization. Discussing the depersonalization that stems from bureaucratic dysfunctions, Katz (1971) and Kuhlman and Hoy (1974) have documented empirically the extent to which control for the sake of control has become predominant in secondary schools. Clearly this is a far cry from the humanistic ideals of Progressives. It is, however, consistent with the Weberian premise regarding the effects of rationalization and bureaucracy, its instrument.

The final test of the validity of the Weberian thesis as it applies to physical educators and their programs can be made by a brief analysis of program outcomes. To what extent have these formally rational programs served substantively irrational outcomes? Commenting on the outcomes of school and recreation programs, Spring observed summarily that "while the goal was mass participation, the result was mass spectatorship" (1974, p. 483). Additional justification for this conclusion can be found in the literature. Not only is there a paucity of actual participation in physical activities during leisure (Robinson, 1967), there is also the proclivity toward viewing the performances of specialists as opposed to participation (Kenyon, 1966). There are also examples of the adverse effects of school physical education programs (Gallon, 1958; Keogh, 1964). Moreover, despite the intentions of Progressive reformers, who were in large part responsible for physical education programs, the participation that exists in physical activities has more often than not cemented rather than alleviated social class–based barriers (Griffiths, 1970; Gruneau, 1975; Baltzell, 1964). Thus the final irony of these programs lies in the fact that they reflect and reinforce the very ideational factors and material conditions that they were designed to help change.

What of the future possibilities for these programs? In keeping with the onrushing tide of rationalization, the following predictions and observations appear to be warranted.

1. Physical educators will continue to rely upon what Ellul (1964) calls technique. Individualized instruction and other forms of instruction technology, although viewed by physical educators as the answer to their problems, can be viewed more appropriately from this perspective. In other words, forms of technology when applied piecemeal to previously existing forms not only will not suffice to solve problems that existed previously, they often produce new problems. These new problems then become objects of attention as well and require new technologies. Aside from cul-

minating in such cycles, technique pursued for the sake of technique leaves fundamental assumptions and program structures unchanged. A reliance on technique also obviates the need for a knowledge base that, ironically enough, constitutes a remedy for the problems encountered by physical educators. Any change in the very structure and purposes of programs must be accomplished in relation to a viable systematically organized knowledge base. What appears to be happening instead is that splinterings by the various subdisciplines, e.g., sociology of sport and psychology of sport, have proceeded to the point where the few applications made to programs are themselves piecemeal and hence a form of technique.

2. The absence of a systematically organized knowledge base will continue to hamper the quest of physical educators for professional status (Henry, 1964; Morford, 1972; Ritzer, 1975). Three adverse consequences will persist as a result of the failure of physical educators to recognize the true meaning of professionalism and to remedy the situation. First of all, the trend toward what Janis (1971) labeled "groupthink" will continue. Groupthink is an emphasis on ability and esprit de corps among a policy-making in-group such as physical educators. By sacrificing independent, critical thinking that comes from a systematically organized knowledge base, irrational and/or dehumanizing actions can result in relation to those whom the program is directed to serve. Where discrepancies do exist between stated goals and actual outcomes, the tendency is to "blame the victim," to use Ryan's (1971) terms. The fault is preceived as residing not with physical educators but rather with those who are exposed to physical education programs and who fail to take advantage of program offerings.

Second, the absence of a knowledge base will foster additional ends-means inversions. As Locke (1969) aptly noted, it is a misunderstanding of ends and means when children are trained to be physically fit and yet learn simultaneously to hate physical education and physical activity.

Finally, the absence of a systematically organized knowledge base will continue to preclude the establishment of a monopoly by physical educators over the activities that they deem to be within their jurisdiction. Insofar as they are governed by and represent in themselves forms of technique, this failure on the part of physical educators constitutes no apparent tragedy. On the other hand, if professions are to be guardians of their selected spheres of human activity, as I think they should be, and if this protective posture rests on knowledge, then physical educators could be placed in a position whereby they protect play, games, dance, sport, and the like from outside influences. Yet the overwhelming conclusion with regard to past action and future possibility is that outside agents have in the past and will continue in the future to be most influential in the directions and design of programs deemed important by physical educators. Parenthetically, had physical education programs indeed educated their clientele, lay persons might also be more protective of these forms.

3. The dual failure of physical educators to establish monopoly over their activities and to respond to changing conditions by altering their programs might be viewed as largely responsible for the mushrooming number of extraschool sport instruction-participation programs. There is every likelihood that both community- and club-sponsored programs will increase over the next three decades. In addition they will offer stiff competition for advocates of physical education because lay persons will not be able to distinguish adequately between these sport programs and school physical education programs.

4. Throughout this century, interscholastic programs have superseded in importance physical education programs (Spring, 1974). No small part of this problem is attributable to the domination of technique in both programs, a domination that has served to mask the necessary conceptual and practical distinctions between the two. The continued domination of technique in both programs promises to produce in the future the same imbalance between them. Moreover, this preoccupation with technique serves to reflect and reinforce the dominant ideational network that permeates the larger society. This relationship has been depicted by Webb (1969, pp. 177-178). The structural and value similarities of sport programs and the urban industrial milieu (especially the economic system) not only produce professionalized play attitudes but also foster the specialization that is characteristic of rationalization. Unfortunately, these very ties to the larger ideational network are instrumental in defeating the altruistic goals of physical educators, among them the goal of mass participation.

To recapitulate the discussion thus far, the process of rationalization and its concomitants have been traced in relation to two exemplary forms, international sport and school physical education programs. In both examples the substitution of instrumental rationality for types of social action formerly determined by tradition, affect, or value rationality was observed. While instrumental rationality has obvious advantages when viewed as an ideal type of social action (in which both ends and means are continuously readjusted), this form of rationality has been distorted in practice and has brought with it disadvantages. Foremost among these disadvantages has been the short-circuiting of ends and means to the point where what once were means have become ends in and of themselves. This paradoxical inversion, which culminates in substantive irrationality, has been observed in relation to international sport and school physical education programs and, if this analysis were to be lengthened, doubtless could be extended to other forms of sport and physical activity. Thus in preparing a normative forecast for the future, a major challenge that must be confronted is that of transforming programs to the point where the Weberian ideal type of instrumental rationality can be made real.

A NORMATIVE FORECAST*

This country's astonishing rate of technological progress has been responsible for widespread economic and social change. Daniel Bell (1973) has contended that the United States has in fact entered a postindustrial era, an era in which continued technological progress can be expected. According to Bell, two major features of the postindustrial society that differentiate it from industrial society are the increasing fragmentation and specialization of roles as well as modes of life that hinge on cognitive and theoretical knowledge. Insofar as the process of rationalization produced both specialized roles and expertise based upon knowledge in industrial society, Bell's argument for postindustrial society on these bases alone is rendered suspect. Bell continues, however, by pointing to new social structures and new social relationships that are distinctive in their form, processes, and functions.

> Industrial society is the coordination of machines and men for the production of goods. Post-industrial society is organized around knowledge, for the purpose of social control and the directing of innovation and change; and this in turn gives rise to new social relationships and new structures which have to be managed politically.†

Furthermore, aside from new social relationships and new social structures, a key feature of postindustrial society is that it is a service economy; this shift from production to services has been made possible by exponential increases in technological capacity. It is equally possible that new belief systems will emerge from within this changing milieu (Platt, 1974).

Bell's prognostication on the whole is congruent with assertions of other futures-oriented social scientists. The increasing primacy of theoretical and cognitive knowledge and the continued reliance on machine technologies will continue to transform both the characteristics of workers and the meaning of work itself. It is in this context that the various human social services (e.g., schools, mental health agencies, and recreation pro-

*Typically normative forecasting begins with some idealized view of the future and subsequently identifies the necessary mechanisms for achieving the future ideal. In this section of the chapter I am mixing normative judgments with a depiction of material conditions which already exist. Unfortunately, the ideational lag produced by schools and other socializing institutions has precluded in many instances the recognition by lay persons of changing material conditions.
†From Bell, D. 1973. Five dimensions of post-industrial society, Social Policy 3:10.

grams) merit extensive analysis and subsequent reconstruction. Consistent with Bell's characterization and in the interests of serving broader portions of the population, social services must begin to rely on cognitive and theoretical knowledge to a greater extent than custom has dictated. Such a shift will necessitate a departure from narrow credentialism and a preoccupation with technique. It must also include modes of planning and decision valuing that contrast sharply with those traditional modes utilized at present (Bell, 1973).

At the outset, four working assumptions should be specified to avoid misunderstanding and misinterpretation. The first of these assumptions is that human beings have a predisposition toward play forms, among them participation in physical activity. This predisposition is currently subjected to socialization pressures that often lead to its extinction. Consequently, social services designed both to aid in the process of socialization into physical activity and to provide outlets for participation will have to be adjusted to accommodate and encourage this basic impulse toward play.

Second, I am assuming that while physical educators may be placed in a position in which they can effect changes in school physical education, athletic, and recreation programs, the professional athletic model is beyond their jurisdiction and control. What merits recognition is that the professional sport system has served to mask the deficiencies of the participant system. In a postindustrial society this participant system should assume greater importance and hence requires major alterations.

A third assumption relates to the nature of social services. Services (and those outlined herein constitute no exception) are designed to provide solutions to problems of the human condition. In this manner, the quality of individual and ultimately of group life is enhanced. An integral tenet in the operation of social services is that they be individualized, i.e., offered on a person-to-person basis. Moreover, recipients of services voluntarily seek aid in modifying their behavior toward some objective or goal. Whether this goal is determined individually or in concert with a professional, this voluntary aspect of behavioral change is indispensable to an understanding of the delivery system outlined in this discussion. Such a volitional element serves to distinguish this form of personal change from the more stereotypical mold of external coercion for purposes of social control. Likewise, it is not intended that these social services should give license to elitist professionals to modify behavior in accordance with a restricted system of norms and values. Indeed, a major challenge confronting teachers, social workers, etc. is that of determining the difference between professional definitions of client needs and the actual needs (or expectations) of clients themselves.

A final assumption pertains to the notion of cybernetic systems. These steering or guiding systems have traditionally been linked with mechanistic views of society. The use of cybernetic systems for social services, however, should be an attempt to utilize theoretical and cognitive knowledge prudently. To borrow from Berger and Luckmann (1967), knowledge and its social base should be viewed as a dialectical relationship; although it is a social product, knowledge should be capable of producing social change. As Weber knew so well, the rational uses of knowledge pose no apparent difficulties if there are procedures for adjusting both means for goal attainment and the goals themselves. The cybernetic system depicted in the following discussion is directed toward this ideal.

The label "delivery system," while not entirely novel, suggests new structures and modes of operation for services such as schools and physical education and recreation programs. Unlike the fragmented or segmentalist approach to problem solving that has been ushered in by specialization and credentialism, the concept of a delivery system points toward modern counterparts of the Greek *paideia*, in which all institutional components are utilized for their complementary educational contributions. Delivery systems, then, represent holistic rather than segmentalist approaches to problem solving. In the case of participation in physical activities, a delivery system would attempt to turn the ideal of mass participation into a reality.

Indeed, the need for such complementary and overlapping networks in postindustrial society has already been identified. Kanter and Zurcher (1973) have summarized concisely the organizational needs of the present, needs that can be applied directly to new delivery systems. These needs include (1) overarching systems of commitment, (2) organizations and services with greater flexibility, i.e., capacity to adapt, (3) democratic social systems capable of confronting the challenge of the technocratic expert, and (4) redistribution and decentralization of power in organizations and services (1973, p. 382). A new delivery system for physical activities would be directed toward satisfying each of the above needs. It is to a more thorough characterization of this delivery system that our discusison now turns.

The quest for a new cybernetic system and the emergence of new structural-functional realignments provide the bases for complementary relationships between and among school programs of physical education, recreational programs of physical activity, and various other service agencies. The system proper would be designed to perform a number of related functions for a variety of users. By sharing information and information systems, these agencies would be bonded by design. The advantages of such a cybernetic system will be apparent after a discussion of four of its primary modes as they apply to a delivery system for physical activity in urban communities.

The first such mode, provided by the typical research-to-practice schema, requires that professionally relevant theoretical knowledge be assembled in a form that can be transmitted to and used by practitioners in the field. Obviously, the initial prerequisite that must be met is the establishment of a knowledge base in undergraduate professional preparation, a measure introduced earlier in this discussion. Having granted the need for additional knowledge as it becomes available, then a research-to-practice paradigm becomes invaluable to both physical education and recreation. In the absence of research institutes centered around the study of physical activity, universities will no doubt continue to bear the brunt of the responsibility for the conduct and subsequent dissemination of research (Bell, 1973). The professional literature, especially in light of its current state, cannot be expected to serve as a primary link. Especially necessary are insightful reviews of related literature and research as they pertain to practitioners' problems. In concert with the literature, the so-called knowledge-linking function can be performed by persons who are equipped to apply knowledge to existing roles and social structures (Havelock, 1971).

A more central solution to the problem would appear to be automated information retrieval systems that provide updated information a moment after it is requested. Local terminals emanating from a multipurpose computer center would tend to make such a possibility much more practical and possible than would initially appear to be the case. Rather than depending on sources or mechanisms outside the system, professionals in the strictest sense of the term would be relatively independent once it became possible to ensure the continuous input of new data into the retrieval system. National and international data banks that may be tapped for a nominal fee can alleviate many such local problems associated with updating and coding novel information.

A second mode that can be identified in the new cybernetic system is that of the identification of researchable problems. If it can be assumed that practitioners cannot be expected to undertake extensive and sophisticated research entirely on their own, then problems they confront must be communicated to investigators in the professional schools. The practitioner is in the unique and enviable position of continuously identifying a host of problems, yet practical problems of time, training, etc. preclude their performing extensive, independent investigations. As in the case in the first mode, a symbiotic relationship between professional practitioners and professional educators affords a mutual compatibility of theory testing and data generation that are the mark of viable professions. Recall one earlier suggestion that field placement and supervision afford exactly the mechanisms for this mode of information exchange.

The information exchange between teacher (professional) and student (client) constitutes the third mode. Although research may focus the practitioner's effort, it in no way obviates the need to obtain information regarding the individual and collective characteristics of clients. Indeed, one of the major examples of the mishandling of information is the self-fulfilling practice of making the client(s) fit the data. Such mishandling likewise marks the difference between effective social services and the ominous Orwellian stereotype of knowledge used for social control. Individualization in instruction and programming is contingent on an information base derived from practitioner-client interaction. Indeed, human social services in any sphere are after all relational in character, i.e., on a person-to-person basis. Thus behavior modification becomes possible only when the teacher or clinician has some clue as to the agents or environmental conditions that affect the student's or client's behavior. While the information gathered by the professional will inevitably be incomplete, individual change and overall programming would appear to be more effective to the degree that such information is furnished. At the same time, collection of salient information supplies a fertile source of data, which when fed into the data banks of the computerized system, can be recalled periodically for comparative purposes or utilized longitudinally to depict more permanent patterns. Longitudinal data are especially necessary in all professional fields, for they allow continuous scrutiny of the same student or group of students over a period of years. Solutions to many problems confronting practitioners in all fields await such an analysis, given the limitations of short-term comparative studies that utilize heterogeneous groups of students.

The fourth mode, which combines elements of the preceding three, encompasses efforts to analyze the effectiveness of the service and guide necessary adaptations in it. Did it meet its stated objectives? Were there other, unintended outcomes that resulted from the treatment or programming? Are future alterations in procedures, structures, and functions necessary? What is the locus of the dysfunction? These and similar questions are best attacked multilaterally. The measures inherent in the first three modes of the cybernetic system, in concert with special institutional research procedures for determining effectiveness, offer the most complete approach to internal problems. Social indicator data and other measures for societal monitoring are invaluable sources for stimulating adaptation to external societal trends. Aside from its use for evaluation and corrective purposes, such information can be used to answer questions which pertain to the accountability problem.

To reiterate, the vast amount of information handling involved in the new cybernetic system necessitates automated or computerized procedures. Services can begin to conform to their individualized, relational character to the extent that practitioners are given both the information and the necessary time to work with clients. Vondracek et al. (1974) have presented a cogent description of how such an automated procedure would operate in relation to all three modes in the system. Thus if information flow is the remedy for problems in personal and organizational effectiveness, then the automated technologies provide the vehicle for the dissemination of the antidote. As Vondracek et al. (1974) have explained:

> In sum, it appears that the judicious use of technology in the human services field holds great potential for releasing humanitarian concern where it has been buried under red tape and paper work, and for giving it new life where it has been pushed aside by excessive workloads and other demands.*

New cybernetic systems for services and programs necessitate in turn new structural-functional relationships. A prime example of how new structural-functional relationships may be established between and among programs focusing on physical activities and those providing other social services is constituted by the community school. Although the community school concept is hardly new, the normative forecast offered here includes in this concept not only the new cybernetic system, but also a consolidated, multilateral approach to social services. By further elaborating on the delivery system for school-based and recreational physical activity, both the intricacies and advantages of this consolidation shall become apparent.

The redefinition of physical education programs in the school leaves three remaining topics for discussion: (1) the use of computer-based information retrieval in physical education and recreational program design, (2) the inclusion of individualized instructional technology, and (3) the establishment of a school-based referral system such as that identified earlier. The first two elements may be discussed concurrently in that the quest to individualize subject areas in the schools and in service programs in municipalities has dominated the literature for the past decade. While most of the literature has been directed toward methods (i.e., as forms of technique) of individualizing instruction and autotuition in physical education (e.g., programmed instruction, film loops, video tapes, and holograms), the pivotal factor is the use of information to guide efforts to modify be-

---

*From Vondracek, F., et al. 1974. Feasibility of an automated intake procedure for human services workers, The Social Service Review 48:277.

havior. Methodological orientations have provided devices for students to differentially acquire the same skills in physical education. Informational utilization provides pairings of skills and content with a student's learning aptitudes, personal physical activity preferences, and extraschool agents and agencies that affect a student's behavior. Such information can be adopted for utilization by all subject areas in the school and by municipal programs that are school based, as well. Indeed, integrated planning of an entire educational experience can be individualized within this framework.

Discussion of the retrieval of information for use in programming assumes that it has been gathered. Professionals in the true sense customarily perform these tasks (Morford, 1972). Vondracek et al. (1974) noted the ease with which such information may be secured and recorded. Ultimately, methodological and informational approaches to programming complement one another. Methodological procedures allow students to proceed independently at their own rate, thus freeing teachers for performance analysis and individual counseling and assessment. By providing information, assessment and retrieval systems help ensure a realistic program for students, individually and collectively. The uses of such data in longitudinal studies and in determining organizational effectiveness have been noted already.

Moreover, both elements can be utilized equally effectively in recreational programming. If physical activities are learned and performed by students and adults under optimal conditions in and around community schools, and if this interest is supplanted by an adequate knowledge base that guides such activity planning and participation, then the patterns of inactivity depicted by Robinson and others might well be reversed. Necessary for such a reversal is the provision of leisure demand systems in city recreation programs. Fortunately, Wagner and Hovis (1974) have piloted such a system for Seattle, Washington, a system that conforms nicely to the cybernetic and delivery systems just described. Their computer-based system provides easily retrievable information about characteristics of clients in relation to sources of the recreation agency. Such data, when geo-coded, aid in program planning and resource allocation. Furthermore, data from local agencies can be pooled for city-wide analysis; consequently, where there is insufficient interest for facilities and programs for judo, in one locale, for example, a city-wide assessment might well reveal such a need in another area. The facility can therefore be identified and programs planned in relation to the bulk of the users. The decentralized community school can be a local hub around which such a system operates.

The community school's function as a local referral agency enables prospective recipients to pinpoint the exact location of the program they require. The current inability of clients, especially those who are poor, to make such a determination in the face of inadequate knowledge and the overlap and confusion of modern bureaucracy was identified earlier. While programs may well be offered in the local school, there will no doubt be cases in which more esoteric services and specialists are required. By first requiring a referral, such special programs would not be overburdened by clients who could have been accommodated locally. For students and adults who require concurrent, multilateral programming, the facilities are so arranged to provide such services.

In the case of the student who prefers additional options beyond the school, clubs, appropriate organizations, and additional sources of instruction can be supplied. In instances where no such extraschool outlet exists, there is the built-in procedure for determining novel needs of the clientele. Such a procedure helps to avoid the self-fulfilling tendencies of physical education and recreational physical activity programming by providing a basis for feedback and adaptation. By the same token, the functions of the community school just described make it possible for people to receive instruction throughout their lives. The influence of situational variables in determining interests and participation in physical activity warrant such a system. By coupling recreational and physical education programs and their resources, such a system can become a reality. Adults may utilize the same individualized methods of learning physical activities that were described previously. Such learning may take place at any time without the need for additional personnel. Only the facilities, materials, and equipment need to be provided. Entire families can be accommodated by such a plan, whether locally or by referral to another locale.

If people utilize the social services of the community school at the very least for referral and in many instances for personal change and general programming, then lateral articulation among services becomes possible. Clerical positions may become pooled for greater effectiveness and efficiency. More important for the consumer, however, is the possibility of multilateral and simultaneous treatment. For example, if an alcoholic treatment team suggests participation in physical activity, whether for a family or an individual, then the necessary personnel can be secured immediately. Programs can accordingly be individually tailored. If a student's emotional problems with physical education demand a special program, then a caseworker can be contacted who can in turn work through other service agents and agencies. The possibilities for such multilateral and simultaneous programs are legion. Cross-fertilization between and among professionals in education, social work, and other areas can become commonplace. By the same token, specialized and extensive treatment where necessary can be provided by referral. The result therefore is an incredible savings in facilities, supportive staff, equipment, and basic expenditures when social and educational services become amalgamated. In the face of such consolidation and on the basis of current expenditures alone, the chances are quite good that there is sufficient funding to provide the automated technologies needed for such a delivery system.

The features of the delivery system for physical activity alleviate current pragmatic and conceptual difficulties that impede program effectiveness in schools and in social services, especially in the case of participation in physical activity. A compatibility likewise results among formerly discrete services and programming in a structural-functional arrangement that is decentralized and localized in the community school. The utilization of a novel cybernetic system carries with it advantages in treatment and programming heretofore impossible. These advantages include the following:

1. Consumers can acquire instruction in or opportunities to perform physical activities of their choice throughout their lives.
2. Overlapping and competing interests for physical activity have been consolidated.
3. Programming in both physical education and recreation can be individualized from both informational and methodological perspectives.
4. Instruction and/or treatment takes place in the local environment, enhancing opportunities for permanence in personal change.
5. Data can be collected to better describe the collective characteristics of each region and/or the city for planning purposes.
6. Entire families can be grouped for treatment simultaneously.
7. Services can be provided concurrently for problems that require such treatments; mental health counseling, manpower training, and recreational rehabilitation can be planned conjointly and provided locally and simultaneously.
8. Data are provided for and by professional schools by means of the interchange depicted in the course of the discussion.
9. Services are allowed to assume a relational character, whereby one-to-one interaction provides effective treatment and/or immediate referral to a more specialized or appropriate agency.

Consequently, from the vantage points of fiscal and social accountability, the public is getting the most for its money in terms of optional service effectiveness. Urban communities can begin to solve their problems by means of educational institutions. Rather than constituting a terminal process, education, consistent with the progressivist ideal, becomes lifelong. Finally, the delivery system represents the Weberian ideal typology of instrumental rationality, in which both ends and means can be readjusted and are substantively rational.

The etymology of our word "school" dates back to the Greek *schole,* meaning leisure. The concept of the community school and its various uses and functions would appear to be consistent with this archetype. By utilizing automated technologies and by relying on theoretical and cognitive knowledge, the complementary institutional relationships that emerge are reminiscent of a modern-day counterpart to the classical *paideia.* The focus on physical education programs in the schools and programs of recreational physical activity provided by municipalities has served to clarify the many advantages of such a holistic approach to individual, community, and societal needs and problems. By planting the seeds for such an approach, my intent has been to indicate how eminently feasible and useful such an amalgamation of services can become. The fruits harvested by the careful cultivation of this concept are represented by the enhanced effectiveness of social services and, by design, sociocultural change. Such fruits, when harvested, represent the natural foods of any healthy sociocultural system.

TOWARD FUTURES CREATION

Thus far I have endeavored to identify the accidental yet adverse consequences of rationality and the process of rationalization. In addition, I have tried to emphasize that there is nothing insidious about instrumentally rational social action per se. For insofar as instrumental rationality corresponds to Weber's ideal type, in which both the mechanisms for goal attainment (technique) and the goals themselves are subject to alteration, it constitutes an efficient and helpful way to reproduce behaviors. Indeed, the delivery system outlined previously exemplifies the prudent utilization of knowledge in an instrumentally rational fashion for goal attainment and goal adaptation. Unfortunately, in practice instrumental rationality often has been undercut by an ends-means inversion. Thus the challenge that confronts physical educators and other interested planners in their efforts to create the future is one of redressing the balance between technique and goal analysis-adaptation.

In addressing themselves to the current imbalance between ends and means, many writers have identified the increasing need for planning processes that provide what Wheeler (1971) calls "intentionality" (Kahn, 1969; Slater, 1970; Meadows et al., 1972; Michael, 1973; Galbraith, 1973). In using terms such as intentionality, these writers have wished to emphasize that society and its institutions should be planned by people to the point

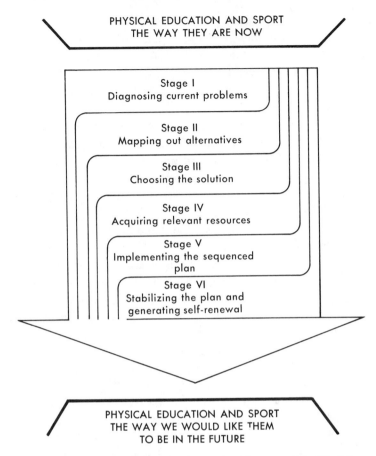

Fig. 2. A planning model for physical education and sport. (Modified from Havelock, R. 1970. A guide to innovation in education, Ann Arbor, Mich., Institute for Social Research.)

at which they correspond with the desires (intentions) of their architects. Consistent with Weber's concepts, these writers have emphasized further that because the goals of institutionalized programs were and are anchored in human values, they should remain subject to alteration as human values and aspirations change. In other words, new normative ideals, when collectively agreed on, should be translated pragmatically to the point where they become real-world targets. This process of moving from ideal to real is futures creation. Both individual and societal development are perceived as stemming from these intentional activities of individuals who forge real-world counterparts of an idealized state of affairs.

Fig. 2 is a planning model for physical education and sport that embodies the concept of intentionality. Furthermore, it serves to link futures forecasting to futures creation by providing an idealized, instrumentally rational model for planning. By adhering to such a model, physical educators and other program planners may remain in the mainstream of the dissemination of knowledge. This knowledge in turn may be applied subsequently to not only the means by which goals are accomplished but also to the analysis of goals themselves. A more detailed discussion of the model should serve to clarify the above and additional advantages.

The portion of the model entitled "physical education and sport: the way they are now" is that which includes futures forecasting via extrapolation. Critical assessments of past and present reality produce information that reveals the extent to which the original intentions for programs have been realized in practice. In addition, the use of a sociohistorical perspective helps to explain these results and provides a basis for extrapolating from existing trends to forecast the future. This method assumes, of course, that the same outcomes will emanate from programs in the future so long as key variables are held constant.

Although extrapolation describes the extent to which idealized intentions were realized in practice, the method proper includes nothing that suggests either corrective action or the advisability of entertaining new goals. This latter function can be linked to that portion of the model labeled "physical education and sport: the way we would like them to be in the future." Normative forecasts such as the one I provided in this chapter belong in this part of the model. While reflecting human values, normative forecasts present an idealized vision of the future, one that is subject to change as human values and aspirations change. Thus a dialectical relationship exists between present (extrapolated into the future) and the normative ideal. Much like a driver in a car, planners must periodically utilize the rear-view mirror while at the same time remaining ready to revise not only the initial routing, but also their very destination.

The various stages which link the present with the normative ideal constitute steps toward future creation. In other words, where discrepancies exist between the ideal and the real, the six stages of the model provide a corrective path toward creating the idealized future. That these steps are related rather than mutually exclusive is suggested by the feedback relationships depicted between and among them.

Stage I, the diagnosis of current problems, is of course linked to assessment of the present. Yet facets of this diagnosis are sufficiently important and independent to warrant separate consideration. In discussing this diagnosis of current problems, Michael (1973) has observed that organizations have in the past eschewed specialized mechanisms that could be utilized to detect errors in both goals and functioning. Clearly, the reluctance to uncover error, i.e., to seek it out and reward those who detect it, can be viewed as a correlate of the common ends-means inversion. Because organizations do not exist apart from their members (Greenfield, 1973) and because goals are taken for granted or petrified, the failure to achieve goals has resulted in negative sanctions being leveled against organizational members. In such a context, it is better for organizational members to conceal rather than to reveal error.

Improvement of services in the emerging postindustrial society, as Bell contended, rests on knowledge. One of the primary uses of knowledge, whether in basic or applied contexts, is in validating or debunking current practice. In discussing the need for new cybernetic systems, I identified four modes that must be used to diagnose current problems. To reiterate, these included the research-to-practice schema, the diagnostic efforts of individual practitioners, and the establishment of specialized procedures for intra- and interinstitutional research. Especially noteworthy in this light were corrective feedback mechanisms that could be used by practitioners to diagnose client needs, demands, and expectations rather than to rely on tradition-bound, occupational perceptions and prescriptions of client needs. Implicit in that discussion were the assumptions that (1) organizational structures and reward systems would have to be adjusted to the point where the efforts to locate errors and dysfunctions would be ongoing and (2) successful location of error or dysfunction would be rewarded.

After diagnosing current problems and presumably either reaffirming or readjusting goals, the task in *Stage II* becomes one of mapping out alternative solutions and their possible and probable consequences. In this second stage the role of futures forecasting is also an important one because the choice of one solution as opposed to others rest not only on present but also on anticipated future consequences. This emphasis on possible alternative solutions to what may be a single class of problems is consistent with instrumentally rational social action. Indeed, the fundamental recognition of two aspects of reality—first, that institutions influence and are influenced by other institutions and, second, that second- and third-order consequences are as important as primary concerns (e.g., goal attainment)—warrants a search for the best alternative from all of these perspectives. In other words, when criteria other than expediency or custom are utilized in the problem-solving efforts of practitioners and their clients, the search for the best solution is frequently riddled with a host of contingencies. While they are indicative of the complexity of the process, these contingencies also emphasize the need to consider a variety of alternative solutions.

Stage III, that of choosing the solution, rests on a combination of normative judgments, applicable social knowledge, and the extent to which one solution vis-à-vis others satisfies mutually acceptable criteria. In the past these decisions customarily have been made by practitioners. Regardless of the area of professional endeavor, the assumption has been that the professional is in the best position to determine client problems and to select the best solution. Clearly, there are self-sealing and self-fulfilling tendencies that are the by-products of this practice. Furthermore, there is in the present and in the near future the need to preserve democracy in the face of the onrushing technocracy (Kanter and Zurcher, 1973).

Habermas (1970), Etzioni (1968), Michael (1973), and others have proposed a pragmatistic decision-making model that is intended to satisfy this need and that is especiallly applicable to this third stage of futures creation. In essence, decision making becomes decentralized to a greater degree, and as a result it becomes more responsive to localized problems and needs. Both the general public and experts alike should be involved in the decision-making process. Lay involvement requires the expert to communicate specialized knowledge (using appropriate language) and to spell out the justification for the expert's recommended solution. Lay persons, once they have the same information possessed by the experts, are in a position to question its validity and applicability. Moreover, once the knowledge differential has been leveled, the value judgments of lay persons become as important as those of experts. Such direct involvement by lay persons in the decision-making process, aside from sustaining the ideals of democracy, can arrest the self-sealing and self-fulfilling tendencies of professional groups. Indeed, both professional definitions of the problems (and implicitly, professional goals) and the search for the solution (i.e., means or technique) are subject to challenge and alteration by lay involvement. This decision-making model thus constitutes the most important feature in this third stage.

Stage IV is frequently overlooked or disproportionately emphasized. In searching for alternatives and subsequently in choosing a solution, questions regarding what appear to be outlandish demands for resource acquisition and allocation can stifle innovation. Yet, in overlooking the question of resources it is equally possible that a proposed solution may never proceed beyond the drawing board. Certainly trade-offs must be made. Timetables must be established as resources are listed in order of priority by decision makers. Moreover, although there is a tendency to equate resource needs with material and/or technological capabilities, two revealing insights can be drawn from the literature on innovation that suggest that this equation may be overemphasized. First, new roles and new programs require not only extensive retraining but also the cultivation of new norms and expectations. A second and related need rests on creating an organizational structure (including a reward system) that can reinforce and sustain the new roles and programs. Thus in the social services the most important resource need lies not so much in the area of material and technological capabilities but in the need for consultants who can facilitate transitions in personnel and programs.

Stage V involves implementation of the proposed solution. As I indicated above, solutions should be broken down into the most appropriate sequence. This sequence should include a flexible and appropriate schedule for implementation.

At the same time as the plan is being implemented, *Stage VI* is initiated. As a part of this sixth stage the changes involved in the proposed solution are stabilized while at the same time mechanisms are created for self-renewal and adaptation. Not the least among the measures intended to stabilize changes is the aforementioned alteration of the normative and structural components of the organization.

This superficial depiction of the planning model and its stages emphasizes the ongoing nature of program planning. Equally apparent is the importance of the link that should exist between forecasting the future and creating it. To reiterate, the model (1) provides the basis for ongoing planning, (2) requires the application of knowledge, (3) involves lay persons as well as professionals, and (4) generates its own stimuli for self-renewal and adaptation in both goals and means for goal attainment. Insofar as it replaces traditional program planning, the model emerges as another example of the process of rationalization. Yet its intended uses and its integral mechanisms would appear to protect planners from the adverse consequences of rationalization, consequences identified earlier in this essay. In addition to using the results of futures forecasting (whether normative or extrapolative), the model also provides simultaneously a built-in, continuous mechanism for stimulating and effecting innovation.

The model, of course, provides only procedural regularity. A concluding question that must be addressed is what policy guidelines might be utilized by the physical education profession (and other planners interested in physical activity programs) in designing alternatives. In other words, if a normative ideal is to become real, the procedural guidelines provided by the model must be applied to specific problems with regard to physical education's roles, goals, modes of operation, and body of knowledge.

In the interest of avoiding contradictions between the policy statements that follow and the premises that I have endeavored to establish on this point, I want to emphasize that these statements are suggestions, i.e., alternatives that may be accepted or rejected. Clearly, the burden of proof always rests with policy analysts in terms of how well their case has been presented. Nevertheless, policy analysts remain accountable for their policy statements (Iceton, 1974; Holt and Turner, 1974). With these qualifications in mind, the following policy statements are offered in outline form.

1. The profession's goals have been in the past almost exclusively service oriented. Yet there have been few feedback and corrective mechanisms that could be utilized to guide practitioners' efforts to the point where the quality of services could be evaluated. This void prompts the need for three policy statements.

   a. Following the practices of true professionals (Morford, 1972), physical educators must initiate diagnostic efforts in the field for the twin purposes of validating their own efforts and determining client demands and expectations.

   b. As the term "physical education" should suggest, school physical education programs must begin to provide for school-age youth a liberal arts orientation to the study of physical activity, i.e., to cultivate knowledge and understanding over and above the performance excellence that now typifies physical training.

   c. The establishment of delivery systems requires better articulation between and among school physical education programs, community recreation programs, and other social services. These articulations should be cemented by a common knowledge base.

2. The preoccupation with services based on tradition and trial-and-error techniques has precluded the need for a body of knowledge that is unique, codified, and abstract. Yet as Ritzer (1975) and Morford (1972) have observed, professional and disciplinary authenticity hinge on a duly organized body of knowledge. The following policy statements stem from this fact.

   a. To complement and at the same time to fuel the service function, departments of physical education in colleges and universities must endeavor to establish disciplinary authenticity. Analogous to other academic units, the search for truth can be utilized to safeguard valued components of culture and/or to criticize appropriate aspects of society. Intelligence must become synonymous with free intelligence, i.e., the right to inquire without a priori judgments and interference by vested interests.

   b. Basic research efforts that are characteristic of a discipline create the need for specialists who are trained to apply knowledge and to design field research. As links with the real world, policy specialists are also responsible for identifying and/or communicating researchable problems to basic researchers.

3. The establishment of a disciplinary-professional model carries with it

100

the need for alterations in program components. The following policy statements describe some of these alterations.

a. Undergraduate and graduate programs, in lieu of focusing on technical or performance competencies, must emphasize the body of knowledge that marks a discipline.

b. The presentation of a knowledge base in both school physical education programs and in undergraduate programs should serve to alter expectations regarding the physical education major; in turn, this will culminate in prospective majors with academic as well as performance credentials. Undergraduate majors in physical education may then be prepared in a nonvocational manner as well as in the more traditional teacher preparation.

c. The researchers who will push back the barriers of ignorance and thus signal disciplinary progress will be available commensurate with the shift from vocationalism to knowledge and understanding at the secondary school and undergraduate levels. Then and only then can graduate education and training take on greater substance and specialization in lieu of the often superficial, initial exposure to theory and research that is characteristic of many graduate programs now.

4. A new genus of professionals will emerge from appropriately restructured programs. They will possess the knowledge and the ability to modify still other programs in schools, communities, and other agencies.

a. By virtue of their knowledge and understanding, professionals should be in a position to cater to the human variability that surrounds participation in physical activity. Certainly, this safeguarding may include the preservation of value-rational forms of social action in physical activity (Klausner, 1968; Morford and Clark, in press).

b. It is imperative that physical educators as guardians of their selected sphere of human activity cultivate in lay persons the knowledge and understanding that may safeguard them against exploitation by groups with vested, material interests. The education of the consumer in American society is the major way to block the producer. In the cases of international sport, professional sport, and commercialized health spas, all of which reside within our sphere of interest, yet fall outside the sphere of control of physical educators, the optimal way to affect changes is through consciousness-raising techniques (based upon knowledge and understanding) which are directed at large numbers of laypersons.

c. To remain abreast of the production of knowledge and to build in the necessary adaptations in goals and techniques, physical educators must build into their practice ongoing planning models such as that presented in this chapter. In the absence of this and similar models, ends-means inversions would almost certainly occur.

d. We must inculcate within professionals the awareness that democracy as an end cannot be served by undemocratic means. This awareness is the only safeguard for instrumentally rational social planning. Without this safeguard, interlocking delivery systems may be utilized to bring about forms of rigid social control that characterize the Orwellian nightmare (Lynd, 1967).

EPILOGUE

Lambert (1973) reminds us of the ancient Greek legend of Prometheus and his half-witted brother, Epimetheus. The differences between the two brothers were underscored by Hopkins (1974). The name "Prometheus" stems from the Greek *promethia,* meaning "to learn before." Epimetheus (from *epimethia,* which means "afterthought") never understood what was going on around him until it had already happened, and then it was too late for him to do anything about his fate. To borrow from Hopkins:

> So from ancient mythology we have two opposing prototypes for modern man—Prometheus, the embodiment of wise forethought who could see in advance what was likely to happen and make imaginative plans and preparations for man's future, and the unimaginative Epimetheus, who couldn't forsee anything but was guided only by impulse and desire and went bumbling along, getting into more and more trouble.*

Thus the central and concluding question appears to be: Are we to continue to be modern-day prototypes of Epimetheus, or are we in Lambert's (1973) terms to become *The New Prometheans?*

*From Hopkins, F. 1974. Prometheans and epimetheans, The Futurist 8:132.

REFERENCES

Aron, R. 1970. Main currents in sociological thought (H. Weaver, translator), New York, Doubleday & Co., Inc.

Avedon, E. M., and Sutton-Smith, B. 1971. The study of games, New York, John Wiley & Sons, Inc.

Baltzell, E. 1964. The Protestant establishment: aristocracy and caste in America, New York, Random House, Inc.

Bandura, A. 1969. Principles of behavior modification, New York, Holt, Rinehart & Winston, Inc.

Beitz, C., and Washburn, M. 1964. Creating the future, New York, Bantam Books, Inc.

Bell, D. 1973. Five dimensions of post-industrial society, Social Policy 3:3.

Berger, P., and Luckmann, T. 1967. The social construction of reality, New York, Doubleday & Co., Inc.

Berryman, J., and Ingham, I. 1972. The embourgeoisement of sport in America, 1860-1960, Paper presented at the American Sociological Association meeting, New Orleans, Aug. 28-31.

Brundage, A. 1952. Remarks at International Olympic Committee meeting in Lausanne, August 14.

Brundage, A. 1953. Remarks at International Olympic Committee meeting in Mexico City, April 17.

Coser, L. 1956. The functions of social conflict, New York, The Free Press.

Coser, L. 1971. Masters of sociological thought: ideas in historical and social context, New York, Harcourt Brace Jovanovich, Inc.

Cotgrove, S. 1975. Technology, rationality, and domination, Social Studies of Science 5: 55.

Cremin, L. 1961. The transformation of the school, New York, Random House, Inc.

Dreeban, R. 1973. The school as a workplace. In Travers, R., editor: Second handbook of research on teaching, Chicago, Rand McNally & Co.

Duncan, H. 1962. Communication and social order, New York, Oxford University Press, Inc.

Ellul, J. 1964. The technological society, London, Jonathan Cape, Ltd.

Etzioni, A. 1968. The active society, New York, The Free Press.

Festinger, L. 1957. A theory of cognitive dissonance, Evanston, Ill., Row & Peterson.

Galbraith, J. K. 1973. Economics and the public purpose, Boston, Houghton Mifflin Co.

Gallon, A. 1958. Voluntary physical education—a way out. In Proceedings of the College Physical Education Association, New York, National College Physical Education Association.

Goodhart, P., and Chataway, C. 1968. War without weapons, London, W. H. Allen & Co., Ltd.

Greenfield, T. 1973. Organizations as social inventions: rethinking assumptions about change, Journal of Applied Behavioral Science 9:551.

Griffiths, I. 1970. Gentlemen suppliers and with-it consumers, International Review of Sport Sociology 5:59.

Gross, R. 1963. The teacher and the taught, New York, Dell Publishing Co., Inc.

Gruneau, R. 1975. Sport, differentiation, and social inequality. In Ball, D., and Loy, J., editors: Sport and social order, Reading, Mass., Addison-Wesley Publishing Co., Inc.

Habermas, J. 1970. Toward a rational society (J. J. Shapiro, translator), Boston, Beacon Press.

Hambrick, R. 1974. A guide for the analysis of policy arguments, Policy Sciences 5:469.

Havelock, R. 1970. A guide to innovation in education, Ann Arbor, Mich., Institute for Social Research.

Havelock, R. 1971. Specialized knowledge-linking models. In Havelock, R., et al., editors: Planning for innovation, Ann Arbor, Mich., Institute for Social Research.

Henry, F. 1964. Physical education: an academic discipline, Journal of Health, Physical Education, and Recreation 35:32.

Hofstadter, R. 1963. Anti-intellectualism in American life, New York, Alfred A. Knopf, Inc.

Holt, J. 1972. Freedom and beyond, New York, Dell Publishing Co., Inc.

Holt, R., and Turner, J. 1974. The scholar as artisan, Policy Sciences 5:257.

Hopkins, F. 1974. Prometheans and epimetheans, The Futurist 8:131.

Houston, W. R. 1972. Performance education: strategies and resources for developing a competency-based teacher education program, New York, New York State Department of Education.

Huizinga, J. 1968. Homo ludens—a study of the play-element in culture, Boston, Beacon Press.

Iceton, N. 1974. Social development practitioners: training for a new profession, Dialogue 8:43.

Ingham, A. 1975. Occupational subcultures in the work world of sport. In Ball, D., and Loy, J., editors: Sport and social order, Reading, Mass., Addison-Wesley Publishing Co., Inc.

Ingham, A., and Loy, J. 1973. The social system of sport: a humanistic perspective, Quest 19:3.

Jaeger, W. 1965. Paideia, New York, Oxford University Press, Inc.

Janis, I. 1971. Groupthink, Psychology Today 76:43.

Kahn, A. 1969. Theory and practice of social planning, New York, The Russell Sage Foundation.

Kahn, H. 1975. On studying the future, Croton-on-Hudson, N.Y., The Hudson Institute.

Kahn, H., and Weiner, A. 1967. The year 2000: a framework for speculation on the next twenty-three years, New York, Macmillan Publishing Co., Inc.

Kanter, R., and Zurcher, L. 1973. Concluding statement: evaluating alternatives and alternative valuing, Journal of Applied Behavioral Science 9:381.

Katz, D. 1974. Factors affecting social change: a social-psychological interpretation, The Journal of Social Issues 30:159.

Katz, M. 1971. Class, bureaucracy, and schools, New York, Praeger Publishers, Inc.

Kenyon, G. 1966. The significance of physical activity as a function of age, sex, education, and socio-economic status of northern United States adults, Int. Rev. Sport Sociol. 1:41.

Keogh, J. 1964. Extreme attitudes toward physical education, Research Quarterly 34:27.

Klausner, S., editor. 1968. Why man takes chances, New York, Doubleday & Co., Inc.

Kolatch, J. 1972. Sports, politics, and ideology in China, Middle Village, N.Y., Jonathan David Publishers, Inc.

Kroll, W. 1971. Perspectives in physical education, New York, Academic Press, Inc.

Kuhlman, E., and Hoy, W. 1974. The socialization of professionals into bureaucracies: the beginning teacher in the school, The Journal of Educational Administration 12:18.

Lambert, J. 1973. The new prometheans, New York, Harper & Row, Publishers.

Lawson, H. 1974. Physical education and sport: alternatives for the future, Quest 21: 19.

Lawson, H. In press. Goal selection for physical education programs. In Concepts of Personalized Learning, Washington, D.C., American Alliance for Health, Physical Education, & Recreation.

Levine, D., and Levine, L. 1975. Social theory and social action, Economy and society 4:162.

Levine, N. 1974. Why do countries win olympic medals? Some structural correlates of olympic games success: 1972, Sociology and Social Research 58:353.

Lewin, K. 1947. Frontiers in group dynamics, Human Relations 1:5.

Lewis, G. M. 1969. Adoption of the sports program, 1906-39: the role of accomodation in the transformation of physical education, Quest 12:34.

Locke, L. 1969. Research in physical education: a critical view, New York, Columbia University Teacher's College Press.

Lockhart, A., and Spears, B., 1972. Chronicle of American physical education, 1855-1930, Dubuque, Iowa, William C. Brown Co., Publishers.

Loewith, K. 1970. Weber's interpretation of the bourgeois-capitalistic world in terms of the guiding principle of "rationalization." In Wrong, D., editor: Max Weber, Englewood Cliffs, N.J., Prentice-Hall, Inc.

Lukacs, J. 1963. A history of the cold war, New York, Doubleday & Co., Inc.

Lynd, R. 1967. Knowledge for what? Princeton, N.J., Princeton University Press.

MacRae, D. 1975. Policy analysis as an applied social science discipline, Administration and Society 6:363.

Meadows, D. H., et al. 1972. The limits to growth, New York, New American Library, Inc.

Marcuse, H. 1964. One-dimensional man, Boston, Beacon Press.

Mesthene, E. G. 1970. Technological change: its impact on man and society, Cambridge, Mass., Harvard University Press.

Michael, D. 1973. On learning to plan and planning to learn, San Francisco, Jossey-Bass, Inc., Publishers.

Molyneux, D. 1962. Central government aid to sport and physical recreation in countries of Western Europe, Birmingham, Engl., University of Birmingham Press.

Montagu, T. 1951. East-West sport relations, London, National Peace Council.

Morford, W. 1972. Toward a profession, not a craft, Quest 18:88.

Morford, W., and Clark, S. In press. The agon motif. In Keogh, J., editor: Exercise and sport sciences reviews, Santa Barbara, Journal Publishing Affiliates, vol. 4.

Nord, W. 1974. The failure of current applied behavioral science: a marxian perspective, The Journal of Applied Behavioral Science 10:557.

Orwell, G. 1946. Nineteen eighty-four, New York, Harcourt Brace Jovanovich, Inc.

Parsons, T. 1963. Introduction to Weber, M.: The sociology of religion, Boston, Beacon Press.

Platt, J. 1974. World transformations in belief systems, The Futurist 8:124.

Polak, F. 1973. The image of the future (E. Boulding, translator), San Francisco, Jossey-Bass, Inc., Publishers.

Riordon, J. 1974. Soviet sport and Soviet foreign policy, Soviet Studies 26:322.

Ritzer, G. 1975. Professionalization, bureaucratization, and rationalization: the views of Max Weber, Social Forces 53:627.

Robinson, J. 1967. Time expenditure in sports across ten countries, International Review of Sport Sociology 2:67.

Ruffer, W. 1965. A study of extreme physical activity groups of young men, Research Quarterly 36:183.

Ryan, W. 1971. Blaming the victim, New York, Vintage Books.

Salamini, L. 1974. Gramsci and marxist sociology of knowledge: an analysis of hegemony-ideology-knowledge, Sociological Quarterly 15:359.

Sallach, D. 1973. Critical theory and critical sociology: the second synthesis, Sociological Inquiry 43:131.

Sarason, S. 1971. The culture of the school and the problem of change, Boston, Allyn & Bacon, Inc.

Schollander, D., and Savage, D. 1971. Deep water, New York, Crown Publishers, Inc.

Scott, J., and Edwards, H. 1961. After the Olympics: buying off protest, Ramparts, November, p. 16.

Slater, P. 1970. The pursuit of loneliness, Boston, Beacon Press.

Smith, J. 1974. Educational innovations and institutional bureaucracy, Journal of Thought 9:219.

Spring, J. 1974. Mass culture and school sports, History of Education Quarterly 14:483.

Swidler, A. 1973. The concept of rationality in the work of Max Weber, Sociological Inquiry 43:41.

Van Dalen, D., and Bennett, B. 1972. A world history of physical education, Englewood Cliffs, N.J., Prentice-Hall, Inc.

Vickers, G. 1965. The art of judgment, New York, Basic Books, Inc., Publishers.

Vondracek, F., et al. 1974. Feasibility of an automated intake procedure for human services workers, The Social Service Review 48:271.

Wagner, F., and Hovis, W. 1974. The leisure information retrieval system: a report on the utility of the demand component for planning recreation programs, Seattle, Wash., Leisure Services, Inc.

Webb, H. 1969. Professionalization of attitudes toward play among adolescents. In Kenyon, G. S., editor: Aspects of contemporary sport sociology, Chicago, The Athletic Institute.

Weber, M. 1968a. Economy and society, New York, Bedminster Press.

Weber, M. 1968b. On charisma and institution building, Chicago, The University of Chicago Press.

Weber, M. 1963. The sociology of religion, Boston, Beacon Press.

Weber, M. 1958. The Protestant ethic and the spirit of capitalism, New York, Charles Scribner's Sons.

Weiner, N. 1971. The human use of human beings, New York, Avon Books.

Weston, A. 1962. The making of American physical education, New York, Appleton-Century-Crofts.

Wheeler, H. 1971. The politics of revolution, Berkeley, Calif., Glendessary Press.

Wrong, D., editor. 1970. Max Weber, Englewood Cliffs, N.J., Prentice-Hall, Inc.

Who are we?

Carole A. Oglesby

Futurists have proposed that one outgrowth of their work is the creation of alternative futures. This book is filled with alternatives for physical education in the year 2000. In this essay, I begin by proposing that the future of physical education is primarily the future of physical educators. I further suggest that the future of physical educators be viewed as a collective search for professional and academic identity. A professional identity, existing in popular culture as a stereotype, can be viewed as analogous in some respects to the individual's self. The search for selfhood is an individual matter and one's self has a more tangible reality than an abstract collective professional identity. However, there appear to be commonalities faced by physical educators as each searches for professional and academic identity. To the degree that common problems and challenges for physical educators can be identified and to the degree that physical educators perceive themselves and other colleagues to be struggling with these common problems and challenges, it seems reasonable to describe the search for professional identity, in part, by its collective aspects.

Construing the future of physical educators as a collective search for professional and academic identity is an arbitrary choice. The practice of arbitrary choice in building psychological reality is a key characteristic of human thought, but the process often occurs without our notice. As children, we come to accept other people's symbols. We accept that these symbols exist similarly, if not identically, for all and that they can be nothing but what we have accepted them to be. In the context of this essay, the professional identity of physical educators is in varying stages of change. The greatest obstacles in assuming this new identity are the old symbols of what we have been. The arbitrary choice to change is very difficult; this is the struggle that the search demands.

The view of the future of physical education as a search for collective psychological (and hence sociopsychological) identity is presented in three sections: (1) developing a view of the world: the physical educator's cosmic egg; (2) alternative concepts of physical education: old circles or a new cosmic egg; and (3) effects of transformed identity: the year 2000.

DEVELOPING A VIEW OF THE WORLD: THE PHYSICAL EDUCATOR'S COSMIC EGG

I have just suggested that the greatest obstacles in our identity search are the old symbols signifying what physical education has been. To propose that this is so is not to take a position on what is good or bad in physical education history. It simply affirms that human beings tend to perceive the world in such a way as to perpetuate their previously constructed "world view." Pearce used this term to describe our general orientation to the world, an orientation structured by a desire for a logical order in the universe (1971, p. 15). For us as physical educators to substantially change that aspect of our world view called *physical education* would require a massive psychological effort; for some it would be impossible.

In exploring the question of how world views develop, we will consider the following issues: (1) how cognitive structures (world views) develop, (2) why these structures are hard to change, and (3) one process of cognitive restructuring. It is assumed, although not always explicitly stated, that physical educators have experienced these processes in developing their respective world views of physical education.

How cognitive structures develop

Robert Frost saw civilization as a small clearing in a great forest. Joseph Pearce regards Frost's "clearing" to be reality-oriented thinking, reason, logic, culture; the "forest" is the unconscious, the unknown. The clearing is our cosmic egg (world view), structured by our intent to logically order the universe. Pearce states, "Our clearing in the forest is the form by which content is shaped; a content which in turn helps determine the form of the clearing" (1971, p. 19). For Pearce, reality and "logical truth" are variables formed and discarded by cultural agreement.

There are various researchers whose empirical work lends support to Pearce's central thesis. Hebb (1949), in *Organization of Behavior,* makes a case for the existence of structures that provide cognitive facilitation for specific thought processes following frequent repetitions of sensory stimulation. He specifically rejected the notion that human behavior is merely a series of reactions determined by immediately preceding events. The structures that Hebb postulates may be elements of Pearce's world view.

Piaget and Hunt give further insight into the processes by which the individual attempts to comprehend the world. Piaget (1963) identifies a general process that he terms *adaptation*, in which the organism interacts with the environment in such a manner that further interchanges favorable to preservation are enhanced. Adaptation takes two forms: *accommodation*, in which the organism adjusts itself to the properties of the environmental encounter and *assimilation*, in which the environmental sensory data are changed and incorporated into structures of the organism. Hunt (1961) describes the same concept, *assimilation*, as a process whereby thought structures warp sensory inputs to their own pattern and nature. Piaget theorizes that the adaptation of healthy organisms is built on a balance of accommodation and assimilation. Pearce works from the premise that in the adult, who has an established world view, assimilation dominates. That is, cognitive structures tend to modify incoming sensory data to make it consistent with that which is expected in the framework of the individuals' world view. When the assimilation process is dominant, the individuals' "cosmic egg" never cracks or changes. No incongruities, which become needs for concept change, are perceived. Reich (1970) in *The Greening of America* and Toffler (1970) in *Future Shock* both suggest that much of the present social and psychological disorder is the result of adult inability to accommodate and the dominance of assimilation in thought processes.

In summary, the following statements can be used to describe the development of cognitive structures (world view):

1. Through interaction between organism and environment, and especially through interaction with other human beings, a general cognitive structure or world view is constructed.
2. The general form of the world view is arbitrary but is heavily reinforced by cultural agreement.
3. The world view, once constructed, influences through the process of assimilation the world that is actually seen.
4. Individuals are able to perform the processes of accommodation and assimilation to varying degrees.

Why the cognitive structures are hard to change

This essay focuses on the future of physical educators in their collective search for professional identity. After the description of processes we have experienced in acquiring our present set of common agreements (few though they may be) about one particular subset of the world, i.e., physical education, we can now consider the question of resistance of the cognitive structure to reformation.

One element of the problem of restructuring is foreshadowed in the summary on world view development just outlined. In assimilation-dominated thinking, the world view influences perception so that distortion between sensory input and cognitive structure is seldom recognized. An example of a hypothetical "physical education world view" may illustrate the processes of assimilation-dominated thinking. Teacher B has been responsible for a professional preparation program for many years. The program is sport oriented, focusing heavily on advanced skills and coaching and teaching techniques. Other faculty members insist that the professional program should be extensively changed to deemphasize skills and technique classes and make academic subfields predominant. In a faculty meeting, teacher B heatedly asserts, "Physical education is sports and games! It always has been, and no matter how you dress it up, it always will be!"

For this hypothetical individual, the cognitive structure (composed of what "everyone" had agreed physical education was to be) distorted understanding of sensory information in at least two ways. All past conflicts about curriculum were erased, and the possibility of any present or future need for curriculum change was denied.

It appears that the existence of the world view and the assimilation process mitigate against significant conceptual restructuring. Anthropologists Hockett and Ascher (1968) write that even the most innovative behavior change is usually motivated by a conservative purpose (the maintenance of a previous behavioral form) rather than by change for change itself. Kelly (1955) also addresses this topic:

> In seeking improvement in the construct system, the person is repeatedly halted by damage to the system which apparently will result from alteration. Frequently personal investment in the larger system and his personal dependence on it, is so great that he will forego . . . alteration.*

Hockett and Ascher, Hebb, Piaget, Kelly, and Pearce present arguments that, taken together, form an important possibility. Within each of us, cognitive structures are developed which may perpetuate themselves to our detriment and that of social groups to which we belong. Frank has cited Alfred North Whitehead's belief that "those societies which cannot combine reverence for their symbols with freedom for their revision must ulti-

---

*From Kelly, G. 1955. Psychology of personal constructs, New York, W. W. Norton & Co., Inc., p. 9.

mately decay, either from anarchy or slow atrophy by useless shadows" (1967, p. 816). Whitehead's views support the need for institutionalization of, or at the very least, strong social support for restructuring processes of all aspects of the world view.

One process of cognitive restructuring

Pearce and Bruner provide descriptions of a process that enhances the continuing possibility of cognitive restructuring. Physical educators can utilize the process in searching for and creating a new professional identity. After I explore this process, briefly, I will apply it to the search for identity in which physical educators are involved.

Pearce describes a key factor in significant changes in world view that he calls autistic thinking. "A-thinking is unambiguous . . . all things are possible, all postulates are true" (1971, p. 24). For Pearce, autistic thinking is the borderline between reality thinking and the unconscious. Bruner's "creative act" consists of three stages that theoretically appear to demand autistic thinking. These are (1) *detachment* from or rejection of the old concept (the physical education world view as it has been), (2) *replacement* with the new concept, and (3) *freedom* to be guided by the new concept.

We have dealt fleetingly with the formation of a world view, resistance to change in a world view, and qualities necessary for such a change to occur. In the next section, I will consider specifically the physical education world view. This particular "cosmic egg" seems to have been in the process of cracking (cognitive restructure) interminably. If we do not utilize some creative transformation processes, the next 25 years may see us circling the same cosmic egg. Around us is the sound and fury of Title IX debate and the potential energy of the feminist-humanist movement. If we can transform our thought, as in autistic thinking, all things are possible. We can be closer at last to clarity concerning who we are.

ALTERNATIVE CONCEPTS OF PHYSICAL EDUCATION: OLD CIRCLES OR A NEW COSMIC EGG

Certainly every profession and discipline will undergo changes in definition and structure before the year 2000. Physical education, however, has been influenced by a unique social situation that has impaired our abilities to continuously create new symbols to represent our work and accomplishments. Rather, we have consistently been defined by external sources.

The world view of physical educators has been adversely affected by stigma arising from two social stereotypes: attitudes toward the body in dualistic, dichotomized thinking and attitudes of isomorphism between sport and athletics and the masculine principle. I will explore this proposition by drawing two futures for physical education. The first is a simple extension of the present world view of physical education. Without transformations in thinking, physical education in the year 2000 will be as similar to what we know today as the "now" physical education is to programs of the 1950s. The second future assumes transformations in thinking centering around a conceptual reconciliation of both dualistic "man" and masculinity-feminity formulations.

Future one, an extension of the present: stigma and physical education

Goffman describes a stigma as an attribute that disqualifies an individual from full social acceptance (1963, p. i). Any attribute, depending on the identity norms that are operational, may be discrediting and function as a stigma. It is assumed here that the world view of those individuals identified with the profession or discipline called physical education is influenced by a pervasive awareness that in many situations such an identity disqualifies them from full social acceptance. Goffman further describes some of the effects of experiencing stigma: (1) stigmatized individuals feel a conflict between their perceptions of personal humanness and innocence (as regards the stigmatized attribute) and shame because they too incorporate the values of the surrounding society, (2) they may work with extra diligence to master areas of activity ordinarily felt to be inaccessible to them because of the stigma, and (3) they may experience feelings of inferiority, insecurity, and anxiety (1963, pp. 10-11).

Before moving to a discussion of the sources of stigmatization, a case should be made for the proposition that physical educators experience this phenomena. Leonard has described attitudes toward physical education and athletics that indicate stigmatization.

> That an experiencing of the "merely physical" can lead us to fathom life mysteries may seem excessive or even grotesque but it did not to Pindar, Pythagares or any of our ancestors who walked the earth before civilization cast its spell over humanity and led us to believe that the body is somehow inferior to the intellect and spirit.[*]

He also asks, "When did it happen . . . that athletics came to be thought of as mundane or degrading, separate from intellect and spirit?" (1975, p. 7).

In the foreword to Locke's monograph, Foshay describes physical education in the following manner:

> The field of physical education has been rather more vulnerable to the ebb and flow of public preference than others. . . . It draws no support from elsewhere in the educational system; it is not a prerequisite for anything else. . . . Lacking

---

[*]From Leonard, G. 1975. The ultimate athlete, New York, The Viking Press, Inc., p. 3.

support from within the educational system, vulnerable to outside pressures, plagued with lobbying, this group has hoped that research could give them the authority and autonomy denied them from other sources.[*]

The sense of inferiority is treated tongue-in-cheek by Walter Kroll as he comments on the fact that advanced degrees in allied fields (e.g., psychology, neurophysiology) have assumed great prestige in some departments of physical education. "Such a situation is indeed interesting as it must qualify physical education as one of the few fields where direct and specific study of its own subject matter is deemed inappropriate" (1971, p. 69). Even Kroll seems to lapse momentarily into stigma-oriented thinking when he speaks positively of Larsen's proposal that a double major be required from bachelor's degree to doctorate, one degree in the allied field and one in the physical education analog (1971, p. 94).

This sequence of commentary has not been presented from a judgmental position about the accuracy of each author's view. Rather my intent has been to illustrate how the thinking of some of the brightest, most competent individuals in our field is sometimes affected by the stigma attached to the profession. A focal point of this essay is the difficulty involved in collectively creating new symbols for our field when our own world has been constructed with stigma-evoking old symbols. Let us now consider the two main sources of stigma in the physical education world view; these are perceptions of mind-body dualism and stereotypic dichotomous sexuality.

Belief in a "mind," "body," or "soul" is an ancient mode of thought, but the perception of human beings as integrated wholes is not new (Gerber, 1972). The "faculty psychology" of the late nineteenth century is of historical significance only, but the terminology of these outmoded systems shapes our thinking. Pearce states, "The average person picks up his symbols and ideas for imagining them from 'those who know.' Abstract and logically developed ideas seep into the untutored thought only as concrete familiar models are found to picture them" (1971, p. 146). The labels and symbols by which physical education is know are inadequate and uncomfortable for us; they have been our prison but also our home and we have not yet produced satisfactory replacements.

We can catalogue historical explanations for the stigma-evoking nature of our symbols as follows:

1. The body and the physical aspects of our nature are a source of sin.
2. Play and leisure are the source of sin.
3. "Physical" expression is an element of nature; hence it is lower in

[*]From Locke, L. F. 1969. Research in physical education, New York, Teachers College Press, p. ix.

importance than other "art" expression viewed as an element of culture (DuQuin, 1973).

4. Because of the dichotomous nature of dualistic thought, "physical" activity is seen as a category that excludes mental or intellectual activity.

5. Movement is primarily a subjective experience and hence not so important as the rational, objective experience of reason (Leonard, 1975, pp. 34-36).

We have not been successful in escaping the stigma associated with these anachronistic attitudes.

Staley in 1938 proposed that the term "physical education" was a misnomer since it emphasized a separate physical learning rather than organic wholeness (Whited, 1971, p. 22). Our cosmic egg is still labeled physical education.

Podeschi, while affirming that movement is subjective activity wherein the living body is the phenomenological center of an individual's needs and goals, states that physical education is symbolic of the dichotomies that have characterized human history, namely, dichotomies of mind/body, mental activity/physical activity, and emotion/reason (1974, p. 13).

We know these stigma-evoking symbols describe us. As Goffman has proposed, we feel innocent of the inferiority the symbols attribute to us. We feel shame because our own thoughts are structured by these symbols.

It appears also that stigma is experienced as a result of perceptions of dichotomous, stereotypic sexuality. Many writers have proposed that our society is characterized by obsessively polarized conceptions of sexuality (Beach, 1965; DeBeauvoir, 1957; DuQuin, 1975; Felshin, 1975; Maccobey, 1966; Weisstein, 1971). Felshin has stated that "the rituals of sport are the *rites* of manhood . . . the styles of sport express an ethic of competition, power, dominance, and male bonding" (1975, p. 33). Sports and games, seen as the central core of physical education (Whited, 1971; Kroll, 1971), have been a cornerstone of the conceptualization of masculinity (Oglesby, 1975b).

The stigma-evoking properties of women's association with sport and physical education have been clearly demonstrated (Hart, 1972; Felshin, 1974; Griffin, 1973; Oglesby, 1974). It is indicative of the inherent joyfulness of play and sport that many women maintained their association with some form of "physical education" throughout the darker periods of harshly stereotyped concepts of sexuality (Gerber, 1974). This relatively high level of participation was also due to the profession's efforts to shield women's activity from public view and to "conceptual gymnastics," which defined women's sport and women athletes as "much different" from that of their male counterparts (Felshin, 1974; Oglesby, 1975a).

Strangely enough, the isomorphism between the "masculine principle" and sport creates stigma-evoking problems for men as well. The athlete symbol, like Jung's Warrior-King, has mythic dimensions. He (and the symbol is He) personifies the masculine principle as described by Roszak and Roszak. However, the old symbol is false and damaging. There is general agreement that just as no human male embodies all aspects of the masculine principle, no woman embodies all the feminine aspects (Beach, 1965; Parsons, 1955; Sanford, 1966). Yet every male athlete, and those male physical educators who deal with games and sport daily, stand in the shadow of the myth. They also suffer in that they may perceive personal shortcomings when they compare themselves to the myth.

Consequences of future one. To the degree that dichotomous, stereo-typic social attitudes toward the "dumb jock" and masculinity as opposed to femininity are perceived as discrediting by physical educators, their collective world view is stigma oriented. The important element of stigma orientation here is other directedness. As Goffman states, "The stigmatized is always told who he should be by virtue of his group identity" (1963, p. 124). Those who experience stigma suffer varying degrees of embarrass-ment, anxiety, overly compliant "passing" behavior, and outer directedness (Goffman, 1963; Leonard, 1975; Wrightsman and Brigham, 1973).

Goffman describes clearly how the individual who is "passing" (striving for full acceptance) is much more sensitive to the demands of the social environment than others. Two basic problems have evolved from the sensi-tivity of physical educators to external demands on the profession and external definitions of the profession itself. First, there is support in physical education literature for a view that overemphasis on the diverse educa-tional service functions has contributed to a lack of theoretical substance and clarity (Singer, 1972; Kroll, 1971). In service functions, physical educa-tors have tried to say yes to everyone. The second problem might be labeled our reactive scramble for academic respectability. In the years after Sput-nik, the Conant report, and Franklin Henry, a few physical educators seemed to swing with customary enthusiasm to the opposite pole and begin the pursuit of "substance" with abandon. Leonard states that to study physical education today "is to display boldly your academic bent" (1975, p. 6). Kroll comments on the "flight from teaching/service responsibilities to the pinnacle, all research-no students" (1971, p. 23). Both Kroll and Lawrence Locke propose that "bridge builders" who would link the worlds of research and teaching would benefit physical education. Beyond their suggested ameliorative measure are the central issues; these are lack of perceived collective autonomy and lack of perceived freedom to create symbols for our field of study and our service profession that serve our own purposes.

At this point, you may feel that this discussion has dwelled exclusively on the distressing aspects of defining physical education. We cannot deal with a complete development of the physical education world view. Our focus is only on those elements of our world view that have limited us in past restructuring and recreating. If we allow stigma-oriented thinking to freeze us in inhibiting stereotypes, future one will be our reality. We will carry the present state of affairs, with its uneven successes, ambivalences, and frustrations, into our future. With a greater understanding of the present constraints of our world view, we can transform that view and build a new future.

Future two: a transformed egg

To bring our collective search for identity to a new level, we must take it under our own control. We must step away from our old symbols, respectfully and without rancor, for these symbols enabled us to survive and they were the best we could create at the time. We can achieve this transformation by utilizing Bruner's creative process (Pearce, 1971):

1. *Detachment* from old concepts
2. *Replacement* of old concepts with new symbols
3. *Absorption* of the new symbols

As we move through this three-stage process, be aware of the potential we have to serve as a model for other aspects of society. The experiences of social disqualification, excessively dichotomous thinking and alienation from self are not unique to us in physical education. Gilbert, for example, has stated that universities have dissolved into a large number of different disciplines that promote specialized learning but not "education, which demands the image of Man at the center of all questions" (1974, p. 16). Gilbert sees the humanities as a central synthesizing force. New symbols for what we have called physical education can lead us to an important role in this integrative process. Leonard (1975) proposes that "the physical education department stands at the center of the campus, the foundation stone of the educational enterprise" (1975, p. 19).

Pearce and Leonard agree on the need for new myths and mythic beings to further reconcile ancient dichotomies. Leonard is the more direct: "Why not look to sport, physical education and the body for our transforming myths?" (1975, p. 249). Thanks to the source materials provided by feminist philosophy, our mythic models will not be exclusively "masculine." We can honor the full complement of human potential in our symbols. "Sport can provide an arena in which we can practice calling off the masculinity-femininity game" (Oglesby, 1975b).

As we transform our "physical education cosmic egg," awareness of the potential to serve as a model does not mean we must let ourselves be seduced by this vanity. We must not continue to allow a by-product to become our goal. Our goal must be a process, a continuing identity search concerning ourselves and for ourselves as we move toward the year 2000.

EFFECTS OF TRANSFORMED IDENTITY: THE YEAR 2000

If physical education is transformed, what will it become? In this concluding section, we consider specific possibilities relating to modes of operation and organizational changes.

Modes of operation

Physical education and physical educators will consistently utilize internal criteria for decision making. Physical educators will hold a highly positive view of themselves as they function in their professional role.

An internal locus of control and a positive self-concept are two aspects of individual psychological health. It is possible to characterize groups by the degree to which their members reflect these characteristics. During the period 1976 to 2000, the physical education professional associations and teachers will make specific efforts to enable current and future physical educators to effect therapeutic changes designed to achieve these two goals.

Such efforts will take place in two stages. Professional associations and programs will offer simple testing services in which individuals can assess the degree to which they exhibit autonomy in professional decision making and a high positive regard for their chosen profession or field of study.

Then, where necessary, professional associations and programs will arrange for or provide training techniques for developing the desired psychological changes. Even here in the year 2000, it is possible to hear some laughter about a whole profession needing "shrinks." That is of course an exaggeration, but there does appear to be a special kind of psychological strength that is demanded of physical educators, yet never explicitly developed. The values of society reinforce a belief in the insignificance of play, and physical educators then must make their life work out of insignificance. We do not believe that play is insignificant, but how do we cope with the discomfort that results from the discrepancy between how we feel about our work and how others view us?

In the year 2000 we shall learn psychological skills for coping with this problem. Across our profession and discipline, we shall learn anew the stages of assertiveness:

1. To acknowledge our understanding of the beliefs and attitudes others hold about us and our field
2. To be able to clearly state our own views about ourselves, our field, and what we need
3. To outline steps for mediating differences and meeting our needs

Physical educators will end sex stereotyping in play, sport, and dance. As proposed earlier, the potential contribution of participation in sport to the development of traditional masculine qualities has long been recognized. By the year 2000, other insights will also be gained. It will be recognized that women and men can benefit from and need participation in those activities that contribute to achievement and personal transcendence. We will also affirm that women and men can benefit from and need participation in those activities that contribute to the development of caring and nurturing qualities. We will recognize that play, sport, and dance are contexts in which these qualities can be developed.*

The common or shared experiences of boys and girls or men and women in play, sport, and dance will also lead to open and honest communication between the sexes rather than the limits imposed by stereotypes (Kanter, 1974). Ending the inviolable rule of sex-segregated sport will greatly weaken the patterns of communication and behavior that have led to boys developing out-group attitudes toward girls and denigration of females by boys and girls alike (Johnson, 1974).

Physical educators will end age and skill stereotyping. Declaring an end to age and skill stereotyping is not to declare an arbitrary end to differential treatment of people in different age and skill categories. It is to affirm that the work of physical education must not be limited to only this group or that. The scope of the profession and discipline must include all people, whatever their age or skill, and wherever they may be found. Graubard (1974) and Frankel (1974) have described the limited view that has prevailed regarding the proper locale of "education." In the past, we often acted as if "physical education" only dealth with the kindergarten through college school population and the elite in skill and body type. "Seventy percent of body types are not represented at the Olympics. Traditional, highly competitive sports are appropriate only for a certain number of people. But there are activities for every body type" (Leonard, 1975, p. 138).

In the year 2000, master physical education teachers will be attached to units of government, industry, businesses, and rural, suburban, and inner-city communities. Teaching and learning will take place wherever

---

*See Reich's discussion (1973) of a team as a circle of affection and Ogilvie's discussion (1966) of the relation of coach to player characterized by trust and care.

117

there are people. In our transformed future, we will diversify program offerings in school and nonschool settings along many dimensions of performance. We will also develop specialized centers for intense skill development in traditional sport and dance forms where needed. This is not a dilemma. Both types of needs (diversification and specialization) are legitimate, and we will establish means to meet them.

Organization and body of knowledge

The transformation of organizational structure and body of knowledge are pivotal points in the identity search we have begun. This is the toughest aspect of our cosmic egg to crack. Two assumptions must be made explicit before examples of transformed organizational structure can be set forth.

It is assumed that there is both a discipline and a profession focusing on agonistic and ludic movement studies.* In the mid-1970s the most popular choices for identity symbols for physical education seemed to be sport, movement, or exercise. Good and bad cases have been made for each. Whited (1971) and Singer (1973) have dealt with the problems of "movement" as our generic symbol. Briefly, the term lacks definitiveness and is too inclusive. The terms "sport" and "exercise" have some appeal but are too limiting as a disciplinary focus. As Whited points out, sport signifies contesting. There is too much left out in the space between "sport" and "movement."

The term "agonistic and ludic movement" has certain advantages. The Greek terms for struggle and playful expressiveness hint at the transformation of ancient idealized forms by virtue of the knowledge, understanding, and insight of more than 2000 years of experience. The term encompasses behavior that is contesting, playful and joyous, and expressive. It brings together in an abstract sense athletes, children, and dancers (with no implication that only athletes contest, etc.) in terms of what they share through in specific movement forms. This label is unfamiliar and would have to be painstakingly explained, but if transformation is to occur by the year 2000, we must be about that process whatever we call ourselves. Perhaps there is no way to know what we will call ourselves by the year 2000. The important thing is that we function to unify human dichotomies.

It is also assumed that academic organization in the year 2000 will be influenced by what Campbell (1969) has called the "fish scale model," in which the various disciplines are seen as very broad and ever expanding. Conversely, each scholar's expertise and related interests are narrow, and

---

*I am influenced in my use of these terms by Hal Lawson and John Loy. I wish to credit them but also free them from any responsibility for my suggestion that we name ourselves by these terms.

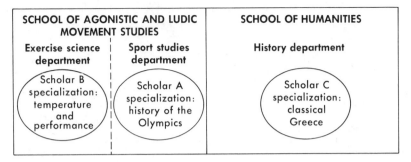

Fig. 3. Diagram of "interdisciplinary closeness."

the demands of specialization create a tendency toward increased narrowing of interest. This configuration results in a good deal of "interdisciplinary closeness." A classic case is diagrammed in Fig. 3. The usual university structure would place scholars A and B in closer interaction than scholars A and C, although in terms of background, interests, and expertise this grouping is illogical. Secondary school departmental structures often create a similar situation. Organizational structures that take into account interdisciplinary closeness as well as disciplinary and departmental origin should be encouraged.

Let us now approach the central question. What programs of study and what professional preparation programs will produce the individuals who will lead us in transforming our identity?

As an integrative profession and discipline, we will need to shift our emphasis to a postgraduate orientation in the pattern of medicine and law. Baccalaureate degree programs that emphasize acquiring skills in analysis of data, synthesis of theory, and verbal and physical communication and expressiveness will be the first stage of professional or disciplinary studies.

Through professional efforts, many technician tasks (that currently devour the professional's time or remain undone) will be delegated to support personnel. These support personnel will be certified as competent in various ways and will handle such tasks as arranging for equipment and uniforms; planning, care, and design of facilities; general supervision of teaching space open for individualized instruction; direct teacher and researcher aid; interpretation of previously designed individualized instruction packets; athletic training; sport officiating; computer programming for skill instruction; game strategy models; monitoring of student needs and interests; and research. Depending on the nature of such support positions, certification patterns might vary from brief, direct apprenticeships to 2- or 4-year training programs.

Those who want to be master teachers or researchers will enter a 3-

College of agonistic and ludic (A & L) movement studies*

Biophysical foundations	Social and behavioral foundations	Performance studies	Professional studies
Council on biomechanics	Council on A & L history	Council on dance	Council on teacher certification
Council in exercise physiology	Council on A & L psychology	Council on athletics	Council on sport administration
Council on motor integration	Council on A & L sociology	Council on sport instruction	Council on teacher behavior studies
	Council on A & L philosophy		Council on support services certification

*The councils included are examples and are not intended to include all possibilities.

to 4-year postgraduate program. Such individuals would combine knowledge in specific movement forms with biophysical, social, and behavioral bases and studies of human development through agonistic and ludic movement forms.

The undergraduate program will encompass both training programs for the certification of support personnel and opportunities for the development of the skills necessary for postgraduate work.

An academic structure for programs such as these is presented above.

Difficult issues are raised even by a structural diagram so simple as this. For example, how can subelements as disparate as the natural and behavioral sciences and humanities be included in one discipline? Camille Brown has commented succinctly on this problem. "Such an approach is a reduction of the discipline to a 'wholeness' starting point. The fields of psychology, physics, physiology, sociology, and others have become so highly specialized that as starting points their materials are too fragmented for use in human movement study" (1967, p. 54). While Brown has chosen different symbols (e.g., human movement), the essential point is clear. The form of the discipline must reflect the form of that which is studied. If agonistic and ludic movement structures are influenced by human biology and sociology, then appropriate elements of human biology and sociology must be represented in the agonistic and ludic structures' discipline. Thus the question of whether one element of a natural and one element of a social science can coexist in the same integrative discipline is irrelevant.

The form of the discipline I have termed agonistic and ludic movement structures is integrative and complex. Administrative and other organizational structures (e.g., professional associations) must be creatively developed. In the year 2000, this may be exciting and challenging and not in the least embarrassing. We have now taken a few steps on the journey toward a transformed identity. First, we considered how people develop their own world view, including concepts of identity. We dealt in more detail with selected factors that shape the physical education world view. We imagined futures with and without significant world view changes. To the degree that we have been able to adopt another world view, if only momentarily, our old cosmic egg is healthily cracked. It will never be quite the same again.

REFERENCES

American Association for Health, Physical Education, & Recreation. 1974. Towards program excellence: the physical education position papers, Journal of Health, Physical Education, and Recreation 42:41.

American Association for Health, Physical Education, & Recreation. 1973. The new physical education, Journal of Health, Physical Education, and Recreation 44:23.

Beach, F. 1965. Sex and behavior, New York, John Wiley & Sons, Inc.

Beisser, A. R. 1967. The madness in sport, New York, Appleton-Century-Crofts.

Brown, C. 1967. The structure of knowledge in physical education, Quest 9:53.

Campbell, D. T. 1969. Ethnocentrism of disciplines and the fish scale model of omniscience. In Sherif, M., and Sherif, C., editors: Interdisciplinary relationships in the social sciences, Chicago, Aldine Publishing Co.

De Beauvoir, S. 1957. The second sex, New York, Alfred A. Knopf, Inc.

DuQuin, M. E. 1975. The philosophic effects of culture on women's experience in sport, Unpublished paper.

Felshin, J. 1974. Triple option for women in sport, Quest 21:36.

Felshin, J. 1975. Sport, style and social mode, Journal of Physical Education and Recreation 46:31.

Frank, L. 1967. The need for a new political theory, Daedalus, Summer, p. 809.

Frankel, C. 1974. Reflections on a worn-out model, Daedalus, Fall, p. 25.

Gerber, E. 1972. Sport and the body: a philosophical symposium, Philadelphia, Lea & Febiger.

Gilbert, F. 1974. Reflections on higher education, Daedalus, Fall, p. 12.

Goffman, E. 1963. Stigma: notes on the management of spoiled identity, Englewood Cliffs, N.J., Prentice-Hall, Inc.

Graubard, S. 1974. Thoughts on higher education's purposes and goals: a memorandum, Daedalus, Fall, p. 1.

Griffin, P. 1973. Whats a nice girl like you doing in a profession like this? Quest 19:96.

Hart, M. M. 1972. Sport in the socio-cultural process, Dubuque, Iowa, William C. Brown Co., Publishers.

Hockett, C. F., and Ascher, R. 1968. The human revolution. In Montagu, A., editor: Culture: man's adaptive dimension, New York, Oxford University Press, Inc.

Hebb, D. O. 1949. The organization of behavior, New York, John Wiley & Sons, Inc.

Hunt, J. M. 1961. Intelligence and experience, New York, Ronald Press.

Johnson, K. P. 1974. Human values through sports: a sociological perspective. In Development of human values through sports, Washington D.C., American Association for Health, Physical Education, & Recreation.

Kanter, R. 1974. Women in organization: change agent skills, Unpublished paper.

Kelly, G. 1955. Psychology of personal constructs, New York, W. W. Norton & Co., Inc.

Physical education: a view toward the future

Kroll, W. 1971. Perspectives in physical education, New York, Academic Press, Inc.

Leonard, G. 1975. The ultimate athlete, New York, The Viking Press, Inc.

Locke, L. F. 1969. Research in physical education: a critical view, New York, Teachers' College Press.

Maccobey, E., editor. 1966. The development of sex differences, Stanford, Calif., Stanford University Press.

Ogilvie, B., and Tutko, T. 1966. Problem athletes and how to handle them, London, Pelham Books, Ltd.

Oglesby, C. 1974. Future directions and issues. In Women's athletics: coping with controversy, Washington D.C., American Association for Health, Physical Education, & Recreation.

Oglesby, C. 1975a. The role of women in the development of university sport. In Proceedings of the seventh international conference on student sport, Helsinki, International Federation for University Sport.

Oglesby, C. 1975b. The forest must be planted all at once, Paper presented at American Association for Health, Physical Education, and Recreation convention, Atlantic City, March.

Parsons, T., and Bales, R. F. 1955. Family, socialization, and interaction process, Glencoe, Ill., Free Press of Glencoe.

Pearce, J. C. 1971. The crack in the cosmic egg, New York, Pocket Books, Inc.

Piaget, J. 1963. The origins of intelligence in children, New York, W. W. Norton & Co.

Podeschi, R. 1974. The farther reaches of physical activity, Quest 21:12.

Reich, C. 1970. The greening of America, New York, Random House, Inc.

Roszak, T., and Roszak, B. 1969. Masculine/feminine, New York, Harper & Row, Publishers.

Sanford, N. 1966. Self and society, New York, Atherton Press, Inc.

Schimel, J. 1970. The sporting and gaming aspects of love and war. In Contemporary issues in sport psychology, Chicago, Athletic Institute.

Singer, R., et al. 1972. Physical education: an interdisciplinary approach, New York, Macmillan Publishing Co., Inc.

Toffler, A. 1970. Future Shock, New York, Randon House, Inc.

Weisstein, N. 1971. Psychology constructs of the female or the fantasy life of the male psychologist. In Gornick, V., and Moran, B. K., editors: Women in sexist society, New York, New American Library, Inc.

Whited, C. 1971. Sport science, Journal of Health, Physical Education, and Recreation 42:21.

Wrightsman, L., and Brigham, J. 1973. Contemporary issues in social psychology, Monterey, Calif., Brooks/Cole Publishing Co.

CHAPTER FOUR

EDUCATIONAL FORECASTS

"The future promises to reinforce the emerging role of physical education as the art and science of human movement. . . . Physical education in the future will deal [also] with the enhancing of the movement experience outside of the formal atmosphere of the school. . . . It would seem that human movement will finally be acknowledged as central to the body of knowledge that is physical education. . . . The future promises to provide substantial change in the organization of sport and physical education in the United States. . . . The competitive disaffiliation aspect of sport will be reduced and emphasis will be placed on affiliative, cooperative interactions. . . . Physical education will be "more than movement," larger than sport, and greater than physical education." By extrapolating from current trends, past history, and contemporary postures both in education and physical education and by combining a bit of imagination with insight, Celeste Ulrich presents these and other views regarding the future of physical education.

In the second essay of this chapter, Dean A. Pease argues convincingly that due to a host of factors operating in the larger society, the trend toward imposing the industrial model as a means of structuring educational practice will continue into the foreseeable future. As a consequence of this trend he further argues that physical education must of necessity begin seriously to restructure its programs and practices in accordance with the industrial mode. Pease also suggests ways this might best be accomplished without doing violence to the traditional humanistic concerns of physical education.

In the concluding essay, Charles B. Corbin cautions us about the futility of instituting change for the sake of change. Later he presents a rather personalized view of what physical education should be like in the future. His view of the future is highly humanistic, and he argues that in order to proceed toward this "ideal," physical education will have to develop and apply a new wisdom regarding professional programs and practices.

The future hour: an educational view

Celeste Ulrich

One of the few absolutes that may be ventured is that the future will foster change. Change is usually frightening, for it tests the basic underpinnings of a structure. Thus as the future fosters change, so it promotes anxiety.

To reduce anxiety, many people avoid change and thus try to ignore the future. These people believe that in one way or another the future will take care of itself. Heraclitus' admonition that "nothing is permanent except change" subtly reinforces the feeling that the future need not be studied; indeed, it need hardly be anticipated. That type of philosophical resignation has resulted in the static teaching and learning atmospheres that currently threaten the viability of educational institutions. Physical educators cannot tolerate such ennui.

The prologue for the future of physical education may be found in its history and its contemporary postures. An examination of the trends and torques relevant to physical education, coupled with a bit of imagination and insight, might lead to rational prognostications regarding anticipated change. Such predictions are usually restricted to a specified time span, and for our purposes this period will be the last quarter of the twentieth century. Thus the influence of education on physical education from 1975 to 2000 will be the focus of our concern and will be analyzed with respect to the role of physical education, its body of knowledge, its organization, and its modes and methods of operation. Each issue will be surveyed relative to past and present antecedents and future expectations.

THE ROLE OF PHYSICAL EDUCATION

Human totality must be acknowledged by all those who work with people. For the sake of analytical expediency, it may be convenient to talk of the human mind, the human body, or the human soul, but it is the human being who is the concern of education, and that being is always a whole. Thus the interrelationships among cognitive, affective, and motor behaviors are the central focus of any teaching and learning process. Such an understanding, however, has not dictated the relative importance of each of these behaviors, and when they are arranged in a hierarchy, the usual pattern has viewed the preservation of the soul as primary, the nourishment of the mind as secondary, and the health of the body as tertiary.

The soul's well-being has been delegated traditionally to the care of the church, the mind's well-being has been tended by the school, and the body's well-being has been the province of the individual, to abuse or glorify. The traditional hierarchy has implied value by determining position. The soul has represented the highest worth, finding itself in faith and depending on passion to reveal truth. The mind is valued next to the soul; it is manifested in intelligence and relies on reason to ferret out truth. The body is the least important of the triumvirate. It is revealed in structure and is beholden to function for its validity.

As the school has tended the mind, it has depended on cognitive recall to establish intelligence and to employ reason. Thus regurgitation of information has been rewarded with educational plaudits, and the prosaic emulation of ancient and documented reasoning has been touted as desirable. Only as the body was viewed as the "temple" of the mind and soul was it considered important by schools and churches. In the past the body was considered as "object," an edifice constructed by genetic circumstance and functional only at the discretion of the soul and mind it housed.

It was therefore not unusual to find physical education as an adjunct of the scholastic curriculum. If the individual was able to function with ease, it was assumed that fitness prevailed. Fitness ensured a reasonable structure and abetted both faith and intelligence.

Such a frame of reference suggested that the best that could be done in the teaching and learning environment would be to "train" the body. Thus attention was focused on the development of strength, agility, flexibility, and coordination. Such functional attributes helped to ensure a structural integrity that was both aesthetically pleasing and operationally sound. Historically, education tolerated the education of the physical to the extent that such education did not interfere with the more important capacity of abstract reasoning and the imprinting of information.

It was therefore not surprising when those who thought of the body as more than a residence for mind and soul began to press for education *through* the physical rather than the training *of* the physical. A slow but persistent effort stressed that a change in anthropometic measurements was not the sine qua non of physical education. Function became a truth in itself and was valued, not as a means to an end but rather as a basic aspect of education. The pragmatic emphasis suggested by John Dewey and his followers stressed that education was life rather than preparation for life and that life was "doing."

Physical educators had no difficulty in adjusting to such a philosophical design, and they began to emphasize functionality as the goal of their educational mission. The vehicles used to offer arenas of function were extended beyond the training pits and began to encompass patterns that required the attainment of motor skills. These patterns took the form of games, dance, gymnastics, sport, and aquatics. Thus the individual became functional through the use of ordinative activity, activity that was sufficient to itself and that produced its own disciplinary organization of knowing through doing.

Concurrently, the understanding of "body" fostered an attitude that the body was more than a genetic temple kept ready for worship by training regimens; the body became the functional attribute of reality, and it was claimed that the self was enriched by education through the physical. It was further suggested that physical education was a viable method of education and that the techniques and tools used by physical educators were unique to the educational world and thus offered an additional life experience. The ideal body was a product of a bevy of activities "selected as to kind and conducted as to outcome."

Because there were other academic areas that also claimed physical function as being in their realm of interest, the administrators' inclination was to join all concepts that viewed the physical being as the core of human understanding. Thus health and recreation became "natural" allies of physical education, and a collegiate organization of practitioners was formed. State departments of education, colleges, universities, and national organizations reflected health, physical education, and recreation as a single concept, often taught by the same person.

Almost simultaneously, it was insisted that the *techniques* used to educate through the physical be identified as independent and discrete bodies of knowledge. Notably, dance and sport had strong adherents who believe that the dance and sport techniques used to educate *through* the physical were sufficiently unique that they were deserving of recognition in the educational world. Sport was organized outside curricular offerings into intramural and interscholastic athletics. Sport within the curriculum was a technique, a method of physical education. Sport outside the curriculum was an entity, a phenomenon that demanded peculiar organizational patterns and needed a clientele who believed in the primary importance of athletics in life.

Dance remained a part of the physical education curriculum but it was divorced from the sport techniques used in physical education curriculums. Thus dance educators were different from physical educators, even as coaches were different from teachers. In some instances, all interactions between dance and physical education were severed, and those involved with dance sought visibility and recognition for it as a fine art rather than a part of the movement arts and sciences.

With sport and dance in the vanguard, those involved with other methods used to educate through the physical, e.g., aquatics and gymnastics, also attempted to establish rationales for autonomy. The effort for such

126

autonomy did not have the cultural support enjoyed by dance and sport, and consequently both gymnastics and aquatics have remained within the organizational purview of physical education.

As each of the patterns of movement used in physical education was analyzed, there was the implicit understanding that each experience offered distinct and discrete outcomes to the individual. Specific motor behaviors sponsored specificity in cognitive and affective behaviors. Thus basketball did something for and to an individual that was different from what tap dance did. Diving offered outcomes that were significantly different from tennis. Wrestling produced behavioral interactions that were unlike those produced by free exercise routines.

The individuality of these behavior responses forced physical educators to consider a new definition of body. The body was a part of existence and thus a phenomenon subject to personal understanding and evaluation. That point of view has sponsored the idea that the body may be "subject" instead of "object" and thus may be thought of as "the radical root of reality." Teaching and learning experiences must be structured to enhance the experiential facets of being in the body and the affective and cognitive domains of human behavior must be joined to the motor domain as a tripartite adventure into reality.

There is currently an attempt to change the curricular offerings in scholastic physical education from the simplistic acquisition of motor skill patterns to the complex design of experiencing being in the body. Leonard, in *The Ultimate Athlete,* speaks of finding oneself and suggests that the revelation of the ultimate athlete is a fundamental experience for each person. The discovery of the self through a revision of physical education is Leonard's formula for preparing an individual for an encounter with the "game of games," which is life itself.

Many others, notably Metheny, Abernathy, Kleinman, Jewett, and Barrett, are suggesting that the role of physical education is to provide the individual with understanding that will build on generic movement patterns and utilize ordinative and creative movement designs to help with self-realization. That many of these ordinative designs will come from sport, dance, aquatic, and gymnastic techniques is usually acknowledged. That there will be greater opportunity for the development of individual movement style and innovative movement tactics is the hope of contemporary physical educators.

To highlight the emphasis of the "new" physical education, there have been several attempts to rename it. Names such as "movement arts and sciences," "kinesiology," and "homokinetics" are among the many that have been suggested. The renaming effort is an attempt of physical educators to free themselves from the uneasy alliance with health and recreation and to distinguish their basic concern (human movement) from the techniques used in attending to the concern (dance, sport, aquatics, and gymnastics).

As the struggle for identification goes on, physical educators are coming to realize that their search for disciplinary integrity must grow from existing products and processes and that the history of the "physical" of education cannot be ignored. Recognition of the validity of such an approach has gained subtle encouragement from colleagues in academic circles. Physical education no longer is considered an adjunct to formal education; it is considered instead an integral part of it.

The future promises to reinforce the emerging role of physical education as the art and science of human movement. The attention to humanism within education mandates an understanding of motor behaviors as well as an understanding of the body. Concern with Eastern philosophies, theories of meditation, and phenomenological experiences all suggest that physical education will play an increasingly significant role in the total educational process.

There is evidence that extreme curricular changes in physical education are in the offing. Courses designed to assist individuals in adaptative procedures will be paramount. Study of nonverbal behavior patterns, the geneses of human movement, the functional aspects of human movement, and theories of human movement will be woven into the existing matrix of sport, dance, techniques gymnastic, and aquatic skills and techniques.

Physical education as we now know it will be separated from health and recreation both organizationally and administratively. There will be a tremendous effort to dissolve the traditional walls that have isolated one discipline from another. As those walls dissolve, physical education will take its share of responsibility for the education of the whole person. This scholastic evolution will begin in primary schools and institutions of higher learning and then gradually permeate the secondary schools of the country.

Physical educators will be called on to be a part of the scholastic team that is now as attentive to adaptive procedures as it once was to cognitive recall. The key to such adaptation will involve problem-solving techniques with an emphasis on function. Such problem-solving will be sponsored with respect to an identified concept. For example, the concept may be aggression, and the school will attempt to program the teaching and learning experience in such a way that all aspects of aggression are considered—socioeconomic implications, biological insights, historical perspectives, behavioral manifestations, emotional expectations, physical stratagems, future inferences. The concept might be techniques of interaction, and the interpersonal strategies found in sport, dance, gymnastics, and aquatics would be primary processes to be analyzed. The concept could deal with the pioneer spirit in the United States, and physical educators would be responsible for information regarding the motor aspects of strength, coordination, flexibility, and endurance and for helping to establish the significance of such movement designs in the essential nature of the pioneer spirit. The possibilities of a tapestry of understanding as all educators come to grip with conceptual understandings is exciting. Physical educators will have a part to play in the weaving of such a tapestry.

An additional role of physical education in the future will involve enhancing the movement experience outside the formal atmosphere of the school. Being in the body is not isolated to school-age people. Programs to enhance such understandings must include preschool and after-school groups. Most of these programs will continue to be offered in the traditional forms of sport, dance, gymnastics, and aquatics. There is some indication that new games will be added to the traditional ones we have known and that have often been a preliminary to athletics. Instead the games will reduce competitive elements and enhance cooperative and affiliative processes. Opportunities for involvement in lifetime sport, in community dance programs, and in human development clinics will proliferate. Such activities will not be reserved for leisure time but will become a focus of individual efforts in self-realization and even self-preservation.

During the next quarter century, it is to be expected that the role of physical education will become blurred insofar as it will no longer present a distinct image that suggests that education by the physical is different or unique. The physical of education will be a muted mode of self-actualization and societal enrichment. Just as the elementary school teacher is no longer identified via subject matter but is thought of as a person interested in all aspects of the elementary school–age child, so too the secondary school teacher will assume an expanded image and will seek to educate the whole person. Only in institutions of higher education will disciplinary identifications still prevail. In those institutions the curricular designs will insist on total understanding, and physical educators will be working with psychologists, sociologists, biologists, communication experts, philosophers, historians, and many others to produce a curriculum that is cognizant of the individual as a unity.

THE BODY OF KNOWLEDGE OF PHYSICAL EDUCATION

The expectation that physical education dealt with the physical aspects of people, which were ranked below the concerns with mind and soul, greatly influenced the body of knowledge espoused by physical educators. Obviously, the role of physical education and the body of knowledge espoused were cyclical phenomena. The body of knowledge was closely related to the role expectations of physical education. The development of physiological integrity was basic to the meaning of the education *of* the physical. Emphasis was placed on the development of a sound and aesthetically pleasing physique. Congruent with the enhancement of body structure was the attention to functional attributes that produced it. Thus activities that involved the development of strength and the attainment of endurance were fundamental to all early physical education programs. There was the general expectation that strength and endurance would augment general well-being and would in fact improve health and perhaps even foster longevity. Gymnastic exercises were used to promote the acquisition of strength and to increase endurance. Agility, flexibility, and coordination were assets that were valued more for their aesthetic than their physiological value, but they were part of a regimen that sought to develop fitness.

Even as fitness was spotlighted as central to the meaning of physical education, it became apparent that the gymnastic-calisthenic process used to attain such a state was boring, demanding, and painful. The introduction of gamelike procedures to the conditioning programs produced the same physiological results but with much less complaining on the part of the participants. Thus, weight-lifting exercises were changed to competitive events in which one individual attempted to excell another. Running exercises became races between individuals. Jumping and hurling exercises became contests to ascertain the best among the participants. Scores were kept, spectators were invited, victors were crowned, and tournaments were organized. Thus the fittest become the best. The social system endorsed strength and endurance as criteria for worth and acclaim. The gaming techniques used to acquire the attributes of strength and endurance produced their own aura, and soon the process of gaming became so important that there were many who forgot what the actual purpose of gaming had been. Instead of the *development* of functional attributes, gaming came to be the *testing* of those attributes; in the testing, the establishment of the superlative was primary. Thus play corrupted training and instead of playing to train, individuals began to train to play.

The play motif cast an additional ignoble light on the body of knowledge that was physical education's concern. Play, a human behavior governed by caprice and participated in during leisure time, defied the tenets of the Protestant ethic, which suggested that hard work, seriousness, and devotion to duty were the bases for attainment of the good life. Since schooling was preparation for life, it was suggested there should be little time or concern for play during school. To accommodate the natural inclination of children to avoid work, it was arranged that during the school day there should be some planned recesses from the work theme. During such recesses, it was anticipated that play would occur, but it was an unguided, unorganized, purposeless activity and its chief purpose was seen to be cathartic.

As physical educators capitalized on play as a process for fitness and transformed play into planned activity to acknowledge the fit, it became even more difficult to get physical education accepted as an integral part of the teaching and learning situation. Consequently, sport play, organized as athletics, was administered outside the school program. As athletics grew in popularity, it was claimed that such playing experiences might indeed serve as a behavioral laboratory and offer for the participant an experience with life in microcosmic form. The reasoning was that if one was able to handle real life on the athletic field and in the sport and gaming arena then there would be positive correlation between such abilities and the ability to handle the reality of living. Thus behavioral attributes fostered by play were claimed to be "carry-over" values for life, and play gained a degree of academic respectability as it catered to the formation of desirable behaviors.

It soon became obvious that play was capable of sponsoring undesirable behaviors as well as desirable ones. It was also apparent that behavior in *all* situations was important as a "carry-over" value. There was no way that it could be claimed honestly that sport play was of greater significance than participation in a physics class.

As the development of physiological fitness and the formulation of desirable behavioral responses became subject to questioning and skepticism, it was obvious that the time had arrived for physical educators to finally affirm the core of their professional concern. Until the middle of this century, the body of knowledge of physical education had been identified by articulate self-proclaimed prophets, but there had never been a concerted professional effort by the practitioners within the field to ferret out the body of knowledge with which physical education was primarily concerned.

The work done by Rudolph Laban regarding movement, the adaption of the movement theme as the motif of physical education in England, and the philosophical research of Eleanor Metheny and Lois Eldfeldt brought into focus a concept that had never been identified by professional physical educators as their responsibility. The human movement theme began to gain attention and to create interest. As special groups of professionals such as the American Academy of Physical Education, the National Association for Physical Education of College Women, the National Association of Physical Education for College Men, and the American Association for Health, Physical Education, and Recreation began a systematic exploration of the human movement theme, an acute interest in that concept mushroomed. This crystallized as selected leaders within the physical education group met together to explore the interpretation of physical education. In a conference at Allerton, Illinois, under the leadership of Ben Miller, it was finally agreed that the body of knowledge around which physical education was structured was "the art and science of human movement." The disciples of the fitness motif and the disciples of the play motif both acquiesced to the arguments that human movement was central to all experiences that physical education sponsored.

Consequent meetings and conferences tended to reinforce that assertion, and only recently has there been evidence of second thoughts regarding the adoption of that point of view. Meanwhile, the "movement movement" gained strength. Attention was focused on movement theory, schemes for curricular decision making were concocted relative to the art and science of human movement, methodologies to make movement theory operational were developed and tested, and courses were developed to promote the idea that human movement was indeed the essence of the body of knowledge identified as physical education.

Almost as if it had been deliberately programmed, the area of motor learning blossomed, psychologists became interested in movement as a means of human communication, and sociologists and anthropologists became attentive to movement patterns found in gaming and sport. In addition, increased attention was paid to the notation of movement, and computers were employed to record movement patterns.

The proponents of play began to insist that the special organization of play, called sport, was the unique responsibility of physical education. They argued that many facets of education were interested in human movement patterns but that sport was a distinct and unique responsibiliy of physical education.

As the movement theorists and the sport theorists argued their points, philosophical confusion resulted. Such confusion was ultimately manifested in the creation of departments of human movement and departments of sport. Often these departments had gender identifications, with women suggesting that human movement was central to physical education concerns and men countering with the argument that sport was the core of the body of knowledge identified as physical education.

Physical educators are in the midst of resolving the arguments regarding physical education's body of knowledge. The movement adherents have developed an imposing portfolio of both theoretical and practical material that argues well for the primacy of "the art and science of human move-

132

ment." The sport adherents have spent great time and effort in establishing the relationship of sport with psychology, history, philosophy, anthropology, and sociology, but they have yet to develop material relative to play theory that must be antecedent to the sport theme.

What does the future hold with respect to the body of knowledge that is physical education? It would appear that there will be no "winner" in the interaction between sport and movement. Undoubtedly, future physical educators will insist that both ideas have merit and will seek to synthesize the differing points of view. It is not anticipated that both views will emerge as opposite sides of the same coin. Instead, there probably will be attempts to incorporate one point of view into the other. As the wider and more encompassing concept, it would seem that human movement will finally be acknowledged as central to the body of knowledge of physical education. Consequently, it is anticipated that there will be name changes of physical education that will reflect this decision. The study of sport will be absorbed gradually by those disciplines whose attention has been courted. Thus, it is to be anticipated that sociologists, psychologists, philosophers, historians, and anthropologists will become more sensitive to the science of sport and will incorporate that sensitivity into their subject matter. The practice of sport will continue to be a part of the physical educator's method. In curricular contexts, such practice will deal with acquiring sport skills and tactics and in the extracurricular context, the practice of sport will provide entertainment, sponsor behavioral situations, and structure playing opportunities for those who wish to participate in sport.

As the art and science of human movement becomes more sharply identified with the term "physical education," curriculums will change, learning theory regarding motor input and output will be developed, and professional physical educators will become more attentive to the recording of human movement patterns. Baseball swings will be notated to diagnose the differences between two hitters. Less attention will be afforded the "how many" statistics, while more attention will be accorded the "why is that so" understandings. There will be both theorists and practitioners in physical education. Both groups of people will work as a part of teams of people who are attentive to a holistic approach to learning. Movement ideas will be accepted as an essential component of human understanding.

ORGANIZATION OF PHYSICAL EDUCATION

The bonding of people with like interests into organizations and associations provides solace, power, and opportunities to share concerns and determine future direction. For all of these reasons, physical educators in the United States have found professional associations desirable. The establishment of the American Association for the Advancement of Physical Education reflected the organizational imperative felt by a group of people who needed each other to establish understandings, position, and power. The subsequent changes within that original organization reflected the temporal conditions and the professional physical educator's appraisal of the cultural milieu.

During the 1930s the American Physical Education Association finally capitulated to the classifications deemed expedient by administrators and officially included both recreation and health in its title. From 1939 through 1974, the American Association for Health, Physical Education and Recreation (AAHPER) was the national professional organization promoting the interests and influence of its membership. It was allied with the National Education Association.

Because athletics had never been a real part of the educational curriculum and had been shunted to extracurricular status, it could be anticipated that "athletics" (which were organized mainly for male participants) were not included as an essential part of the operation of AAHPER. The National Collegiate Athletic Association (NCAA) had been organized in 1906 to give guidance to collegiate athletics for men. High school athletics for boys were under the auspices of the National Federation of State High School Associations (NFSHSA). AAHPER did concern itself with the direction of athletics for girls and women, and its affiliates, the National Section on Women's Athletics (NSWA) and the National Section on Girls and Women's Sports (NAGWS), were attentive to the control and guidance of sport for women.

Organizations outside the purview of education were formed to cater to special interest groups. Sport clubs were prolific and were organized as private groups or community projects. The Amateur Athletic Union (AAU) was organized to sponsor national competitive events. In addition, individual groups were attentive to the interests of hockey, football, volleyball, golf, tennis, lacross, softball, and a host of other sport activities. In some cases, recreation programs limited their activities to a sport orientation and became quasieducational institutions for the promotion of sport. The YMCA and the YWCA assumed such roles and served many individuals who were not able to participate in sport in school because of the exclusivity of the athletic programs. Often scholastic athletics catered only to the proficient.

By the 1960s it was apparent that the AAHPER would no longer be able to accommodate the diverse interests it supported unless reorganization occurred. After 10 years of study and planning, the American Association for Health, Physical Education and Recreation became the American *Alliance* for Health, Physical Education and Recreation, and significant component parts of the Alliance assumed Association status. The group attentive to the interests of physical education and sport is known as the National Association for Sport and Physical Education (NASPE). It represents the majority of the Alliance membership and is concerned with interests of all physical educators and coaches.

Because the AAHPER had been responsible for the organization and administration of athletics for girls and women, and because the social climate was just awakening to the discrimination that had been exercised against women, some members of the Alliance felt that the continuation of a group designed to be attentive exclusively to the athletic interests of girls and women was necessary. As a result, the National Association for Girls and Women in Sport (NAGWS) was organized. Within that association was constituted the Association of Intercollegiate Athletics for Women (AIAW), an organization that focuses exclusively on the governance of women's collegiate sport.

Legislation, litigation, and expediency are all suggesting that the gender orientation of sport is a thing of the past. Consequently, there are power struggles going on with respect to the governance of scholastic and collegiate athletics for men and women. The National Association for Intercollegiate Athletics (NAIA) was formulated to protest the fact that the NCAA is controlled by the large and monied universities, and to attempt to keep collegiate athletics within the bounds of propriety. The National Junior College Athletic Association (NJCAA) was formed to attend to the special interests of junior college athletes. The AIAW was formed to guarantee that collegiate athletics for women would remain amateur and not be perverted to professionalism. The AIAW was also concerned that women should have a voice in planning their own destiny.

The NCAA considers itself the most powerful and relevant organization dealing with collegiate athletics. The NFSHSA considers itself the spokesman for high school athletics. The NFSHSA recently moved to include girls within its jurisdictional domain and was able to make that move with minimum resistance from women's groups. The fact that the governance of the NFSHSA, and indeed of the majority of the public school system, is controlled by male principals gave the AAHPER little opportunity to be involved in the decision affecting girls' athletics and gave the NSGWS no vantage point from which it could speak. On the other hand, the move of the NCAA to organize and administer women's collegiate athletics has been resisted by the AAHPER, the NAGWS, the NASPE, and scores of special interest groups who suggest that the "takeover" is more to serve the interests of the NCAA in its drive to monopolize collegiate sport than it is to serve the woman student athlete.

Physical education: a view toward the future

The future promises substantial change in the organization of sport and physical education in the United States. It is apparent that there must be some resolution of the athletic organization problem. That resolution will not be easy, and it is quite possible that arbitration from the government will be required. As the federal government becomes more and more alert to the problems of sport, it would appear that intervention is indicated. There is the possibility of the establishment of a Secretary of Sport, who will be a part of the presidential cabinet. There is also the possibility of the establishment of a Bureau of Sport, which would be under the auspices of the federal government and will be responsible for both amateur and professional sport concerns. There is also the possibility that the amateur sport organizations (NCAA, AAU, AIAW, NAIA, NJCAA, and NFSHSA) and committees such as the United States Olympic Committee (USOC) will be willing to band together voluntarily into a consortium for sport. A great deal will depend upon the legislation affecting sport and the litigation regarding the power of sport governance organizations.

The organization of physical education will reflect the body of knowledge to which physical educators lay claim. The Alliance will continue its enabling role in support of its historical interests in all areas dealing with human health and maintenance. It will be the obligation of NASPE to reflect the area of concern designated by physical educators as their responsibility. The future will reinforce the interest of NASPE in the processing of physical education knowledge. Splinter groups that have organized to focus on specific areas of physical education will ultimately find their home in the NASPE organization and will be dependent on that association to provide enabling procedures. Meetings, conferences, and symposia, the publication of journals, newsletters, and reviews, and the survey of trends and forces will be germaine to the NASPE charge. The continued concern with pushing back the frontiers of physical education knowledge will be served best by individuals and groups who are less interested in power and visibility and who are more interested in scholastic interaction. Groups such as the National Association for Physical Education of College Women (NAPECW) and the National College Physical Education Association for Men (NCPEAM) will eventually unite and, together with other associations such as the American Academy for Physical Education, will be concerned with exploring new areas of endeavor as academic descilines.

There is nothing in the future to suggest that proliferation of interests will be curtailed. Economics may limit the ability of people bonded by like interests to function in all of the ways that they might wish, but it would appear that the groups will continue to exist regardless of limitations on their operations. Such groups not only will reflect the future; they will shape it.

OPERATIONAL METHODS OF PHYSICAL EDUCATION

The operational modes and methods of physical education have historically been influenced by formal education. Most of the professional organizations concerned with physical education have been tangential to the formal education process. However, the people outside the schools, those too young to go to school and most especially those who have finished their formal education, have demanded some attention to their activity needs. The school program of physical education has paid little attention to these individuals and continues to act as though sport belonged to the young and that movement behaviors are the perrogative of those within the first quarter century of their lives. Little has been done by teacher education schools to prepare individuals to be more than teachers of youth. Within the patterns of teacher preparation for physical education there have been a number of stereotypical approaches. Traditionally, physical education has been segregated as to sex, has been built around the acquisition of sport skills, has tended to teach skills at a beginning level, and has treated students in terms of behavioristic conditioning methods. Physical education has seldom carried academic credit, has been a required course for all students, has catered to motor behaviors while ignoring the affective and cognitive aspects of human behavior, and has been contained within the class period, never making demands for out-of-class preparation or out-of-class enrichment.

Presently, physical education's operational methods are being influenced by legislative edict and fear of litigation and changes are being sponsored. The guidelines for Title IX of the Omnibus Education Act of 1972 have insisted that opportunity in both physical education classes and on athletic teams be made available to men and women and that one group should not be accorded advantages that another group does not have. In practical terms this has meant that physical education classes, which were organized according to sex, are being reconstituted. Football is no longer male and field hockey is no longer female. Dance is for both sexes, and the combative arts must accommodate both men and women. Title IX guidelines have been opposed strongly by the NCAA, the NFSHSA, and other interest groups who believe that including women in sport programs will destroy patterns of operation that are time tested and desirable. Title IX has also been opposed by some physical education teachers. Some women believe that by including men in their programs the educational value of the program will be diluted. Some men believe that including women in their programs will damage the charismatic image of the male athlete, and they fear the programs will have to be altered so drastically to accommodate women that the values of strength and endurance training will be obviated.

The fear of liability suits has made many physical educators remove from their programs some of the activities that involve substantial risk. Boxing was an early victim of such concern. Gymnastics, swimming, contact sport, and intense conditioning programs are also suspect areas and are under constant scrutiny.

The future methods of operation available for physical education will reflect social conscience to a greater degree than they have in the past. Educational methods that are being tested daily will undoubtedly influence the future operational modes of physical education.

The great push toward humanistic interaction will be felt ultimately in the last stronghold of behaviorism, sport. The organization used to structure sport will change to include teacher-learner and coach-athlete planning. Rules governing conduct will reflect the social environment, and there will be a greater push toward the involvement of many in sport rather than the exclusive planning for the elite. Opportunities for post-school individuals will proliferate, and older citizens will make demands for opportunities to exercise their motor techniques. Municipal courts, links, and playing space will be reserved for the elderly and the mature as well as the children and youth.

The physical education curriculum will reflect the adopted body of knowledge, and attention will be afforded the cognitive and affective aspects of human movement patterns. These curricular opportunities will be available to all people regardless of their sex, age, and skills. There will be more attention to the needs of the individual and prescribed activity programs geared toward the nature and desires of each person will be available. Physical education will be "more than movement," larger than sport, and greater than physical fitness.

The competitive disaffiliation aspects of sport will be reduced, and an emphasis will be placed on affiliative, cooperative interactions. Efforts will be made to suggest that numerical position need not represent a value judgment. Hence being number one will not be of greater value than being number five; it will merely indicate a different position with respect to goal attainment.

Physical education will take its rightful place in the school and will no longer be delegated to second-class status. Overt recognition of this fact will come about as physical education courses are accorded the privileges of the academic payoff. Credit for course work will sponsor attention to all of the behavioral domains, and expectations for cognitive behaviors will emerge. Students concerned with bowling may be reading research about speed and accuracy, may be observing the notated patterns used in ten pins and duck pins, may be experimenting with interpersonal aggression as a part of a bowling team, may be describing the feeling and meaning of the bowling phenomenon in terms of the fine arts, and surely will be understanding the self through the bowling experience.

Prospective practitioners of physical education will be able to concentrate in specific aspects of the area. There will be room in the future for the movement theorist, the teacher of motor skills, the coach, the dancer, the exercise physiologist, the kinesiologist, the sport sociologist, the athlete, and many, many more proponents of the art and science of human movement. These people will be interacting with all people, and physical education and sport will assume an equalitarian approach to understanding and participation.

CONCLUDING STATEMENT

The change that the future will foster for physical education is less frightening than it is exciting. At the beginning of the last quarter of the twentieth century, physical education is on the verge of the great breakthrough or its final breakdown. The transitory character of our culture insists on change to accommodate the future. For those who are unwilling to make such change, there is only oblivion. For those who are willing to risk anxiety and who are qualified to institute the change, the future is promising. There will be times when the direction for change is not clear, when the incentive for change is not strong, when the reason for change is not known. But there will be many more times in the future when reason, incentive, and direction have a lucidity that transcends both anxiety and ennui. Those will be the times when physical educators will know "enough if something from our hands have power, to live, and act and serve the future hour."

Physical education: accountability for the future

Dean A. Pease

It would be simple enough to look at the future, determine as accurately as possible the human needs at that time, and make some projections about what schools should begin to do to prepare. While that must ultimately be done, education must also contend with present conditions if it is to adjust today's practices to meet future needs.

PERSPECTIVE ON THE PRESENT

Three distinct trends have been evolving in this country, each with its interdependent effects on current school practice: (1) advancements made by industry, (2) increases in government services, and (3) inflationary economic conditions. To understand how these trends have affected current school practice, each will be discussed briefly.

There is no need to elaborate on the advancements made by industry during the past half century. Science, technology, and cybernetics have brought about overwhelming changes in all aspects of life: communication, transportation, space exploration, health and medicine, etc. We have benefited directly from these changes. Our standard of living has risen and our life is easier and basically more pleasurable. Because of these changes, the industrial model of comparing output (productivity) to input (resources) has become considered an efficient and effective system of operation.

Out of this success, however, we have grown to expect similar advances in other areas as well. In education, wide publicity has been given to such negative topics as the relatively large percentage of high school graduates who cannot read and the decline of college entrance examination scores during the past few years. When this publicity is coupled with such widespread volatile topics as drug use among our youth, campus unrest and student militancy, and forced bussing, the tax-paying public has become quite disenchanted with the schools.

The second trend concerns a continued increase in government services in an attempt to ensure equality among all people in our country. Program after program is being developed and funded at local, state, and federal levels in an attempt to assist the disadvantaged. Social security programs, Medicare, housing and urban development programs, food programs, welfare programs, programs for the retarded, prison reform programs, and health and rehabilitative service programs are but a few examples that require government financial support, and all are demanding more money. Since tax dollars are required to conduct these programs, public education must compete against all of these services for its share of the tax dollar. As government services increase, and indications are that this trend will continue, either taxes must be raised to meet the increase in costs, or competition must become greater for a lesser share of the tax money that is available.

The third trend concerns the continuing inflationary economy. Because of inflation, the cost of living has increased: it takes more money to purchase the same amount of merchandise, and sales, property, and state and federal incomes taxes have all soared. At the same time, it costs more money for schools to operate.

These trends have combined to have a significant influence on education. At a time when there is public disenchantment with current school practices and when rising taxes have forced economic restrictions on all people, taxpayers are looking very critically at education. They are exerting pressure on government officials to cut back on spending at a time when more money is required to operate and when government is increasing its services.

Because of industry's accomplishments during the past half-century, and because of the need to control government spending, politicians have yielded to this public pressure by more or less imposing the industrial model on education through accountability legislation. As a result, educators are being forced to be accountable for their efforts.

Accountability means being held responsible for the realization of systematically stated goals and objectives. Emphasis on accountability in education is just beginning, and it appears as though this emphasis will continue indefinitely. Also, it appears the industrial model will continue to be implemented to ensure that accountability is maintained.

Accountability, however, will not be the only criterion educators must satisfy. Schools also will be forced because of increased operating expenses to teach only toward those goals and objectives deemed desirable by society. Schools that fall short on either count simply will not be supported.

Therefore the decisions we are making today about what to teach will be critical. More accurate than "today's decisions will determine our future" is "today's decisions will determine whether or not we have a future." While accountability will be a necessity, care must be taken to ensure that the goals and objectives of physical education remain relevant, that they continue to satisfy the needs of people and society in the future. To suggest only what is needed now would be to prepare people for a world that does not exist. Therefore a brief look at what futurists say will be happening during the next 20 to 25 years is in order. Only after we explore future alternatives can we make statements about what society will deem desirable.

TOWARD 2000

The year 2000 seems like a fantasy, and predicting life at that time seems unimaginable. On the other hand, 2000 is only 20 or so years away. Somehow, predicting 20 years ahead does not seem so fruitless.

It is fairly safe to predict that society will become considerably more complex between 1980 and 2000. It has been estimated that the sum total of human knowledge will double twice by the end of this century (Morris, 1974). Paul Nash (1973) argues that advances in cybernetics will result

141

in a second industrial revolution, producing machines to control machines. This revolution will have several effects. People will become increasingly dependent on, and thus subservient to, the machine, a condition that may well have a negative affect on our self-concept, ego state, and self-identity. Leisure time will increase as technology increases. It is estimated that the work week will be phased down to about 30 hours by 2000. This reduction may lead to a 4-day work week or some other combination of work and rest. Also projected is that retirement will likely drop in stages from ages 65 to 60 to 55 (Buchen, 1974). Almost certainly the society of the future will see a dramatic increase in the percentage of older citizens.

As our technology and our knowledge increase, so will our potential for incurring stress. It is further anticipated that the emphasis in the future will no longer be on producing enough but on choosing wisely. This change of emphasis will require decision making in determining alternatives, selecting from among alternatives, making a commitment to a choice, and taking responsibility for those choices.

Trends also indicate that the United States will increasingly become a planned society. As this occurs, the potential will be even greater for us to lose our identities. Our need to develop a strong self-identity for the purpose of defending our rights and making wise decisions thus will become increasingly important in the future. In addition, it is anticipated that as society becomes more planned, the potential to let professional decision makers make the decisions will become greater. This eventually would tend to depersonalize us even more, besides opening the door to the possible tyranny of the minority over the majority (Orwell, 1961).

TOWARD 2000 IN EDUCATION

Schools alone will not be capable of preparing people to live adequately in the future. Society will come to realize that it has been placing too great a responsibility on its schools. Jencks et al. (1972) were accurate when they said that schools have been asked to do what parents either cannot or choose not to do. While it is obvious that schools are not accomplishing their objectives, Dean C. Corrigan (1974) explains this dilemma by suggesting that the quality of educational output has not declined but that society has increased its expectations to the level that schools cannot comply. The result appears as school failure.

Regardless of the cause, schools are in trouble. Because schools are being held responsible for many of the existing social conditions over which they have no control and because of the resultant mass exodus of students away from public schools, public education as we now know it may cease to exist. Public education may exist only to serve the disadvantaged. The more advantaged may seek education as they currently seek their physician (which in itself has merit).

If the trend is away from public education, industry may enter the educational marketplace en masse. Industry already has contracted with some school systems (Asbell, 1970). Using specially trained personnel, sophisticated research, and updated equipment, industry is in a position to dominate the field. Given the current state of the art in education, industry might be able to accomplish in 5 years what would take the education profession 20 years.

If formal education is to survive, some dramatic changes must occur. Decisions must be made regarding what education can and cannot do. Teachers must be held accountable; they must state what they plan to do and then be made responsible for seeing that it is done. Those who do not perform adequately should be replaced.

While the industrial model is more a political tool to keep resource allocations in check than it is an educational strategy, actual practice in education must become more aligned with the medical (pathology) model. Teachers must begin to diagnose needs based on criterion-referenced pre-assessments, prescribe learning experiences both in and out of school utilizing all available community resources including the family, and be accountable for the results based on criterion-referenced assessments of accomplishment. Assessments are not limited to traditional written examinations. On the contrary, assessment can be any data collection technique, including teacher observation and professional judgment. Regardless of assessment techniques, the diagnosis and prescription model must be implemented in education.

While use of the medical model may ensure accountability, educators will never be able to bring about desired results systematically until they operate on a research base. A rationale for decision making in education must be based on a scientific body of knowledge. If decisions by teachers regarding desirable changes in student behavior are not based on some scientific framework, the intended results of those decisions will be left to chance. Operating on a scientific base will improve the results of decisions from chance to a high probability of occurrence.

The body of knowledge is already available. Teaching is a behavioral science and teachers must begin to become well-versed in knowledge of human behavior. All teachers should be experts in various learning theories. Learning theory should provide the underlying knowledge base for all decisions about learning. All teachers should be able to recognize abnormal behavior characteristics. If educators are going to talk about meeting individual needs, they must consciously be able to identify these needs and

143

either treat students systematically or refer them to proper professionals who are better prepared to treat such conditions.

If education is to become research based, the attitude of educators toward research must change. This notion holds for all educators, from researchers to teachers. Educators must become familiar with the scientific method and learn to value it as the ultimate method of knowing. (Even those teaching for humanistic goals must ultimately learn to systematically assist students to identify their own feelings and needs.) Educators must begin to understand, value highly, and be able to utilize theory in daily decision making. The use of theory can no longer be Ph.D.-level content. Theory must become the basic framework for teaching, the body of knowledge that distinguishes professionals from technicians, paraprofessionals, and parents. Currently this distinction is not evident, a condition that explains why education finds itself in an accountability crisis.

Other practices must also change in education. Education must begin to prepare people for the future, to accept change, to tolerate differences, to make decisions, to be responsible for decisions, and to anticipate future conditions when making decisions. Education must become more meaningful and relevant by including more experiences related to, and in, the real world. Education must emphasize stress reduction, and it must emphasize intelligent use of leisure time. Schools have not performed adequately in any of these areas in the past, and the need will be greater in the future.

I am not naive enough to think that schools alone have the power to produce these desired outcomes. There are too many intervening variables. Then, too, these outcomes are often not demonstrable, measurable, or even definable, which makes it extremely difficult to establish accountability for their achievement. This does not change the desirability of the goals, however, nor will it reduce the pressure on educators to be accountable.

TOWARD 2000 IN PHYSICAL EDUCATION

All of the responsibilities relative to education in general are equally the responsibility of physical education. No one discipline is powerful enough, nor should it be held accountable, to teach for such humanistic outcomes as anticipatory thinking, decision making, tolerance of differences, and acceptance of change. Teaching for these outcomes requires the combined efforts of all educators. Yet each discipline must teach for specific outcomes, and every educator should be held accountable for his efforts.

In order for accountability to be possible the stated objectives and goals of physical education must be demonstrable, i.e., subject to empirical observation. Many of the humanistic objectives referred to earlier cannot be defined or measured adequately, and teachers cannot systematically contribute to those outcomes sufficiently to be accountable for their achievement. For teachers to be accountable, the learning outcomes must be stated in advance and they must be attained by all students. Teachers alone simply are not powerful enough to influence to a significant degree such outcomes as attitudes, values, emotions, and character.

This is not to suggest that affective objectives should be ignored. On the contrary, they are important and the teacher should create and take advantage of every opportunity to teach for these outcomes. Realistically, however, if physical education were to rest its worth on producing such objectives, there would be no evidence available to support the inclusion of physical education in the school curriculum. Providing such evidence is required for accountability, and accountability is the primary criterion against which the ultimate fate of physical education will be determined.

Physical education is nevertheless in an exceptionally good position to satisfy both accountability criteria as well as many short- and long-term needs of people. *The primary goal of physical education should be for each student to be well skilled in several different lifetime, leisure-oriented sport skills.*

Motor skills can be determined in advance; they are demonstrable and they can be measured. There is a body of knowledge based on research pertaining to motor learning, and there is increasing knowledge being generated on teaching for motor skill acquisition. These conditions satisfy accountability criteria, and because of the orientation of teaching and learning toward research, learning sport skills can be influenced greatly by teaching.

Being well skilled and thus able to participate in leisure-time activities also prepares an individual for the future. One of society's great problems, even today, is the intelligent use of leisure time. Prolonged idleness is wasteful and unsatisfying. Leisure time will continue to increase as machines continue to control machines, as work weeks shorten, and as retirement lengthens. We must be prepared to meet this crisis, and no discipline will be better able to prepare people for the worthwhile use of leisure time than physical education.

Other conditions likely to occur in the future also lend urgency to the need for skill acquisition. As society becomes more highly planned by professional decision makers, the opportunity for individuality becomes less. This suggests fewer opportunities for us to actualize ourselves. Sport provides an environment in which we can express and experience our feelings, our senses, and our awareness. In a word, sport provides an avenue toward self-actualization. Stress reducers will be needed to a greater extent, and sport has the potential to alleviate stress. The social, emotional, and attitudinal factors discussed previously will continue to be important, and sport affects these factors positively for most participants.

It cannot be assumed that these outcomes will result directly from physical education experiences or from the direct efforts of physical education teachers. These outcomes are nevertheless crucial to society, and sport provides an environment in which they can occur. They will not occur automatically, and they might not occur at all for some, but the potential is great for such outcomes to occur as by-products of participation in sport. That alone makes the acquisition of sport skill desirable, and physical educators can affect such acquisition systematically.

To accomplish the primary learning outcome of sport skill acquisition, current practices must be examined and alterations must be made accordingly. Perhaps the single most important condition that must be altered is recommitment to a goal. We all must work for the same goal, and all efforts should be coordinated to attain it.

Once commitment is made to motor skill acquisition, the primary learning outcome for which physical educators will be held accountable, other practices can then be examined. Greater emphasis, both by the classroom teacher and by the researcher, must be placed on research in learning and teaching motor skills.

Great progress in this area has been made. Robert M. W. Travers (1973) has edited a fine collection of monographs, each chapter synthesizing the research on various aspects of teaching. Within this collection, John E. Nixon and Lawrence F. Locke have compiled an outstanding synthesis of the research on teaching physical education, and Michael Rosner and Steven W. Keele have teamed on the topic of skill learning. Similarly, A. M. Gentile (1972) and H. T. A. Whiting (1969) are pursuing skill acquisition models, and Terry R. Tabor and I (1976) have presented a skill acquisition teaching model for scientific investigation. These efforts are only a beginning.

All teachers should know as a baseline the basic research in their particular area of specialization. "What the research tells the . . . ," "Theory and practice of . . . ," and "Principles of teaching . . ." are all examples of being one step removed from knowledgeable, thinking professionalism. Teachers should be able to form their own conclusions after reading the research themselves. Until that time, educators will be "faking" it. Again, that is precisely why we are in an accountability crisis today. As research on learning and teaching continues, the success of teaching for skill acquisition will increase. The more knowledge on which decisions about teaching can be based, the greater the probability that those decisions will be accurate.

If the primary learning outcome is to be skill acquisition and if physical educators are really serious about attaining this goal, i.e., if they are going to be accountable for its attainment, then learning experiences in the total physical education curriculum must be systematically coordinated toward that end. Further, all physical education teachers must be accountable for contributing to their segment of the process, for attaining their specific objectives. This suggests that learning be defined behaviorally rather than by a fixed unit of time and that learners either advance or recycle, based on their ability to perform the objectives.

Ironically, changing from a time orientation to a learning orientation is a rather major conceptual difference in current school practice. The concept is in line with futurist thinking, however, and the transition would not pose that much difficulty. While some persons may "graduate" from physical education at the age of 12 years, others may be involved in physical education instruction throughout their lifetimes. Margaret Mead (1969) and Peter Drucker (1957), for example, suggest that in the future no one will ever complete an education. This trend is supported by the fact that the number of learners 35 years of age or older enrolled in some form of adult education has increased 30% during the past 2 years (*U.S. News and World Report*, 1975). The current trend in the development of the community school concept (Gores, 1975), in which the public school and the city recreation department combine to provide increased recreation facilities, not only makes the learning rather than the time orientation feasible, it makes it desirable.

Designing the total physical education curriculum for the purpose of producing a well-skilled individual requires coordinating all learning experiences for the purpose of obtaining the goal. It simply is inadequate for a child to experience "drop the hankerchief," "throw and go," and other cat and rat games in the primary grades, kickball and relays in grades four through six, and football, basketball, softball, and track from grades six through twelve. Probably none of these experiences assist the student with acquiring higher order objectives, and probably none of these experiences assist in preparing students for the future. Each day is an end in itself. Unfortunately, at the end of grade twelve, after more than 6 years of practice, many students cannot even perform simple skills such as picking up a routine ground ball and throwing a runner out at first base, dribbling a basketball around an opponent and shooting a lay-up, or running a predetermined pattern against a defense and catching a pass. Some cannot even throw or run! This is the equivalent to not knowing how to read after the same amount of schooling.

While there is not a great deal of evidence available to support the claim, logic suggests that the total physical education curriculum should be systematically designed according to a psychomotor taxonomy. Although research is needed to validate Anita Harrow's taxonomy (1972), it nevertheless appears to be a logical framework on which to base the design of a physical education curriculum for obtaining skill acquisition. Initial physical education experiences would concentrate on basic fundamental movement. These would be followed by perceptual experiences and experiences designed to develop physical abilities, respectively. Once physical abilities are fairly well developed, learning experiences would then concentrate on skilled movements.* The same taxonomy might be utilized to further coordinate learning experiences within each taxonomical level.

Other current practices in physical education must also be reexamined if physical educators are to become more relevant and competent. Greater specialization must occur within teaching. The world consists of specialists. Specialization has caused our society to advance as it has in medicine, space exploration, law, and technology. Education simply has not become specialized in tune to the world around it.

All teachers, regardless of discipline, must become more competent in the area of research. Research itself has become highly specific but teachers are not knowledgeable enough to use it. As a genetic competency, if you will, all teachers must be able to interpret and apply formal theory and research literature.

Another specialization that *all* teachers must develop is the ability to effectively use the medical model. If educators are truly going to be accountable, each child must be diagnosed in terms of educational needs, prescriptions must be written in terms of learning experiences that are to be conducted at home, at school, at work, during leisure, or wherever and however the objectives can be attained, and criterion-referenced post-assessments must be given to determine whether the child is to recycle or to be rediagnosed. The responsibility for learning is then more equally shared between the learner and teacher. This system would probably de-emphasize the need for grades. Also, research would become more vital in linking prescriptions with diagnoses.

Within physical education, specialization should focus on the most effective and efficient ways to attain the intended goals. For the reasons cited earlier, our primary goal against which every client should be diag-

---

*I suggest that the goal for physical education be skill acquisition rather than nondiscursive communication. I am not debating the existence of the latter, I am arguing that it cannot be defined or measured adequately at this time (accountability), that there is no knowledge base (research) on which to teach for it, and that the ultimate value of sports lies in participation, not in communication. Where possible, I do recommend pursuing nondiscursive communication objectives. Perhaps through nondiscursive communication, self-actualization in sport can be facilitated.

nosed, is skill acquisition. Other aspects of education should not be ignored, and where possible physical educators should either refer students elsewhere or diagnose and prescribe accordingly. The primary diagnosis and prescriptions in physical education, however, should lead toward skill acquisition.

To accomplish this task, all teachers should have a solid command of applied biomechanics and kinesiology, applied physiology of exercise and rehabilitation, and applied sociology and psychology of sport. While all teachers must be experts in applying the available knowledge in these fields toward the ultimate goal of helping learners become well skilled, I do not see teachers as specialists in these areas. These are generic competencies for teachers. Specialists, on the other hand, are either doing specific research or interpreting it for teachers. This suggests that the mainstream of research in these areas ought to be directed toward applied learning outcomes.

Before credibility can be established around the more sophisticated and intriguing areas of our business, we must first be well founded in the basics. At present, physical education programs in our schools across the country are not performing adequately, physical educators are not operating on a research base, and they are not being held accountable. While it is legitimate to "flirt" with research that has as its primary outcome the advancement of knowledge only, the thrust of research must be generated toward outcomes that can directly assist teachers in our schools. Similarly, academic prestige resulting from presentation of papers and journal publications must shift away from research for its own sake toward research that can be applied. For financial and political reasons we should not build out, we should build up. To do this we must recommit ourselves to shoring up the foundation.

To solidify our base or support, i.e., to become accountable for having all of our clients well skilled in several sport activities, teachers must become specialized on a different front, the psychomotor taxonomy. If research supports Harrow's taxonomy, then teachers might become specialized either at the lower levels of the taxonomy or at the skill acquisition level. Eventually, as new knowledge is generated, each taxonomical level might become an area of specialization in which separate diagnosis and prescriptions are conducted.

If professional popularity is an accurate indicator, it appears that movement education has great potential for teaching for the lower levels of the taxonomy. If evidence supports this trend, then teaching specializations should utilize movement education models as frameworks for teaching for the lower taxonomical levels and skill acquisition models as a framework for teaching for the goal level.

This difficulty in defining and measuring the lower levels of the psychomotor taxonomy suggests that teacher accountability at these levels is difficult if not impossible to obtain. In fact, accountability may be impossible to obtain as long as any movement education teaching models are used. I feel confident enough that movement education contributes to these lower level objectives and that these lower level objectives in turn transfer positively to overall skill acquisition. Therefore I would be willing to determine the accountability of movement education teachers, at least until more knowledge is generated, by whether or not their students ultimately obtained the overall goal of skill acquisition.

Research, then, should concentrate on motor and perceptual development and on motor learning. Equally important, research should concentrate on means of teaching for those outcomes.

It would not be too difficult for schools to reorganize their structure to accommodate this curriculum model. Ultimately, it would mean no grade levels. Each person would go through physical education (on a diagnosis-prescription basis) until he has satisfactorily completed the goal level. Grade levels are irrelevant. Utilizing the community school concept, people could always have access to facilities, instruction, and practice, regardless of age. Note here that the goal is learning, not grades or time.

The suggestion that research might center around movement education and skill acquisition teaching specializations assumes that there is ultimately a potential theoretical base for teaching for each of these outcomes. Just as there is a theoretical base for learning in general (called learning theory), it is assumed that there are theoretical bases for the two types of teaching. The research should be designed to develop these theories. A teaching specialist, then, would be an expert at applying the research and theory in diagnosing needs and prescribing learning experiences directed toward these outcomes.

This discussion centers around teaching and knowledge specializations. If we are to be accountable, these specialized areas must be developed. Another type of specialization, differentiated staffing, may also develop into a useful teaching aid. Differentiated staffing will give the specialists more time to do what they are best able to do, diagnose and prescribe. Other types of staff (most likely volunteers such as parents, the elderly, ex-athletes, and even parolees and first offenders convicted of certain nonviolent crimes) could assist in clerical duties, equipment repair and storage, monitoring practice sessions, officiating, and organizing field trips and facility use. In some cases, small wages might be paid for such services. However, there are many responsible persons in the community who would very much enjoy joining a teaching team to assist toward the goal of developing well-skilled people.

There has been nothing mentioned so far about sex roles in physical education. That is because they are irrelevant! Everything that has been discussed applies to all people regardless of sex. Men's physical education and women's physical education are duplications of expense, services, equipment, facilities, and brainpower. The problems facing education, and specifically physical education, are too great for us to be concerned with trivial questions such as "power of the sexes." All physical educators must come together to solve the real issues. If we do not, the present accountability crisis in physical education will continue.

Teacher education

Many of the current deficiencies in education point to inadequacies in teacher education. Teacher education should not be condemned too strongly, however, not because it has performed its intended functions inadequately, but because teacher education, as it now exists, may not be able to perform these functions adequately.

To date, there is no evidence to suggest that formal teacher education is powerful enough to affect the behavior of teachers once they have exited from the reward system of the university. The reward system in teacher education requires a certain set of trainee behaviors in order for trainees to survive that process. Trainees must learn to respond within the reward system of teacher education; once success has been achieved, both the teacher trainer and the trainee feel a mutual satisfaction. The reward system is completely different in the schools than in teacher education, and the behavior required to receive these rewards is also completely different. The rewards in the schools are determined by the students and fellow teachers, whereas the reward system in teacher education, through use of the final grade, is determined traditionally by each teacher educator. The trainee learns to behave one way to become sanctioned, and then must learn to behave another way after becoming sanctioned. No wonder so many people say, "I learned more my first year of teaching than I did in four years at the university," and "Those people up there in their ivory towers need to get down here where the action is." This also suggests the accuracy of the notion that students, rather than teacher educators, teach teachers how to teach. Unfortunately, the intentions of students and teacher educators are not the same.

Until now a primary criterion for being a teacher educator has been teaching experience. The rationale for this criterion has been logic: How else can people teach other people to teach unless they have been there first? The assumption, of course, is that personal experience is the best method of knowing about teaching, and that the same personal experience is somehow useful in teaching teachers how to teach.

Both of the above assumptions have probably been true in the past, but that is because personal experience has been the *only* method of knowing about teaching children and therefore about teaching teachers. Closer observation of teaching children and teaching teachers suggests that experience is often detrimental and irrelevant. An explanation is in order.

When teaching children, the only base a teacher apparently has to rely on is "what has worked before." There lies the power of experience. It is true that experience separates the veteran from the novice teacher. Success in teaching, i.e., what works for the teacher, is determined primarily by how the teacher *feels* about his efforts. The teacher gathers intuitive data, centering mainly around how the children respond, and formulates a judgment as to whether or not the teaching behavior actually worked.

In keeping with the notion mentioned earlier, i.e., that the reward system for teachers is determined primarily by students, it is the students who determine whether a given teaching behavior is successful. If students do not like what has been designed for them, they will respond negatively. Because that feedback is immediate, because it is difficult to obtain feedback that directly tests stated objectives, and because most teachers are sincere in their efforts to satisfy their students, teachers are vulnerable to being shaped by their students. This socialization process (Burlingame, 1972) is a classical example of operant conditioning—the influence of positive and negative reinforcements on human behavior.

Learning to be a teacher (after teacher education) can be viewed as a subtle process of negotiation between teacher and students until both are satisfied. Teacher satisfaction is measured in terms of the amount of positive reinforcement received, and student satisfaction is often measured in terms of the amount and nature of the work required. Too often, the negotiation ends in mediocrity, which explains, in part, the existing public disenchantment with schools and the current accountability crises in education.

Nevertheless, teachers end up *feeling* they are successful teachers. When this experience later becomes the primary (or only) body of knowledge on which to teach teachers, teacher educators are sincere in their efforts and are convinced that what they pass on to their trainees will work. Because reward systems in teacher education are determined by each teacher educator, trainees are forced to comply in order to survive. Both the teacher educator and the trainee feel successful at their individual missions. However, the experience-based teacher educator has not had much effect on the trainee's teaching behavior. Teacher educators' experiences relate to their own personalities in interaction with other personalities. What the teacher educator considered initially to be "successful" experience was the behaviors students wanted to reinforce, and "success" was determined by the teacher's own subjective observations, selective perceptions, biases, needs, and other personal idiosyncracies.

More than likely, what has been most meaningful in learning to teach, both positively and negatively, are the teacher trainee's observations (modeling) of former teachers and teacher trainers. The trainee is continuously formulating a model of how to teach based upon good and bad personal experiences as a student. The accountability crisis and the public disenchantment with education suggest this not to be a very effective method of teaching teachers. At any rate, it is not until the trainee begins teaching, *after* being officially sanctioned, that the adequacy of the perceived model is actually tested.

What is desperately needed is research on teaching. Until there becomes a scientific body of knowledge about teaching, or as long as teaching remains an art and not a science, then the behavior of teachers will be subject to the behavioral reinforcers operating at any given moment. Only when teachers can work from a knowledge base can they put their intellectual abilities above their own needs and interests. Until teacher education predominately emphasizes the science rather than the art of teaching, methods courses will probably have little permanent effect on teacher behavior.

This discussion suggests that teacher education should consist primarily of knowledge about human behavior, understanding the behavior of others and knowing how to behave toward others in order to bring about desired changes. A "course" in human growth and development, or behavior modification, or even "Methods of . . ." are unrealistic approaches to permanently affecting teacher behavior. Teachers must be experts in learning theory and experts at detecting individual needs. The training of teachers should concentrate predominantly on the science of human behavior from psychological, sociological, and cultural points of view.

Another aspect of education so desperately needed is research on teaching teachers. While it is easy to list those teacher education practices that are not successful, it is more difficult to determine what techniques might be successful. Competency-based and performanced-based teacher education, relatively new attempts at teaching teachers, both appear fruitful (*Phi Delta Kappan*, 1974). Competency-based teacher education (CBTE) was designed primarily as a system to satisfy accountability legislation rather than as a system to prepare teachers to teach. CBTE emphasizes the competencies needed by successful teachers, and unfortunately this has forced many teacher educators into believing that the best (or only) way to teach teachers how to teach is by providing them with what they need to *know* about teaching.

It seems reasonable to view teaching as one would view a motor skill to be learned as well as to view it as a cognitive function.* Pease and Tabor (1976) have argued that in the absence of any real knowledge about teaching teachers, viewing teaching as a motor skill to be learned does provide a preliminary theoretical framework from which to teach teachers. Using the motor skill acquisition model provided by Gentile (1972), prospective teachers must not only gain knowledge about teaching (identify the relevant stimuli in the environment and formulate a motor plan), but they must try it, attend to the results, alter the motor plan accordingly, and make another attempt. Using this model as a base, practice over an extended period of time with accurate, immediate feedback throughout is crucial to affecting teacher behavior.

If teaching resembles a motor skill to be learned, then the performance-based teacher education (PBTE) model appears to be a more fruitful design for teaching teachers. PBTE satisfies accountability criteria, it establishes the competencies to be learned, *and* it requires the trainee to perform the desired competencies to observable satisfaction.

There are two basic differences between teaching teachers from this motor skill framework and teaching teachers from the traditional knowledge-centered plus student-teaching framework. First, practicing the skills of teaching is done before a person is sanctioned to teach rather than after. Second, immediate feedback relative to teaching behavior is provided by persons whose intent is to improve the process rather than by persons whose intent is to alleviate work. Traditionally, the student teaching experience has served only as a random introduction to the socialization process rather than as a systematic experience to improve teacher behavior effectiveness.

Teacher education in physical education

If what is to be taught in physical education, as well as how it is to be taught, are determined individually by each teacher with no common framework for making decisions about teaching and learning, then no teacher education program will have any significant effect on teaching teachers. Practice without such a framework will serve only to familiarize the trainee

---

*Before the humanists completely discredit this argument, the affective element of teaching is a constant rather than a variable. The idiopathic (personal) dimension of behavior will always be an influential factor in teaching. However, I am arguing that (1) teachers must rely less on affective factors (art) and more on cognitive factors (science) if we are to be accountable and (2) looking at teacher behavior as a motor function yields much greater insight into effective teaching of teachers than does looking at it as a cognitive or an affective function.

with the rules of the game (socialization) and feedback from teacher educators regarding teaching behavior by necessity will be inconsistent.

Before teacher education can be an effective force in shaping teacher behavior, there must first be teaching models, based on research, that serve as a common framework for making decisions about how best to faciliate learning. It seems logical that teaching models should reflect learning models. Learning difficulties can then be diagnosed, and the prescriptions will center around the corresponding teaching behaviors.

In keeping with motor development, basic fundamental movement, and motor skill acquisition as the goals of physical education, research learning and teaching for these outcomes are vital. Because of difficulties in defining and measuring, research on learning and teaching in the lower levels of the psychomotor taxonomy will be difficult. Nevertheless, systematic teaching models for motor development and basic fundamental movement must be generated and substantiated if physical educators and teacher educators are ever to become accountable in these areas.

For the goal of motor skill learning, the skill acquisition model of Gentile (1972) may provide a good beginning for the development of a skill acquisition teaching model. For each stage in her learning model, Pease and Tabor (1976) have suggested a corresponding stage of teaching. Such learning and teaching models might provide a common framework around which knowledge, performance, and feedback all center.

Once these teaching models are substantiated, teacher education can then concentrate its efforts on teaching teachers to learn about learning (for diagnostic purposes) as well as to learn to implement the teaching models effectively (for prescriptive purposes). These same learning and teaching models provide the teacher educator with a common framework from which to provide feedback to trainees regarding their teacher behavior.

Determining how best to teach teachers is the next crucial question. Research must be conducted on various teacher education learning experiences to arrive at methods that are most conducive to teaching teachers how to teach. Using the Gentile skill acquisition model as a learning framework and their corresponding skill acquisition teaching model as a teaching framework, Pease and Tabor suggest a systematic C/PBTE model for teaching teachers for skill acquisition. This and other teacher education models must be subjected to close scrutiny. Not until research provides a systematic model for teaching teachers will teacher education be accountable for having a significant affect on teacher behavior.

While generating systematic models of learning, teaching, and teaching teachers from a research base is crucial for the survival of physical education, the development of such models alone does not provide a panacea. To suggest otherwise is to admit political and economic naiveté.

Other practices must also change if teacher education is to become an effective agent for producing teachers. The current lack of support of education and the oversupply of teachers has both positive and negative effects on the status of physical education.

On the negative side, preservice training of teachers is not the avenue of pursuit that will change present teaching practices in our schools. Tight economic conditions, increased competition for a share of the tax dollar, and increased public disenchantment with schools on the one hand, and the fact that physical education is presently among the lower budgetary priorities on the other hand, suggests that few new physical education teachers will be employed each year. Thus preservice teacher education will have little impact on current physical education practices, and this trend more than likely will continue into the 1980s and perhaps into the twenty-first century.

Improving current teaching practices will be difficult. If higher education is to have any influence on changing present school physical education practices, it must enter the retraining business, and this must be done with as much or more vigor as is currently involved in pursuing preservice teacher training. Retraining must become an ongoing systematic process.

Because feelings of animosity and distrust between higher education and public school personnel are so prevalent today, implementing a systematic retraining program will not be easy. A total team approach toward accomplishing the goal must be initiated. Cooperation, trust, and mutual dependence must permeate the entire process and involve those teaching the various levels of the taxonomy, those teaching the teachers, and those conducting and interpreting the research. In the political arena in which education and physical education finds itself, no faction can stand alone. The sooner we realize this, the sooner we will begin to join forces to accomplish our common goal.

On a more positive note, now is an ideal time to take advantage of conditions that have produced a current oversupply of teachers. Reducing supply will eventually increase demand. Teacher education should be exceptionally selective in the teachers it sanctions. Either only the "A" trainees should be sanctioned to teach, or prospective trainees should be more rigorously screened and fewer be permitted to enter the teacher education program (Hoffman et al., 1975). A greater effort also should be made to recruit quality students.

Now is the ideal time to cut back on supply and redirect our energy toward quality. Concurrently, we must take advantage of this opportunity to generate knowledge from research about teaching teachers. In sum, physical education should come out of this present period of political and economic hardship with knowledge about how to promote desirable teacher behavior that will withstand socialization pressures to a situation that finds physical education in a high demand–low supply market.

Reducing supply will reduce the number of full-time equivalent university faculty positions. To compensate, many universities have expanded from the traditional teaching of teachers to other areas of the sport world. Sport journalists, athletic trainers, and sport administrators, for example, are being produced in the name of physical education. At the University of North Florida a person can negotiate all learning experiences from inside and outside the university, including one or more internships, to prepare for any career he might select. While this thrust within various departments is probably necessary for their survival and probably beneficial to society, care should be taken not to let these efforts interfere with teacher education resources.

CONCLUDING STATEMENT

Because of the great technological advances of the past few decades, society has come to value the industrial model as a successful basis of operation. Because of the inflationary economic conditions and the increased expense of operating schools, government officials favor the industrial model as a means of gaining control over educational resources. Whether it is favorable or unfavorable for education, in the future the productivity of schools will be closely monitored and all people in education will be held accountable for their efforts.

Striving for humanistic outcomes will not satisfy the accountability demands being placed on education. While these outcomes are important, and teachers should take every opportunity to teach for them, physical educators must look to the future and establish their goals accordingly.

Accountability will not be the only criterion for determining what is to be offered in the school curriculum. Offerings must also be viewed as desirable, they must meet human needs now and in the future. Meeting future needs requires planning now.

For years one of the primary goals of education has been the development of constructive uses of leisure time. Physical education, possibly more than any other discipline, has had the potential to contribute to this goal. While it may be a little harsh to suggest that physical education has failed miserably in its attempts to satisfy this goal, it is safe to say that physical education has not begun to approximate its potential.

If physical education is to survive the political and economic hardships that lie ahead, we must recommit our efforts to the basics: coordinate all efforts to produce well-skilled persons in several sport activities. No persons should exit from physical education without having attained this goal.

To accomplish this goal, the total curriculum, beginning at the preschool level, should be reexamined to provide a sequence of learning experiences designed to produce well-skilled individuals. Physical education must become learning centered, not the time- and grade-centered program it is now.

To accomplish this goal, research in learning and teaching must be expanded. What motor development and basic fundamental movement components, if any, transfer generally to motor skill acquisition? Which transfer specifically? How do students learn best, and what teaching styles facilitate these components? What teaching behaviors best facilitate acquisition of motor skill?

To accomplish this goal, research on teaching teachers must also begin with vigor. How do teachers learn to be teachers? How can inadequate perceptual models of teaching in trainees be broken down and replaced with more adequate perceptual models? How can the socialization process be reversed so as not to influence teacher behavior negatively? What training experiences have long-term affects on teacher behavior? No longer can the doctorate be a primary criterion for qualification as a teacher educator. Teaching teachers must become an area of specialization with special training and its own body of knowledge.

To accomplish this goal, physical education must begin to specialize. I suggest specialists in motor development, basic fundamental movement, and motor skill acquisition. Further, physical educators must begin to diagnose their clientele relative to the position of each individual in motor or skill development and prescribe learning experiences accordingly.

At a time when all of education is struggling, physical education is in a position to emerge in a leadership role for all of the educational disciplines to follow. Teaching for motor skill acquisition satisfies accountability criteria and it meets human needs now and in the future. Motor skill acquisition lends itself nicely to research that can make learning models and teaching models a reality. From this research base, diagnoses and prescriptions can also be implemented into educational practice.

REFERENCES

Asbell, B. 1970. Schools hire out the job of teaching, IBM Think, September-October, p. 5.

Buchen, I. H. 1974. Future focus: social trends, 1959-2020, Intellect 103:109.

Burlingame, M. 1972. Socialization constructs and the teaching of teachers, Quest 17:40.

Corrigan, D. C. 1974. The future: implications for the preparation of educational personnel, Journal of Teacher Education 25:100.

Drucker, P. 1957. America's next twenty years, New York, Harper & Row, Publishers.

Gentile, A. M. 1972. A working model of skill acquisition with application to teaching, Quest 17:3.

Gores, H. B. 1975. The future file: schoolhouse 2000, Phi Delta Kappan 56:310.

Harrow, A. J. 1972. A taxonomy of the psychomotor domain: a guide for developing behavioral objectives, New York, David McKay Co., Inc.

Hoffman, H. A., Bowers, L. E., and Klesius, S. E. 1975. Selective admissions: a first step in professional preparation, Journal of Physical Education and Recreation **46:** 29.

Jencks, C. 1972. Inequality: a reassessment of the effect of family and schooling in America. New York, Basic Books, Inc.

Mead, M. 1969. Culture and commitment, New York, Doubleday & Co., Inc.

Morris, J. 1974. Visions of education in 2000 A. D., School and Community **60:**24.

Nash, P. 1973. Education 2000 A. D., Journal of Education **155:**3.

Orwell, G. 1961. 1984, New York, The New American Library, Inc.

Pease, D. A., and Tabor, T. R. 1976. Teaching teachers for skill acquisition: a competency-based teacher education model, Briefings **2:**41.

Phi Delta Kappan. 1974. January, entire issue.

Travers, R. M. W., editor. 1973. Second handbook of research on teaching, Skokie, Ill., Rand McNally & Co.

U.S. News and World Report, 1975. **78:**7.

Whiting, H. T. A. 1969. Acquiring ball skill, Philadelphia, Lea & Febiger.

A new wisdom for physical education

Charles B. Corbin

Once upon a time, the animals decided they must do something heroic to meet the problems of "a new world." So they organized a school.

They adopted an activity curriculum consisting of running, climbing, swimming and flying. To make it easier to administer the curriculum, all the animals took all the subjects.

The duck was excellent in swimming, in fact better than his instructor; but he made only passing grades in flying and was very poor in running. Since he was slow in running, he had to stay after school and also drop swimming in order to practice running. This was kept up until his web feet were badly worn and he was only average in swimming. But average was acceptable in school, so nobody worried about that except the duck.

The rabbit started at the top of the class in running, but had a nervous breakdown because of so much make-up work in swimming.

The squirrel was excellent in climbing until he developed frustration in the flying class, where his teacher made him start from the ground up instead of from the treetop down. He also developed "Charley Horse" from over exertion and then got C in climbing and D in running.

The eagle was a problem child and was disciplined severely. In the climbing class he beat all the others to the top of the tree, but insisted on using his own way to get there.

At the end of the year, an abnormal eel that could swim exceedingly well, and also run, climb and fly a little had the highest average and was valedictorian.

The prairie dogs stayed out of school and fought the tax levy because the administration would not add digging and burrowing to the curriculum. They apprenticed their child to a badger and later joined the groundhogs and gophers to start a successful private school.*

---

*From Reavis, G. H. 1953. The animal school, Educational Forum **17:**141. By permission of Kappa Delta Pi, An Honor Society in Education, P.O. Box A, West Lafayette, Indiana 47906, owners of the copyright.

This is a well-known parable that has many implications for the future of physical education. Although many valuable lessons can be learned from it, I use it here to dramatize one basic but important point. *Education, including physical education, should not be focused on the "things" we want students to accomplish but on helping students to become fully functioning, healthy individuals.* Learning to swim, climb trees, play volleyball, or whatever is not the substance of physical education; helping people to fulfill their potential and become fully functioning individuals is!

A FOCUS FOR THE FUTURE

Toffler (1970) has estimated that seven of 10 people in the world do not live in the manner to which we have become accustomed. This estimate is based in no small part on the large populations of the world's emerging nations, but it does have implications for educators. Just as the majority of the world's population live a different life-style, so too do educators often operate in a less than current manner. In physical education, we too are often not up with the times. Before we can effectively focus on the future, we must unshackle ourselves from the past; we must not only be willing to look forward, but we must want to look forward.

Two possible explanations for operating in the past, conventional wisdom and the Titanic effect,* have been suggested by Watt (1974). Conventional wisdom is a willingness to accept tradition or opinion on faith rather than fact. To accept and operate on the basis of conventional wisdom would be to live in the past, relying on outdated information to solve current or future problems.

It is my belief that because of conventional wisdom, physical education all too often has operated in the past. This suggests that the focus for the future of physical education should be to develop a "new wisdom." Change for the sake of change may have tragic consequences as illustrated in the parable of the animals. To merely make program changes is not the answer for the future of physical education. The new wisdom in physical education must not be program oriented but must focus on goals and objectives. Program changes for the future will take care of themselves if a new wisdom is created and goals for the future are based on this new wisdom.

---

*The Titanic effect, although not of principal interest in this paper, is another deterrent to change. The Titanic effect indicates that the magnitude of disasters decreases to the extent to which people believe that they are possible and plan to prevent them. In physical education we may refuse to change programs because we do not believe that there is any threat of losing our programs in the school. Only if physical education programs began to be dropped in some school districts would we feel the compulsion to change what we are doing.

Fig. 4. Conventional wisdom continuum.

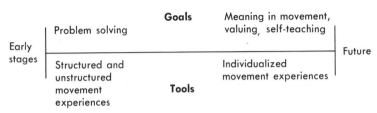

Fig. 5. New wisdom continuum.

THE CONVENTIONAL AND THE NEW WISDOM: WHAT ARE THEY?

Because this essay focuses on the development of a "new wisdom," it is appropriate that the concept be more fully outlined. Also it seems appropriate to clarify the nature of conventional wisdom and how it differs from the new wisdom, specifically within the discipline of physical education.

As stated previously, conventional wisdom is the willingness to rely on tradition or opinion rather than fact. Within physical education, the concept of conventional wisdom could mean many things. The focus here will be on the goals of physical education and the tools* selected to help learners meet those goals. My concept of conventional wisdom is shown in Fig. 4.

Although there are obvious exceptions, the thrust of the conventional wisdom is and has been the achievement of physical fitness, the acquisition of sports skills, and in general the attainment of a specific state of well-being or a specific performance level. Under conventional wisdom the blurring of means and ends (i.e., tools and goals) has made it difficult for the profession to differentiate one from the other. Activity and the immediate benefits of activity seem to be the *goals as well as the tools of the conventional wisdom.* This blurring of tools and goals, if allowed to continue, will tend to have a negative impact on the profession's future.

The new wisdom, according to my concept, is shown in Fig. 5.

---

*As I see it, the tools of physical education are the means we use to accomplish the specific ends we seek. Our goals are the ends. Our means, or our tools, are our programs, our curriculums, and the experiences we use to help students attain goals.

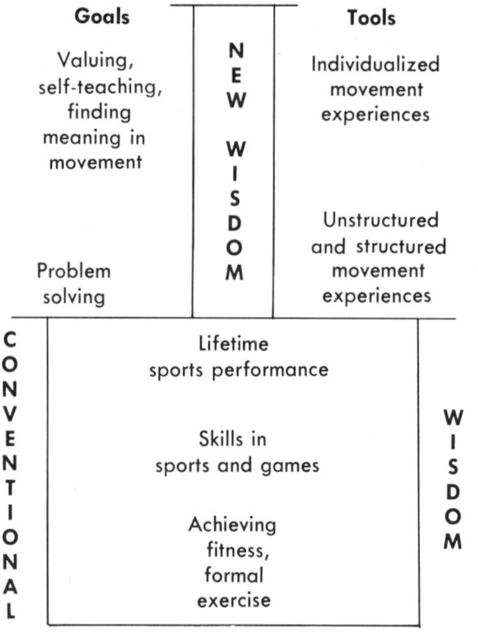

Goals		Tools
Valuing, self-teaching, finding meaning in movement	N E W W I S D O M	Individualized movement experiences
Problem solving		Unstructured and structured movement experiences

C O N V E N T I O N A L	Lifetime sports performance	W I S D O M
	Skills in sports and games	
	Achieving fitness, formal exercise	

Fig. 6. An integrated wisdom.

There is a clear distinction between goals and tools. The goals are the central aspect of the new wisdom. While I have argued that many if not most of the current programs in physical education operate on the basis of conventional wisdom, there are exemplary programs that have already pushed to the dawn of the new wisdom. These programs focus on problem-solving abilities (i.e., ability to determine for oneself how to move efficiently and effectively and the ability to solve one's own exercise problems, including exercise program planning and evaluation) and have used innovative movement experiences, frequently of an unstructured nature, to achieve these goals. But the ultimate goal that characterizes the new wisdom is the creation of a desire within the individual to value life, to find meaning and joy in existence through the medium of physical education and human movement. Subgoals of the new wisdom include understanding and living with one's own movement limitations and the ability to self-teach to accomplish one's fullest movement potential. In the broader educational context, Leonard characterized the new wisdom when he wrote, "One of the first tasks of education, then, is to return man to himself; to encourage rather than to stifle awareness; to educate the emotions, the senses, the so-called autonomic systems; to help people become truly

162

responsive and therefore truly responsible" (1968, p. 127). To meet these goals, creative and innovative individualized movement experiences (tools) must be developed (of course creative and innovative teachers will also be necessary). However, the emphasis is on the goals rather than the tools of the discipline.

All of this seems to suggest an urgent need to change from the conventional wisdom to the new wisdom. This is not exactly the case. The new wisdom does *not* supersede the conventional wisdom. The conventional wisdom is *not* to be discarded; rather it forms the basis for the new wisdom. Conventional wisdom by itself is shortsighted, but without it the new wisdom probably would never exist. Fig. 6 illustrates the integration of the conventional wisdom *with* the new wisdom.

Early learning based on the conventional wisdom can be of value, but the value of the physical education experience is not limited to performing tasks and achieving skills. Beyond achieving skill, physical fitness, or whatever, higher order objectives and goals exist. The essence of the new wisdom is to provide innovative experiences for all people so that they may become fully functioning individuals. To the extent that experiences stemming from the conventional wisdom contribute to this goal, it can be said that the conventional wisdom is the basis for the attainment of the new wisdom.

THE NEW WISDOM: WHY?

As previously mentioned, the easiest way to change physical education for the future would be to change our programs. This has already been done in many public schools and universities. Unfortunately, it may be a mistake to plan current or future programs based exclusively on conventional wisdom. For example, to change our activity programs from team sports to more relevant lifetime sports because it is "up to date" may be like teaching flying to rabbits. The real future of physical education lies in the development of goals that are consistent with the needs of people. Though lifetime sports are good means for developing significant new goals, the teaching of lifetime sports for sport's sake is to cling exclusively to the conventional wisdom.

For many years the goals of physical education have been easily and almost universally agreed on. Admittedly, there has been concern as to which objectives to emphasize, but a basic consensus has been reached concerning the principal objectives of the profession. Generally acknowledged as principal objectives are physical fitness, development of movement capabilities, and worthy use of leisure time. Most physical educators have accepted the conventional wisdom of these basic goals, but few have really applied themselves to answering the question of relevant goals for the future. This is not to say that the goals just listed are not important. They are! But as Burt* said, "Viewed from the outside, there is not a 'single vision' in physical education. There are self-serving divisions . . . of your field, but . . . the students of the discipline consistently fail to see how the parts fit together" (1975).

To paraphrase Burt, the conventional wisdom of teaching activities directed toward developing disintegrated parts (such as fitness or skill) rather than the total individual must be rethought. A wisdom focusing on the totally integrated person must be the wisdom of physical education in the future.

Rather than focusing on which activities to teach today or which sports students must learn, Burt suggests that we should direct our efforts elsewhere. The real questions are not "How do I learn a skill?" or "How do I become physically fit?" Instead we must ask, "How can we help people find something to be healthy for?" and "How can we help people find a reason for possessing efficient movement skills?" In other words, the central focus for the future lies in helping people discover themselves and find a meaning in life. To summarize, a fully functioning, healthy individual is aware of his or her own limitations and is capable of being responsible for his or her own success or failure. If the physical education of the future can help *all* people to become physically educated in this context, then we will have become founded in a new wisdom. These physically educated people will have a reason for being fit and healthy, a reason for wanting to learn leisure skills, and they will feel responsible for directing their own futures. In the truest sense they will have no difficulty finding ways to meet their needs through the movement medium.

IMPLEMENTING THE NEW WISDOM
The universities' role in developing the new wisdom

If we as physical educators are to be effective in dispersing the new wisdom, it must be through our teacher preparation programs.† The physical educator of the future must be a partner in the development of the new wisdom and must participate in the study of styles of teaching and

---

*It is interesting to note that Burt, a former physical educator, is now a practicing health educator. As is so often the case, we must look outside our area to find a true mirror for seeing ourselves as we are. Too often we on the inside, possessing a similar image, cannot see ourselves as we really are.

†I am also convinced that in-service education is important and must be provided to enable practitioners to convert to the new wisdom and resulting curriculum modifications. However, the prognosis for future change seems more realistic for future teachers than for practitioners already soundly rooted in the conventional wisdom.

development of innovative programs for implementing the new wisdom. Several important changes must occur in the university system if a new wisdom is to be successfully implemented.

Future physical educators must participate in the planning of their own education. If the core of the new wisdom of physical education is to help students to find meaning in life and to feel responsible for their own success or failure, we must prepare future teachers who are equal to the task. Vaccaro, in looking at the future of American education, suggests the necessity for a ". . . shift in responsibility, from a rigid system in which the college requires detailed adherence to minute degree and course requirements, to a flexible system in which the student is responsible for and, in some ways, shapes his own program of study" (1975, p. 388). If the central goal of physical education is to help people to become fully functioning, healthy individuals, it seems obvious that individualized learning experiences are necessary. Each future teacher has individual strengths and limitations. Just as future students will need to focus their learning in areas of greatest individual need, so too will the future teacher. It seems reasonable to assume that future physical educators must be participants in their own learning process.

Physical educators of the future must be responsible for policing the quality of their own teacher education programs. The licensing of professionals of any type has the problem of a double-edged sword. The negative side is that licensing is restrictive and may discourage creative approaches to education. The positive side is that licensing provides an increased probability* that practicing educators will have the competence and qualities necessary to implement the new wisdom and its accompanying programs.

At last count there were 27 different institutions in Kansas,† a state of approximately 2 million people, preparing individuals for careers in physical education. Many of these institutions *do not* have the resources, the staff, or the "wisdom" to prepare physical educators for the future. It is no wonder that physical education is operating in the past when one considers the number of "physical educators" being "prepared" in substandard programs, many of which are not even soundly based in the conventional wisdom, let alone a new wisdom.

Obviously we are duplicating efforts at many institutions of higher learning. If we could pool our resources so that a few schools would have

---

*Licensing does not ensure quality, it only improves the probability of quality.
†The situation in Kansas is not unique but is used to illustrate a point. Similar conditions exist throughout the United States.

the necessary resources, we would have a much better chance of preparing a better professional physical educator. We would do much better to have a few quality programs than to have many mediocre ones. I advocate an "approved program" approach to licensing physical educators. A national board of physical educators would provide evaluation teams to accredit sound programs. Graduates of accredited programs would be licensed to teach. This system of internal policing is superior to policing from outside and is superior to a system of certification that is based on "taking courses," a plan that all too often forces colleges to plan a rigid program of study.

With all projections for the future indicating the need to reduce the size of the teacher force, it should be noted that any system of approving programs would need to apply to institutions with doctoral as well as baccalaureate programs.

A sound licensing system would serve to reduce the number of future practitioners in the profession as well as to improve the chances of implementing a new wisdom in our schools.

Teacher preparation institutions of the future must develop a system of qualitative rather than quantitative accounting. The recent emphasis on "accountability" has resulted in the development of a quantitative system of accounting. The "number of heads" or student enrollment has become the criterion for determining the worth of a teacher preparation program. New faculty and resources are assigned to programs with large "head counts." To a point, such accountability is good. However, the potential for deterioration in program quality is obvious. As a premium is placed on quantitative enrollments, inducements such as high grades and limited outside assignments are offered. In some cases the quality of physical education teacher preparation programs has already deteriorated, as indicated by the proliferation of cheap credit summer offerings, workshops, etc. The physical education of the future must reward the quality programs with resources by developing a system of qualitative accounting. The Titantic effect must not apply in this case. We cannot continue to use an exclusively quantitative accounting system with the thought that our programs will not be affected. They are, and they will be.

Future physical educators must develop a new set of tools as well as a new wisdom. Just as the physical educator of the future cannot rely on the conventional wisdom, he cannot rely on the tools of the past. Gold has indicated that "we still measure program effectiveness in participation hours rather than what happens to people as a result of participation, and we offer relatively little in the way of meaningful, noncompetitive and innovative activities" (1975, p. 42). Just as we must develop a new wisdom, we

166

must take Gold's advice and direct our efforts toward developing new experiences for implementing it.

As alternatives or supplements to formal activities such as games, organized exercises, traditional sports, and even lifetime sports, which have become the major tools of the physical educator, we must consider such tools or means to accomplish physical education's goals as guided discovery, self-learning activities based on the concept of open-ended achievement, movement exploration, small group problem solving, and sum positive physical activity experiences, to name but a few.

The physical education of the future must be a dynamic as well as a reflective part of our culture. Physical education has been content for too long to stick with the conventional wisdom because it is the easy thing to do. It has been said that in many cases the only thing physical educators must do to keep their jobs is to "give good grades and keep kids from getting hurt." The physical education of the future must not be content to "get by" with what the public permits or even expects. Although change is often painful, educators must create and apply the new wisdom and perhaps more importantly make the public aware of the new wisdom and its potential contributions. Physical education can be a significant contributor to the betterment of future society if only the profession is willing to be dynamic.

Simple solutions to complex problems

As Furst has aptly pointed out:

> The problems of modern education are terribly real and pose [a great problem to the profession]. If educational leaders deal only with the symptoms, as they have so often in the past, no effective cure can be expected. Treatment of the basic problems—in short, a new role education should play in our society—would bring some relief from the trouble that plague the education industry in America today.*

While Furst is suggesting creative visions for the future, he is also emphasizing the fact that there are *no simple solutions to the complex problems education will face in the future.* No single change in philosophy, no innovative program, and no creative educational doctrine alone will solve all of education's problems. It is with this in mind that I offer some "simple" suggestions for the future that might offer some solutions to the problems from which physical education suffers today. Specifically I refer to the problems associated with wasting human beings as natural resources or

*From Furst, L. G. 1975. The educational fifth column: an expanded role for teachers, Phi Delta Kappan **57**:11.

failing to help each person to become a fully functioning, healthy individual.
The physical education of the future must be based on sound, long-range planning. If the physical education of the future is to have any chance of implementing the new wisdom and of contributing positively to a solution of society's problems, programs of the future cannot be left to chance. Programs must be based on predetermined educational objectives. The Titantic effect suggests that all too often we are willing to wait until it is too late to change. The Titantic effect notwithstanding, failure to recognize and plan for future trends, changes in numbers of school-age children, changing life-styles, fuel crises, etc. will thwart the implementation of the new wisdom.

Even such technical things as planning physical education facilities, developing accountability, and scheduling for individualized instruction must be based on sound, long-range planning. However, it should be emphasized that although education must be increasingly planned, plans must be developed in such a way as to allow for the individual differences of all students. Preplanning cannot be allowed to result in inflexible programming.

The physical education of the future must become more personalized. Van Til indicates that, in general, "Contemporary high schools are too large, age segregated, overly separated, [and] quasi custodial" (1975, p. 493). He also indicates his support for "smaller, more diverse, age-integrated and community related" schools (1975, p. 493). If we are to truly implement a new wisdom, the future physical education, whether in schools or out, must place a premium on more individualized learning experiences and less emphasis on the economy afforded by large schools, large classes, and large group learning experiences. Tyler summarizes a personalized educational philosophy based on a new wisdom when he suggests:

> In the school every student is to be respected as an important person, regardless of his background. In the school, justice and fair play dominate a society where people care about each other, and where all have an opportunity to share in planning activities, executing them, and gaining the rewards of what they have accomplished.*

The physical education of the future must extend beyond the school walls. The emphasis for the future must change from "school system to educational system" (Fantini, 1975, p. 10). Many learning experiences can and must occur outside the school environment as society in general becomes more responsible for the education of its youth. Open schools, community school co-ops, noncredit education, nontraditional study programs, and off-campus university instruction are merely examples of aspects of the truly continuing

*From Tyler, R. W. 1975. Reconstructing the total educational environment, Phi Delta Kappan 57:11.

physical education program. Education, especially physical education, must be a continuous process that cannot be limited to a process occurring inside school buildings.

The physical education of the future must be a lifelong process. Physical education is not just for youth; it is for all people. Physical educators, because of heavy work loads and because we "already have more students than we can handle," have been reluctant to conduct programs for students other than those enrolled in school classes. The physical educators of the future must be willing to conduct programs not only for school children but also for preschoolers, adults, and the elderly. We must provide the initiative necessary to organize and implement programs of continuing physical education.

CONCLUDING STATEMENT

As physical educators face the future, we must be prepared to push beyond the philosophies and programs of the past and implement a new wisdom. Programs of the past (although some still exist today) were based on the assumption that activities (including sports and exercises) had value for all people and that mere exposure to such activities would benefit all participants.

Many contemporary programs have been successful in complementing the traditional programs with "problem-solving" approaches to physical education. These programs also emphasize the value of physical activity and movement experiences in the lives of all people but are designed to help each individual to solve his or her own movement problems, including selecting appropriate activities for achieving physical fitness, selecting and learning lifetime sports for enjoying leisure time, and generally gaining an understanding of how to move effectively in daily life.

While it is my belief that there is value in participation in physical activity (past) and that every person should be prepared to solve his or her own movement problems (present), I also feel that the physical education of the future must be based on a new wisdom. The new wisdom emphasizes the need for all educational endeavors to focus on helping every person to become a fully functioning, healthy individual. Inherent in this philosophy is the notion that all of us are responsible for our own futures and that all of us can find a "meaning" in life commensurate with our own abilities and potentials. Physical education then becomes a way of helping people find meaning for their lives as well as being a means to accomplish ends such as physical fitness, movement skills, or even problem-solving abilities.

Thus the physical education of the future must become a part of a total process of helping every person to find meaning and purpose in life. Because of the self-testing possibilities, the concrete opportunities for studying one's own limitations, the possibilities for social interaction, the many alternatives to success, and the tremendous joy which comes to people through human movement, it is my belief that when it comes to developing the new wisdom for helping each individual to become fully functioning and healthy, few if any disciplines have as much to offer as physical education.

By the year 2000 the prairie dogs, badgers, groundhogs, and gophers were back in the public schools. Suffering the effects of inflation they were unable to pay the tuition necessary to support their own private schools. Though the eels, rabbits, ducks, eagles, and squirrels were still unhappy about the activity-based curriculum, they were all encouraged when a bright young skunk was hired as school superintendent.

The skunk, not being particularly skilled in running, swimming, climbing, or flying, knew full well the limitations of the "old" curriculum. The skunk set out to bring the curriculum from the past to the present, but he knew he had to have the support of the constituents who were growing tired of perennial problems in the schools. First he convinced all the parents that while all activities were important, the activities were not as important as what the activities did for school children. He promoted a problem-solving approach to schooling in which each animal learned all activities but selected the methods best suited to his own skills and abilities. He even encouraged the young squirrels to help the other animals with climbing; ducks, badgers, and eels to help with swimming; the groundhogs and rabbits with running; and eagles with flying. To top it off digging was also added with the assistance of prairie dogs and gophers. Everyone acknowledged that all the animal children learned all skills better than ever before.

But the skunk was not satisfied. His ancestors had been barred from the school because of their alleged antisocial behavior. He knew also that the young animals were bright and inquisitive and would want to know "why" they had to learn all of the activities in school. Also too many animal children were still inclined to "give up" in school. Even though they were learning more than ever before they found little meaning in their schooling experience. Some of the animals became dropouts. Children and their parents even felt that there was little they could do about their own future, that the schools and society were responsible for their problems.

The skunk knew that if he and the schools were to succeed in the future, the curriculum must continue to change. He proceeded to use a new philosophy and implement a program based on that philosophy. All of the animals, regardless of their abilities, were encouraged to study their own limitations and strengths. The young animals were also encouraged to study the natural abilities of the other animals so that they could better understand each other's limitations and strengths. The squirrels learned that they would never be great swimmers but such a limitation was not catastrophic. The squirrels even learned to respect the swimming abilities of the ducks and eels and enjoyed an occasional recreational swim.

As more of the animals embraced the new philosophy there was a new respect for the individual abilities of the other animals. Each animal child found new meaning in the school experience and learned to work within his or her own limitations. The skunk children, in spite of their limited abilities in the traditional subject matter, were accepted in the schools and as contributing members of the community.

170

REFERENCES

Burt, J. J. 1975. Comments on realms of meaning in physical education, Paper presented at the American Academy of Physical Education, Atlantic City, March.

Fantini, M. D. 1975. From school system to educational system, Phi Delta Kappan 57:10.

Furst, L. G. 1975. The educational fifth column: an expanded role for teachers, Phi Delta Kappan 57:8.

Gold, S. M. 1975. The Titantic effect on parks and recreation, Parks and Recreation 10: 23.

Leonard, G. 1968. Education and ectasy, New York, Dell Publishing Co., Inc.

Reavis, G. H. 1953. The animal school, Educational Forum 17:141.

Toffler, A. 1970. Future shock, New York, Random House, Inc.

Tyler, R. W. 1975. Reconstructing the total educational environment, Phi Delta Kappan 57:12.

Vaccaro, L. C. 1975. The future look of American education, Phi Delta Kappan 56:387.

Van Til, W. 1975. Reform of the high school in the mid-1970's, Phi Delta Kappan 56: 493.

Watt, K. E. F. 1974. The Titantic effect, Stamford, Conn., Sinaver Associates.

CHAPTER FIVE

TECHNOSCIENTIFIC FORECASTS

Using an exploratory forecasting model, Robert N. Singer makes some rather provocative as well as insightful forecasts regarding the impact technoscientific developments will likely have on the profession of physical education in the years ahead. For example, in a well-reasoned argument based on current trends, Singer forecasts that the present cleavage between the scientifically oriented and physical educationists wings of the profession will increase, causing those scholars interested in the scientific basis of movement to form their own autonomous organization. Singer, in fact, suggests the name Movement Sciences Association for this new organization and believes that such a development will be mutually advantageous for both groups. These and other views into the future are clearly enunciated in this thoughtful essay.

In the second essay of this chapter, Joseph R. Higgins and Susan Arend confront the reader with numerous interesting possibilities from science and technology that they believe will shape the future of physical education. They too see the emergence of a broadly-based science of human movement studies of which physical education will be only one of many applied areas. Of particular interest is the vividness with which Higgins and Arend describe specific scientific and technological developments and how they might be applied by the physical educator of the future.

Technoscientific forecasts

Robert N. Singer

If only we could peer into the future. There is nothing like assurance that we are moving in the right direction. However, it is difficult enough to project events from day to day or week to week in our volatile world, let alone to predict with any degree of confidence what we will be about in the last quarter of this century. Yet, the more distant the focus, the greater the flexibility one has in making forecasts. There is much room for speculation, and of course the forecaster cannot be condemned too severely for an erroneous prediction.

I find the challenge a very exciting one, and not because I relish the opportunity of speculation without consequences. A serious analysis of possible future technoscientific developments as related to physical education also insists that one become more philosophical, introspective, and thoughtful of contemporary circumstances. As present and future threads are tied together in the imagination, a reevaluation of present thinking and goal-directed energies may logically occur. Consequently, I selfishly look forward to the challenge of forcing myself to ponder my own role in the current state of affairs and of attempting to penetrate the future, logically deducing "how things will be," and enjoying my competitive spirit, which finds me betting with myself on the probability of correct projections.

THE TECHNOSCIENTIFIC AREA: THE PRESENT

Technology and science have infiltrated all aspects of our lives. Their impact is obvious as well as subtle, as personal life-styles, occupational demands, manufactured products, and educational procedures change. Alterations of the current status are bound to be met with acceptance, rejection, or indifference. Such is the case in education.

Technoscientific advances have produced the means to manage budgets, curriculums, and students more expeditiously and effectively than ever before. Classroom materials are more sophisticated and yet presumably more compatible with learning or behavioral principles. Research efforts penetrate every conceivable aspect of the school environment and promise better instruction and greater student achievements.

Yet humanists, among others, quarrel with these developments. Will we become too mechanized? Too indifferent to individual students? Too programmed, too formal, and too insensitive to flexible changes as each dynamic classroom situation unfolds? Too dependent on research findings, which in fact may be too inadequate, unimportant, and irrelevant?

These typical but by no means exhaustive arguments by proponents and opponents of some applications of contemporary technoscientific developments are found in every area of education. Our focal point, of course, is physical education. An analysis of the literature outlines the most recent events and issues in our field. One of these is the possibility that we are on the verge of some very sharp internal cleavages. Such is bound to be the case when an area attempts to be both a discipline and a profession. We try to produce our scholarly scientific and philosophical foundation material (although borrowing heavily from the works of others) and at the same time to formulate educational curriculums and prepare teachers who serve

173

in various types of institutional and noninstitutional programs. The coordination of these efforts can be smooth or bumpy. At the present time there are many difficulties, and their resolution is an immediate imperative if progress is to be made. The nature of the cleavage, with causes and outcomes, will be discussed shortly. But first of all, let us see how the technoscientific area relates to physical education.

What is the technoscientific area?

Technological, research, and scientific processes, outcomes, and progress represent an invaluable aspect of our ability to understand human movement behavior. From the practical point of view, improved training and instructional programs relate to the achievement of skills; the quest for organic efficiency; the development of self-image, self-actualization, and personal fulfillment; the appreciation of aesthetics, strategies, and movements in skilled performance; and the enrichment of social interactions.

Research is a formalized process of collecting and analyzing data in order to develop and test theory, or practice, or both. From a scientific point of view, then, research can be undertaken in many fields relevant to physical education. Interestingly enough, most of the fields have usually been termed "scientific" in the physical education literature. Examples of these fields are the following:

1. Exercise physiology (work physiology, ergonomics)
2. Anatomy
3. Biomechanics (kinesiology, biokinetics)
4. Motor learning (skill acquisition)
5. Motor development
6. Sports psychology
7. Sports sociology
8. Instructional design, mediated materials

Although many of these areas overlap, the continued scientific study of human movement behavior from a particular reference point leads to a body of knowledge that can be useful to physical educators, coaches, and others concerned with similar functions. The accumulated body of knowledge contains information on which intelligent coaching and teaching decisions, tempered with logic and common sense, can be made.

Exercise physiologists are concerned with studying the body's systems and how they function. They have suggested scientifically valid training programs that might enhance the health, the working capacity, and the prospect of longevity for individuals throughout the world. Their efforts have included the study of nutrition, body composition, cardiovascular dynamics, pulmonary function, strength, injury prevention, recovery and rehabilitation measures, stress environments, and biochemical changes. Physical education programs, which have objectives for the development of the physical properties of human beings, can be formulated in a sound manner as the result of the efforts of exercise physiologists.

Few people trained specifically in anatomy direct their research efforts especially toward implications for physical education. However, normal or unusual bone growth and muscle development associated with athletic participation or the lack of it is one critical area in which the anatomist can make a real contribution.

The expanding discipline af biomechanics reflects the contemporary view of merging various lines of endeavor for the more effective study of a common area of concern. The study of human motion and movement requires a mixture of knowledge from such sources as physics, cinematography, biology, and mathematics. In order to perform a physical act with minimum effort and maximum potential, appropriate principles of body mechanics and motion should be used. Every act can be carefully analyzed with an assortment of instruments and techniques, and specialists in biomechanics provide information on a variety of gross motor and specialized skill activities associated with sport and physical education.

With an apparent origin in the psychology of learning, motor learning specialists have attempted to resolve issues related to processes of skill acquisition, with consideration of typical, handicapped, and exceptionally proficient individuals. Methods of practice have been compared, and topics related to motivation, feedback, retention, transfer, and abilities have been studied in order to obtain a more thorough grasp of the nature of the learning process and the effect of situational manipulations. Models of skill acquisition and research in motor learning can lead to more effective teaching procedures if the bridge between them is drawn satisfactorily. Motor learning research may be observed in athletic situations or in the laboratory with computer management experiments and recorded physiological and performance measures.

Since the development of children during the preschool and early school years is so important, it is little wonder that the scientific study of developmental processes and behavior should unfold. Physical, emotional, cognitive, biomechanical, psychomotor, perceptual, and sociocultural characteristics that influence the behavior of the child of a particular maturational or chronological age must be identified and understood if physical educators, special educators, early childhood teachers, and elementary school teachers are to enhance their potential to work with children. As is the case in all scientific fields associated with physical education, research on problems in motor development can be pursued in a controlled laboratory setting, in a classroom or gymnasium, on athletic fields, or in recreational settings.

Sports psychology and sports sociology have been established recently in the United States as recognized areas of scholarly activity. Social and psychological parameters of athletic performance as they affect superior athletes as well as the mass of participants are being identified and researched. The result of these research efforts is a more comprehensive understanding of how to analyze, treat, and train athletes. Group dynamics, interpersonal relations, psychodiagnostics, and sociocultural influences are some of the areas in which major scientific thrusts are being accomplished.

The science of instruction is a very new concept. For years we have talked about the art of teaching, as if teaching skills progressed only as a result of creativity and intuition. Yet an increasing number of educator-scholars have supported the notion that there are sound scientific behavioral and instructional principles on which education should rest. Furthermore, modern technology has led to the creation and development of a variety of instructional media, the most sophisticated of which is the computer. Instructional designers attempt to identify the systems that influence behavioral change and in turn recommend the sequence, contents, and nature of instruction that helps to meet preestablished instructional goals and objectives.*

From the preceding discussion it can be seen that a number of identifiable scientific avenues of study constitute a good portion of the "discipline" aspect of the field of physical education. The body of knowledge can provide assistance to physical educators as well as others who might be interested in the psychomotor domain and psychomotor behaviors. There are practical as well as theoretical implications of these research efforts. The scholarly activities may originate with trained physical educators and others representing different fields of study, or from their combined efforts. At any rate, the technoscientific area has continually developed its reputation.

Content and approaches. The technoscientific revolution in industry, business, education, and society in general has emphatically changed approaches to completing tasks and the expected nature of the output. As far as physical education is concerned, we might view this impact in two dimensions: research and teaching. The products of science and technology can be used to improve research endeavors as well as instructional situations. With advanced technology, used logically and appropriately, we can expect improved outcomes.

More sophisticated equipment aids in the conduct of experiments in ex-

*Books in physical education that discuss this subject are written by Singer and Dick, 1974, and Rushall and Siedentop, 1972.

ercise psychology, biomechanics, motor learning, and other areas that involve the collection of data. Data are obtained under more controlled conditions, and a variety of useful measures may be recorded simultaneously. Scientists associated with human movement behaviors, and in turn with physical education, have become better equipped to formulate research problems, design and undertake research, and thus improve research activities, theoretical developments, and practical implications and applications.

Technological and scientific advancements have made it possible for the teacher, armed with a variety of media, assisted by resource specialists, and knowledgeable about human behavior, instructional delivery systems, and instructional design, to be more effective than ever before in handling the vast array of responsibilities associated with the teaching profession. Physical educators, in the classroom or in athletic situations, can improve their teaching effectiveness.

Consequently, the content of and approaches to research dealing with movement behaviors as well as physical education have changed from the more simplistic to the more acceptable from the scientific point of view. This transformation has left some researchers and teachers happy while others feel pressured, imposed on, and resentful of attempts to infiltrate their approaches with scientific and technological processes. It would be profitable to examine the situation in which those who would advance the scientific body of knowledge in physical education confront those involved in the preparation of physical education teachers.

The cleavage. Ideally, a mutually beneficial relationship should exist between the researcher and the practitioner, between the scientist and the professional preparation specialist. Coordinated efforts would lead to a more desirable goal—improved physical education programs and better trained physical educators. Yet resentment and resistance appear among both parties. Why?

First of all, mutual respect for the activity of each appears to be lacking. Specialists view their own work to be of a primary importance, the other to be of less relevance. A complaint registered against researchers is that their work is specialized, intellectual, impractical, and nonmeaningful. A complaint directed against practitioners is that their efforts are naive, superficial, nonacademic, and antiquated. As one group attempts to become more academically respectable, the other attempts to become pragmatic and useful. Will this become a battle or a marriage between those who consider themselves movement scientists and those who feel they are physical education professional preparation specialists? Unfortunately, at the present time, the cleavage seems to be growing greater (Fig. 7).

Second, a proportionally greater number of individuals than ever before

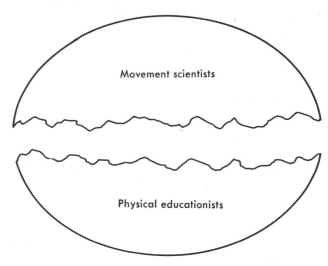

Fig. 7. The cleavage?

appear to be interested in and dedicated to the scientific study of human movement. They are concerned not only with athletic skills but also with all types of movement science behaviors. In the university setting and often in the minds of the public, the intellectual and scientific is more important than the physical, athletic, and recreational. Reward systems are developed accordingly. Academic snobbery can increase the cleavage between the two groups. Although an interest in physical education and sport may have instigated the thrust of academic study, many movement scientists are finding it more personally, academically, and financially rewarding to totally or partially disaffiliate from association with the physical education profession.

Increasingly their research articles and writings appear in journals other than those associated with health, physical education, and recreation. Instead of attempting to appeal to the family that nurtured them, the trend of many movement scientists is toward the particular academic base most related to their work. For example, exercise psychologists publish in journals associated with physiology and sport medicine. Motor learning specialists publish articles that deal primarily or in part with psychology, learning, and movement behaviors. Their research has gained academic respect as methodology has become more sophisticated and content more theoretical and oriented to pure research.

But what of research from these areas applied to curriculum and instruction considerations in physical education? Who would bridge the gap? Is there a need to bridge this perceived gap? Obviously if we believe that education and instruction should be grounded in science and research, there is a need for extrapolating from laboratory findings to the "real world."

Research directly conducted in these "real world" situations can have even more important consequences.

Will those educators who are involved in teacher preparation and curriculum work undertake this research? Will they reject this avenue and instead provide direction based on empirical judgment and common sense? These and other questions are difficult to answer at the present time.

Yet the ramifications of division are obvious. Interdependent efforts can serve mutually beneficial outcomes. What might we predict for the future in this situation? We will return to this problem later.

THE TECHNOSCIENTIFIC AREA: PAST DEVELOPMENTS

An understanding of the present and a rationale for future projections can be enriched through an analysis of historical antecedents. Science, technology, and research have influenced directions in physical education in the United States since the nineteenth century, at times very little, at times a little more, but never to a great extent. Similar trends may be found in all educational fields. Yet the pattern of influence in terms of magnitude and effect has indicated a greater reception and impact on educational fields other than physical education.

A partial explanation may rest with the intention to gear technoscientific efforts to the improvement of instruction and the preparation of teachers in the so-called cognitive areas. Much financial support has encouraged this marriage. Furthermore, the psychomotor domain of behavior contains many barriers to a similar marriage. Research is easier to undertake with cognitive behaviors than with psychomotor behaviors. It is easier to modify environments with the intent of using technology to influence cognitive behavior than psychomotor behavior. Furthermore, the public, school administrators, agencies responsible for the financial support of research, and the government in general have indicated a decisive preference for improving reading, mathematics, science, communication skills, and other classroom activities through scholarly research and functional curricular change models, to the neglect of physical education and other fields of study in which the medium is primarily movement.

Nonetheless, let us trace these developments, if only superficially. We will consider the relationship technoscientific developments have had with the physical education profession in general, the advancement of the body of knowledge, the improvement of instruction, and the advancement or creation of organizations.

Early developments

In the latter part of the nineteenth century the health aspects of physical education were of primary importance. Consequently, methods were created for measuring and developing facets of health and physical fitness. Data were collected to assess positive changes as a function of guided experiences in physical education.

Medical doctors and medical science had a profound influence on programs and objectives at the turn of the century. Education of the physical was the dominant theme. Instruction was oriented to health ends. Equipment to advance the physical condition of students was improved through scientific efforts, as were physical education programs.

As the philosophy of education became influenced by the work of Dewey and the Progressives, a new wave of curriculum changes was supported to deformalize education, to promote the individual and social development of students, and to encourage students to enjoy their learning experiences. The fulfillment of an expanded variety of personal objectives was to occur through the physical medium of physical education.

During World War II and shortly thereafter, technological advances changed societies all over the world. Scientific study was strengthened in institutions of higher learning. Industrial firms produced scientific products and undertook research that would bear on scientific knowledge, instructional content, and educational procedures and programs.

The use of several media in classroom instruction was proposed; the teaching machine and procedures of programmed learning created by Pressey in the 1920s and advanced by Skinner were introduced. Computers demonstrated their potential, and research became a by-word in education.

And physical education? Nearly all students who majored in this field professed an interest in teaching or coaching. Very few indicated an interest to contribute, as scientists and scholars, to a body of knowledge associated with human movement and activity. Those who did continued to work in exercise physiology. Some inroads were made in kinesiology and motor learning. Physical education, however, was associated almost solely with the preparation of teachers. They were prepared in most institutions to teach athletic skills, to organize programs, and develop curriculums, but there was little emphasis on science, research, and technology.

Sporadic attempts at innovating instruction were observed. Basically, teaching was straightforward and traditional. To all intents and purposes, any physical educator considered to be professionally oriented, regardless of specialization, belonged solely to the American Association of Health, Physical Education, and Recreation. The primary publication outlet for those considered to be scientists and scholars was *The Research Quarterly,* the research publication of that organization. Yet those trends were to change dramatically in coming years.

Contemporary times. As we review the developments in the 1960s and

1970s, distinct "happenings" can be identified. For one thing, a new breed of students, more academically oriented and scientifically interested, showed enthusiasm for physical education. Scientific disciplines allied to movement behaviors were identified, clarified, and specialized. Serious scholars carved out niches for themselves.

These thrusts required extensive academic graduate work outside of the usual physical education curriculum and in the specialization of choice. Exercise physiologists enrolled in an exotic array of courses in physiology and chemistry. Would-be motor learning specialists undertook numerous courses in the psychology of learning, research design, statistics, and laboratory equipment. Biomechanics emerged as a sophisticated, multidisciplinary study of human movement based on physics, biology, high-speed photography, and computer applications.

Shortly thereafter, areas described as motor development, sports sociology, sports psychology, and instructional design required special preparation that partially removed students from physical education to associated areas of study. Academic respectability was achieved. A heavy emphasis on research design, statistics, specialized content, and laboratory equipment was promoted. The discipline of physical education and, even further, the discipline of movement science, became established.

Those who were involved in these specialties went beyond an attempt solely to relate their work to improved teaching in physical education and acceptable programs, although this was one major goal. Contributions were directed to theory. Basic research as well as applied research was undertaken. Research investigations were published in a variety of established journals, and new journals were created to absorb the influx of articles. These events were received with mixed feelings by the "establishment," the "pure" physical educators.

Sophisticated technology, research design, and statistics, available to all scholars, became more heavily utilized by these scientists. In fact, they were often adapted to the unique considerations of movement behaviors. New professional organizations were formed to satisfy the special concerns of the movement scientists. The American Association for Health, Physical Education, and Recreation, now an alliance, revised its structure to accommodate these scientists.

And what of their effects on the teaching of physical education activities, on program developments, and on the profession in general? In some places, their reception was warm. In most places, there was distress over these developments. Physical educators viewed the relationship of these new efforts to physical education as nonexistent. The gap between research and the practical was not bridged smoothly or effectively. If blame had to be assigned, should it be directed toward the researchers for not translating and applying their efforts? Was it the fault of those in professional preparation for not being able to interpret and use this body of knowledge? The point is obviously open to argument.

Was elitism being created, together with disdain of practitioners? Did insecurities and resistance encourage the practitioners to reject the work of the movement scientists? Is there a need to completely or partially re-shape the nature of physical education as it is usually interpreted and to ground it solidly in research, science, and technology? Or can the strength of physical education be firmly based in activities and teaching methodologies, regardless of sophisticated scientific developments?

Let us now turn to future forecasting. The question is, Where is physical education headed with respect to a technoscientific framework?

THE TECHNOSCIENTIFIC AREA: FORECASTING THE FUTURE

Our task at this point is to attempt to forecast the impact of scientific developments on physical education, with special regard for the profession, the discipline of movement sciences, instruction, programs, and organizations. How receptive will those involved in pedagogy be to accepting and utilizing the potentials? To what extent will scientists attempt to be influential?

At the present time, there is little indication that the advances and sophistication of technology in general will diminish. We have become more accepting of the products of science in order to simplify and reduce our efforts in accomplishing tasks. Our lives are presumably enriched as we learn how to enjoy the variety of products and processes that result from technoscientific developments. The technoscientific way of life is not only here to stay, it is and will continue to be a dominant force in our work and leisure activities.

But research, science, and technology cannot be forced down the throats of those who believe that their present course is just as effective or even more effective without it. Changes occur when needs are identified and alternative solutions are sought. Changes may also occur when it can be shown that alternatives are better than current practice, as the intellectually enlightened recognize the value of adopting new strategies, products, mediums, and the like. Many educators, in spite of their image as liberated thinkers responsible for the shaping of a variety of thought-provoking processes in others, are themselves remarkably conventional and resistant to change.

Physical educators can no longer sit idly by as attacks on the quality of and even the necessity for their programs in institutions of learning mount.

We cannot defend what exists when it is barely defensible. We understand the values of physical activity and its potential for the realization of many worthy goals. Outsiders do not. By necessity, then, physical education programs *must* be modified within the framework of technoscientific developments if their value is to be truly realized and in turn accepted by the doubters.

The ever-rising cost of education will have a negative effect first on those areas considered to be irrelevant and expensive. They will be reduced in scope, and they may be eliminated. This need not be the case with physical education, however. The public, legislators, and school administrators are convinced of the importance of reading and communication skills, mathematics, and the sciences. They need to realize as well the value of participation in physical activities of various kinds. They need to see that in fact physical education programs can help to produce desirable changes in students. They need to know that the effects of the serious study of human movement can influence a wide variety of programs connected with the psychomotor domain.

A scientifically and logically formulated program of physical education could be the answer. With an organized body of technoscientific scholars to contribute to the supportive structure and intellectual and innovative educators who would shape programs and influence the development of students, physical education might approach excellence and gain respect. I would like to believe that this is what the future holds. Out of the need to survive, we will turn to more streamlined and defensible programs.

Contributing to a body of knowledge

The trend toward an increased proportion of graduate students in physical education who wish to study in an area of the movement sciences and to undertake research will undoubtedly continue. The body of knowledge in the movement sciences will advance at a remarkable rate due to the quality of the students, their numbers, their specialized backgrounds, their reliance on the latest scientific methods and testing instruments, and their ability to contribute to a host of theoretical and practical concerns related to psychomotor behaviors, thereby influencing society and education in a number of ways.

We might even anticipate the development of the Movement Sciences Association (MSA), in which all those scholars with an interest in the scientific bases of movement would belong. A small number would probably belong to the American Alliance for Health, Physical Education, and Recreation as well. Departments of movement science (or biokinetics, or something similar) will spring up in universities. An increased determination by academicians to formulate a scientific body of knowledge related to movement behaviors will necessitate their recognition, independent of the physical education profession, as making a contribution to many other fields in addition to physical education.

As math educators look to mathematicians and science educators to biologists and chemists for the content of their respective areas, physical educators will utilize the information advanced by movement scientists. In turn, these educators responsible for the professional preparation of teachers will concentrate on communicating ideas about teaching skills, class management, and ways of using a wide assortment of physical activities in programs.

The recognition of two distinct bodies, a profession of physical education and a discipline of movements sciences, will be advantageous to both in the long run. Each can autonomously and energetically develop its own interests. Each can make a major contribution to the other. The trend is toward more independent efforts of physical educators and movement scientists as each group sets specific goals and operational procedures for itself. When the identity of each group is formulated clearly and mutual respect is shown, effective communication lines will enable scientists and educators to explore ways in which each can assist and promote the efforts of the other.

Furthermore, the body of knowledge developed by movement scientists will be useful for early childhood educators, elementary education teachers, educators of handicapped children, coaches, performing artists, those involved in medicine, the military, business and industry, industrial and vocational educators, physical therapists, and others interested in psychomotor behaviors. The potential magnitude of influence is unlimited. Movement scientists are beginning to make inroads in sport medicine, the behavioral sciences, medicine, industry, a variety of educational areas, and the military. The general assumption has been that physical educators are people who teach a physical activity or coach a team. Their scientific accomplishments therefore have been misdirected, misunderstood, and ignored.

Although a number of movement scientists will continue to direct their work toward sports and physical education programs and their participants, many others will be concerned with other kinds of psychomotor activities or with psychomotor behaviors in general with the hope of contributing knowledge that will be useful to scientists and practitioners who have some degree of interest in processes related to, the effects of, and influences on movement activity.

Educators, parents, and societies in general will recognize the importance of human movement as we progress into the future. For example, movement scientists will make continued appreciated and recognized contributions with regard to the following areas:

1. Understanding how and why the body responds to vigorous activity, ways of improving the health and organic efficiency of the body, and techniques of rehabilitation following injury
2. Principles of motion and movement relevant to athletic skills, rehabilitative efforts, occupations, the military, etc.
3. Processes and factors related to the acquisition of skill and performances in a variety of movement behaviors, with implications for the instruction and training of groups of persons as well as with respect for individual differences
4. The psychomotor development of children, with special consideration for capabilities, diagnostic tests, perceptual-motor programs, and instruction
5. Sociological and psychological considerations in environments in which individual or small group movement activities occur, with special reference to sport, physical education, recreation, and play situations

In all these areas and many more, theoretical and pragmatic concerns will be addressed. People will learn to appreciate their bodies more, just as they have learned to value their intellect. The skyrocketing costs of being entertained, more available leisure time, and an awareness of how to enjoy and fulfill oneself through recreational, exercise, and athletic experiences will encourage movement scientists to provide scientific guidelines and information with respect to human movement.

Consumer fraud with regard to nutrition, weight loss, fitness, and longevity will diminish as movement scientists become more actively involved in educating the public and contributing to its welfare. This area has been sorely neglected for too long.

The prognosis, then, is for a future that looks bright in many ways for the deployment of movement scientists and their services, contributions to society, and the advance of a discipline associated with movement behaviors.

Contributing to the physical education profession

Movement science specialists, independently of physical education specialists, will develop their own unique organizational structure with dissimilar primary functions. Consequently, their impact regarding the role of science and research in physical education programs may be rather indirect.

Scholars who are presently involved with technoscientific responsibilities associated with physical education have had little influence on the structure, functions, and direction of the profession. The fault may rest with practitioners, professional preparation specialists, or researchers, or all of them. Regardless, an interpretation of the present trend would suggest the ultimate autonomy of each group. The contributions made directly by movement science specialists to the physical education profession, then, would be through means other than personal roles of leadership.

Technoscientific findings will be used to shape curriculum and program content. Developments in instructional technology will serve as a basis for devising instructional media and communication styles. Services can be expanded and varied through the implementation of these products and processes. The willingness of physical educators to accept a strong scientific basis for the content in teacher preparation programs and educational and athletic programs in schools and colleges will obviously determine the nature of these programs. The same is true with regard to technology and class management and communication decisions.

Technology is presently being employed to meet the needs of the profession in terms of data collection and information dissemination. Without the appropriate hardware, these procedures would be tedious and laborious. We must assume that further technological developments will be utilized by the profession to further these objectives. Data banks, retrieval systems, and dissemination procedures reflect the value of computers and other equipment to assist the profession in fulfilling its mission.

Contributing to instruction

Seymour Kleinman (1975) has stated that science, research, and technology are not necessary for and in fact confound the teaching-learning process. Larry Locke (1975) has questioned the quality of research on teaching physical education and any meaningful impact it has on productive outcomes. He is, however, optimistic regarding future potential. I am in total agreement with Locke.

Effective instruction is an art and a science. Good teaching can proceed in a logical manner, firmly based on laws of behavior and sound scientific principles of instructional design, delivery, and management. As we progress technologically and improve the quality of research on teaching in physical education, there is every reason to expect better education for all.

But technology alone is not the answer. There will always be a need for sensitive, enthusiastic, and caring teachers. Indeed, John McHale (1969) may be correct in his observation that science and technology had a major role in changing the past and present, and that the crucial aspects of the future *are not* technological. We will need more social thinking to improve cooperative relationships.

Yet the potential of technology to offer useful alternatives in education is not even close to being realized. As McHale has noted, technology has been used in education primarily for administrative convenience. It stands to reason that science and technology will be exploited more creatively and willingly by educators in the future, thereby offering teachers and students a variety of avenues to worthwhile goals. Teachers will be free from daily chores that consume valuable time and detract from teaching responsiveness. They will be able to concentrate on challenging each student to reach her or his potential in any learning situation as technology provides the media appropriate for such purposes.

Some examples of useful roles of technology in physical education are the following.

Computerized data base on each student. As a student progresses through school, measurements of skills, physical dimensions, psychological features, and the like will be recorded continually. In this way, the characteristics of each student on entry to a new class will be known to the teacher. Class management can then proceed in an intelligent manner, with goals and objectives compatible with the entry capabilities of the students. Performance expectations will be realistic and individualized. Individual goals, with a student attempting to improve on his own performance level instead of competing against others and norms, is educationally defensible as a model of class procedure. Sensitivity is thereby shown for individual differences in present capabilities and future potential. Furthermore, students can be individually guided to a wise selection of activities, activities that make demands compatible with their characteristics, thereby increasing the probability of selection.

Instructional goal orientation through visual media. Words and written material are not as effective as visual materials teaching some physical skills. Modeling procedures can be much more effective in providing students with an image of what they should try to achieve. Yet we need not only rely on live models to demonstrate skills. Technology can produce samples for students to learn from and with which they can compare their performance. Beginners tend to think too much about too many things; they are overinstructed. They are overstressed by external pressures (inadvertently exerted by teachers) or self-imposed pressures. As Adam Smith (1975) has pointed out, they just think too much.

Tim Gallway (1974) may have made a major breakthrough in his analysis of learning tennis, although his observations are applicable to learning all types of sports skills. Learning skills is probably easiest through sight and feel, and the answer is the ability to produce the right images. Observations of the techniques for performing skills must be translated into schema, plans, images, or some type of internalized "comparator" base. Technology can yield many visual presentation modes that can be continuously available to students.

Development of simulators and trainers. If learning activities are highly complex or dangerous, technology can produce modified versions of the learning tasks. They are useful at the beginning stages of learning. There is danger that too great a reliance on them, however, will produce dependence and a crutch difficult to eliminate.

Certain physical education activities require environments not often available to students, at least on a year-round basis. Golf, water- and snow-skiing, and target practice are examples. Simulation through technology permits the introduction of experiences in these activities. Furthermore, skills can be practiced and maintained in the absence of the "real thing."

• • •

With regard to research implications for instruction, we might speculate that research will help to accomplish the following:

1. *Indicate the value of various instructional approaches in fulfilling expected or hoped-for outcomes.* Experimental research demonstrates what is expected when students with specified characteristics are exposed to a specified instructional format. Quality research will provide the data necessary to justify an instructional alternative as the best means to reach particular objectives.

2. *Help to develop technological hardware for instructional purposes.* The utility and usefulness of this equipment will be carefully analyzed.

3. *Suggest the best type of program to produce the necessary skills and intrinsic motivation on the part of students to participate in activities, during school years and afterward.* Perhaps necessary research will be undertaken in the immediate future to determine whether desirable behavioral changes occur in students as a result of experience in physical education. Physical educators will be able to defend their programs with evidence that cannot be argued.

Research, science, and technology hold a variety of interesting possibilities, potentials, and implications for the future of all aspects of physical education. As McHale has observed, "Given his present state of knowledge, social as well as scientific and technological, man now has an enormously enhanced capacity to choose his future, both collectively and individually" (1969, pp. 8-9).

Scientific and technological advances have been most influential in recent years. Education, and more particularly, instruction, has lagged behind. Hopefully, this will not be the situation for much longer.

Contributing to organizations

Professional organizations provide the necessary services that put life into and provide direction for any field. They rightfully assume leadership, motivational, unifying, and policy roles. Suprastructures and substructures create outlets for those with tangential interests and activities in common.

Science and technology enhance communication networks. Capabilities for information storage, retrieval, and dissemination are increased. Organizations thereby become more viable units for the fulfillment of their stated functions. The administration and arrangements of organizations of any type are improved when technology is used intelligently. Consequently, one of the most apparent advantages in the continued use of the latest technological products and procedures can be demonstrated in the functioning of professional organizations.

CONCLUDING STATEMENT

The physical education profession must be more dependent on technoscientific developments as it attempts to realize its potential. Scholarly endeavors and programs cannot proceed in an orderly manner without some technoscientific support. This does not imply the irrational deployment of mechanistic processes and products for the creation of nonhumanistic, unenjoyable, inflexible, and meaningless programs—quite the opposite.

Research efforts can be improved with the use of advanced technology. Research benefits a profession in many ways, with its implications for the design of instruction, the foundation of curriculums and programs, the management and administration of organizations, and the unification of the discipline.

Technology offers viable alternatives for instruction in physical education. There is no one way to teach. All learners do not benefit in the same way and to the same extent from the same instructional approach. The future acceptance and utilization of technology in the management of learning and the organization of classes suggests the widespread support of diverse programs and teaching styles. It also presupposes a greater interest in truly matching learning expectations with student capabilities and hence a genuine respect for individual differences.

Class procedures will be more imaginative, pleasurable, and productive. The growth of the discipline of human movement will be scholarly, logical, and beneficial to a number of teaching professions, training programs, and allied health areas. Programs associated with the psychomotor domain will no longer lag behind the cognitive domain in the development of their integrity, the fulfillment of their potential impact on participants in allied programs, and the respect they are accorded by others.

REFERENCES

Gallway, T. 1974. The inner game of tennis, New York, Random House, Inc.

Kleinman, S., 1975. Who needs research on teaching physical education anyway? Paper presented at the symposium on research and instruction in physical education, American Alliance for Health, Physical Education, and Recreation convention, Atlantic City, March 15.

Locke, L. 1975. Research and teaching: an overview, Paper presented at the symposium on research and instruction in physical education, American Alliance for Health, Physical Education, and Recreation convention, Atlantic City, March 15.

McHale, J. 1969. The future of the future, New York, George Braziller, Inc.

Rushall, B. S., and Siedentrop, D. 1972. The development of sport and physical education, Philadelphia, Lea & Febiger.

Singer, R. N., and Dick, W. 1974. Teaching physical education: a systems approach, Boston, Houghton Mifflin Co.

Smith, A. 1975. Sport is a western yoga, Psychology Today 9:48.

Science and technology of human movement studies: some assumptions for the future

Joseph R. Higgins and Susan Arend

There cannot be a philosophy, there cannot even be a decent science, without humanity . . . the understanding of nature has as its goal the understanding of human nature, and of the human condition within nature.*

By its very nature, science is future oriented; the science of today is the knowledge, understanding, and invention of tomorrow. Experiments in science are predictive, being based on assumptions derived from a body of knowledge born of a pool of past experimental results and human insight. Scientific findings and experimental results have their greatest impact well into the future. In fact, it has been shown that "90 percent of the basic research behind an innovation has been accomplished a decade before development of the innovation" (Thompson, 1969, p. 374). In addition, it is worth noting that scientific research, with a primary goal of knowledge for its own sake, has also provided "a reservoir of understanding essential to subsequent technological innovation" (Thompson, 1969, p. 375). Science should be viewed as an important change agent of the future, contributing to a pool of knowledge from past and present thinking and laboratory research, with its ultimate application being found in the betterment of humankind of tomorrow.

*From Bronowski, J. 1973. The ascent of man, Boston, Little, Brown & Co., p. 15.

We will define and discuss the relationship of science and technology, relate this to physical education, and propose the emergence of an area of study we shall call *human movement studies*. This area will be defined within the context of the science of humankind and the nature of the scientific endeavor, where study and research are directed toward understanding the nature of human movement within the broad context of understanding the nature of our thoughts, our perceptions, and our actions. Discussion will focus first on the science of human movement and on its relationship to the profession of physical education and to the society of the postindustrial era foreseen by the year 2000. Finally, areas of future concern and imminent innovations and directions related to human movement studies and to physical education will be identified.

We submit that the profession of physical education receives partial support for its practice from the science of human movement. The theory that guides practice and program development in physical education is most closely related to educational theory and practice (Curl, 1973). Human movement study makes its contribution to the profession of physical education through technological developments and not by direct involvement in the formulation of principles for practice or curriculum.

Our focus is the science of humankind, the function of which is to enhance the understanding of our nature and to provide increasingly valuable information and knowledge for application without further impositions save the search for truth. In the main, science relates to laboratory sciences that deal with "isolated deterministic systems, [where] future events may be described as certain" (Schumacher, 1973, p. 227). Any statements made about the future should be viewed as conditional, exploratory calculations that provide a framework for talking *"about future events only on the basis of assumptions"* (Schumacher, 1973, p. 227). Thinking and talking about the future are useful only when we act now, in the present, while we can (Schumacher, 1973).

SCIENCE AND TECHNOLOGY

Science is about ideas and has since the time of the ancient Greeks been an approach to understanding the nature of our thoughts, perceptions, and actions (Toulman, 1967). This is what we mean by understanding the nature of humankind. The sciences of humankind are what Piaget (1970) refers to as *nomothetic* sciences,* those that search for generalizations or

---

*Piaget (1970) distinguishes or classifies four categories of sciences of humankind; these are the nomothetic, historical, legal, and philosophical. The distinguishing characteristic of the nomothetic sciences is its experimental research approach. For a more detailed discussion of this distinction, see Piaget, 1970.

laws through formal controlled experimental procedures. They are a mode of gaining understanding through comparisons and classification resulting from direct systematic observation and measurement; the results yield quantitative relations or mathematical functions through statistical analysis. Ideas in science are speculative; they are constantly being altered, refined, and verified through controlled experimental research. When the ideas move from the domain of speculation to the domain of certainty, then science becomes a technology (Hebb, 1975). The formulation of generalizations must precede technological development. The application of any scientific finding must await careful vertification or else risk the imminent possibility of inconsistent, confusing, and often erroneous results. (One does not have to look far in either education or physical education to see that often application has preceded the verification of the underlying theories.)

Technology consists of the techniques and tools by which the human capability is extended (Schon, 1967). The computer, for example, is a technological innovation that has had an almost immeasurable impact on human capabilities. It has improved our ability to analyze problems, to store and process information, to control environmental settings, etc. Teachers are employing a technology that improves the capability of the student and increases their capacity as teachers in developing programs, structuring environments, and deploying sound techniques for instruction. The teaching of physical education is a technology; teachers of physical education, whose primary function is to facilitate the acquisition of skill, are informed, artful, humanistic, and skillful technicians.

Technology has an important and reciprocal relationship with science. There is a circularity wherein the development of technology simultaneously serves and is served by science. The application of computer technology, for example, has in the past several years made very significant influences in instrumentation techniques in the biological and psychological sciences (Sidowski, 1975), the two sciences most closely allied with human movement science. The gains in instrumentation techniques have allowed more sophisticated questions to be answered by the application of technological advancements or developments on the science.

The relationship between technology and science is both pervasive and essential. We only need to be cautious that technology does not overbalance the science—that ideas do not grow out of available technology, but rather from the minds of modern scientists. The important distinction is that through controlled experimental research, science seeks to understand our nature through the world of ideas by formulating knowledge from natural phenomena and information, by generating questions, and by attempting to systematically and precisely establish relationships. Technology provides the tools and techniques for science to answer questions with better control and more precision. We take a positive view of this interaction among science, technology, and humankind. There are dangers and cautions of which all responsible and reasonable people must be aware; the optimistic view holds that scientific knowledge and technological progress should and will serve the positive attributes of humankind. This view is possible only when our values grow out of a broad humanistic sensitivity and concern.

One of our intrinsic needs is knowledge, and much of that knowledge is furnished by science. Technology is primarily the application of knowledge. In part, it becomes the future of the science of today. Both the scientist and the technician must understand the context within which they ask questions, realize answers, and develop applications. Before specialized questioning is valid, we would agree with Lorenz, who says, "One has to know the very particular *structure* in which these elements are put together" (1963, p. 78). The scientist and the technician need a firm grasp on the whole—the gestalt—of the underlying problem and fundamental principle. The technology and science of the future will continue to exhibit a reciprocal interactive relationship and will not be viewed as separate entities as many might believe or wish. The broad function of the nomothetic sciences is, as Piaget (1970) suggests:

> To provide increasingly valuable applications in all spheres of knowledge, but on the condition that basic research is developed without prior limitations imposed for the sake of utilitarian criteria; for what seems to be the least valuable at the beginning may have the most unexpected consequences, whereas initial delimitation with a view of practice makes it impossible to see all the questions at issue and may result in neglecting what is in fact the most important fruitful line of investigation.*

As we look into the unknown future, we can with some certainty note that the humanistic use of scientific knowledge and technological development will improve our lives. We will have at hand those tools and techniques that should have the potential for providing a fully realized existence for increasing numbers of human beings on our small spaceship "Earth." Science, as we know it, is and will continue to be a penetrating and important agent of change. We gain and apply knowledge for the benefit of humankind only when science incorporates humanistic values as essential. Science serves humanity in ways from which all of us are bound to benefit.

THE SCIENCE OF HUMAN MOVEMENT STUDIES

Science is concerned with ideas and with understanding nature. An integral aspect of our nature is movement. As an area of study in the

---

*From Piaget, J. 1970. The place of the sciences of man in the system of sciences, New York, Harper & Row, Publishers, p. 87.

United States, physical education from its inception has drawn from and been supported by the tradition of science. (The early founders of the field received their training in medicine and brought the tradition of science, especially the biological sciences, to the early training programs in physical education.) The basis of physical education draws not only on educational theory but also upon the sciences of physiology, anatomy, physics, psychology, neurology, etc. This information was and still is expected to be integrated in the minds of students of physical education as a basic and necessary foundation for their becoming good teachers. Nixon and Locke (1973) point out that research on teaching in physical education has had little effect in improving teaching and, more to the point, the scientific knowledge gained from the research yields little information about learning and even less about teaching. In other words, knowledge gained from research in motor skills, physiology, and kinesiology has little to show in terms of its impact on teaching and, for that matter, research on teaching. (Recall the point made earlier regarding the dangers inherent in attempting to apply research before the empirical verification and careful evaluation of theoretical positions have been established.)

In essence, there is a gap between physical education and its scientific bases. This gap is one factor that has led to the emergence of an area of study in and of itself—the science of human movement studies, a science separate from physical education, separate from an obligation for immediate utilitarian application, and away from the general mode of education. Human movement studies is a science that has as its overall goal the understanding of human motor behavior; it draws on knowledge from psychology, physiology, anatomy, physics, mechanics, sociology, and anthropology to investigate the underlying structure of movement, the underlying schema for the organization of movement, and the relationship between movement and environment. There is little doubt that the science of human movement studies will itself become an important source of knowledge to the very fields on which it now draws.

The concern of the area is to bring together the knowledge about human motor behavior and the questions that relate to it. Knowledge from these diverse scientific areas can be combined to help identify and answer questions in two broad primary areas, motor behavior and exercise response. For example, human movement scientists might investigate the relationship between environmental conditions, movement organization, and physiologic response in human movement and the acquisition of skill. Human movement studies will provide a theoretical base for practice in many health-related areas, in special education, education, physical education, sports, industry (where movement is an essential concomitant of work), recreation, and leisure. In short, the formalized area of human movement studies crosses many disciplines. It relies on information from these disciplines to pose its questions and in turn has an equally broad range of application through established education, health, and psychological and sociological institutions within our society.

We maintain that physical education derives much of its theoretical base from educational theory and that as both an art and a technology its prime function is to teach motor skills within the schools. The science of human movement studies is conceived as a discipline whose primary purpose is the unencumbered quest for knowledge through scholarship and laboratory research. This knowledge ultimately relates to the broader issues facing society in general and to the more specific concerns and issues encountered in professional fields such as physical education, athletics, and many allied health fields such as occupational and physical therapy.

Aesthetics, self-expression, and creative endeavors are increasingly needed and valued within our society. An important aspect of human movement study deals with the historical, aesthetic, philosophical, and theological domain, that is, the humanistic elements of human movement. This essay focuses on the concern with science and technology; hence we shall say little about the humanistic aspect other than to suggest that it be thought of as a legitimate branch of the area of study. Human movement studies is thus conceptualized as having a scientific branch and a humanistic branch. It is to the humanistic branch that we would turn if we wished to learn about an emotional quality as expressed in a dancer's movement. The choreographer or the writer can answer these questions, questions that defy and are antithetical to experimentation and quantification. If we wish to know about humanistic aspects of movement we go to literature or to philosophy (Langer, 1948; Cassier, 1944). As Hebb has stated, "Science is the servant of humanism, not part of it. Combining the two ruins both" (1975, p. 74). This does not mean that scientists are or should be ambivalent about or unconcerned with humanistic values; on the contrary, responsible scientists and technicians must develop and maintain a sensitivity for humanitarian values. These values are important and invaluable perspectives that must constantly be upheld in the pursuit of knowledge and in the ultimate application of knowledge through technology.

It is well worth considering how in the future these two branches of human movement study can best be drawn together. In physical education, for example, we may see the humanistic and the technoscientific articulating through the act of teaching itself. Perhaps this process of articulation should be a goal of teacher training programs. For example, if teaching is to involve the use of technological innovations, if it is to rely increasingly on machines and automated equipment such as the computer, we must clearly understand the inner feelings of the learner as well as the way he or she might learn in the futuristic learning environment. It may be that by answering questions about movement, environment, and learning, the "mechanistic" trends often perceived in teaching by computer and a computer-controlled machine can be made a more humanistic experience, with learning occurring more rapidly and more efficiently.

In the process of defining the context for this essay we have made a conditional statement about the future; we have identified a trend or direction that seems to us both desirable and inevitable. That is, the future will see the emergence of an area of study that is unique, has its own body of knowledge, and is capable of directly pursuing questions dealt with indirectly in other disciplines. The science of human movement studies will flourish. Physical education will continue to be part of education, part of the school, where the teaching of motor skills, sports, and games will be the dominant feature. The scientific contribution of human movement studies to physical education will be through the application of theories, generalizations, and laws verified through the rigors of science. Physical education will be the technology deriving its support in part from the science of human movement.

THREE SOCIAL ISSUES OF FUTURE CONCERN

As pointed out by Bell, the year 2000 will see us in a postindustrial period of history "where many problems of production tend to be fairly routinized, [and] the major new institutions of the society will be primarily intellectual institutions" (1967, p. 667). Schumacher identifies this as an era of the "Learning Society" (1973, p. 21), where there is an increasing urgency for learning how to live peacefully with ourselves and with nature. Society or "intellectual institutions" in the year 2000 will be idea oriented. Ideas from science will strongly influence the most effective social forces. Science and technology will be used to deal with broad social problems and issues related to *population density,* use of *leisure* time, and *expansion of knowledge.* These are by no means the only issues, but they are compelling and frequently identified as forces of major future importance (Bell, 1969; Toffler, 1974). The issues are sufficiently broad in scope to have important implications for the study of human movement. Looking toward the year 2000, we might ask how scientific discovery and technological innovation in the area of human movement studies will meet the social/cultural needs inherent in these three problem issues.

Population density

Population growth will continue to be a formidable social force demanding considerable scientific and technical resources. Associated problems of health and education provide special questions for study of human movement. The population is not only increasing but at the same time is biologically diverse. This genetic diversity, a long-ignored aspect of population dynamics, as well as population density demand that we "diversify man's environment" (Mayr, 1969, p. 833). We need more varieties of schools and educational settings, more diverse curriculums within these settings, and more diversity in economic and moral rewards (Mayr, 1969). Within this context, questions need to be addressed that relate to human movement needs in densely populated areas, e.g., identifying and meeting differential movement needs and exercises for the maintenance of health and rehabilitation, dealing with extended life expectancy and related problems of aging and its effect on movement and exercise, and dealing with the entire range of movement problems associated with the emotionally, physically, and mentally disabled population.

Leisure

Population growth, automation, and industrialization will continue to contribute to our available leisure time or time freed for the pursuit of non-work-related activity. In addition, separation of work and leisure is increasingly viewed as an arbitrary distinction and will soon become an outmoded notion. The potentially sedentary existence resulting from increased leisure time due to automation works against physical activity and thus poses serious problems for the future. Attention need be paid to basic physiological and psychological factors, since as we become a less production-oriented society and more intellectual or idea oriented, we increase the potential of becoming sedentary to the point where it may pose a serious health problem in the nation. (A recent report issued through the Department of Health, Education and Welfare indicated that one of the leading health hazards in the nation today is lack of exercise.) Certainly we need to confront not only basic questions about physiological responses to exercise but also attitudinal questions—what can we do to motivate individuals to exercise? Furthermore, what types of environments, activities, and instruction are needed? What designs for recreational facilities will maximize their use? What programs will ensure a population physically fit and skilled enough to enjoy active participation in sports and games?

Expansion of knowledge

The expansion of knowledge is one of the more important social issues having direct implication to science and to education. In science alone, 6 to 7 times the present volume of information will be produced, making it exceedingly difficult for any scientist or scholar to "keep up" with anything but a narrow specialization. Knowledge comes only after discovering or establishing relationships between facts and pieces of information. Knowledge is *not* simply the amassing of facts or information; it is the underlying insights, principles, and understandings that come from the process of careful, systematic analysis of information. To facilitate the process of knowledge expansion, science and technology must provide means of improving human information capacity, methods of efficiently organizing information, and methods of retrieving information. The implications for teaching and for education should be obvious. Furthermore, the synthesis of information and of facts is just as important and as valuable as the production of facts; we need not only scientists who can generate information and new facts but also scientists who can synthesize or integrate facts in relation to specific domains.

TECHNOSCIENTIFIC DIRECTIONS RELATING TO HUMAN MOVEMENT STUDIES AND PHYSICAL EDUCATION

To provide a point of departure for viewing science and technology of human movement against the backdrop of the three social issues identified above, we have selected some innovations which have implications for the science and the technology of human movement studies. Kahn and Weiner (1969) identified 100 technological innovations that are likely to occur in the next 25 years or so. With little stretch of the imagination, 23 of these innovations were selected as having either direct or indirect implication for the science of human movement. In selecting and abstracting these technological innovations, we asked ourselves four questions: Was the innovation of primary use or value to science or was science necessary for its development? Was the innovation related to the science or the technology of human movement? Was the innovation specifically related to population, leisure, or knowledge expansion? Was the innovation in any way related to the broad interpretation of education? These selected technological innovations are presented in the list on the opposite page and will serve as a basis for discussion in the remaining section where forecasts are made for study and application in human movement and physical education.

The categories indicated are not necessarily mutually exclusive and are intended to stimulate discussion and thought. The science of human movement must address problems and questions that emerge from social issues and the projected innovations listed. We foresee (1) increased automation affecting learning, teaching and research, (2) controlled learning environments, (3) improved low-cost, integrated living, working, and educational structures, and (4) improved health programs for maintenance and re-

---

Technological innovations with implications for science and technology of human movement studies*

Computers
1. Information in high-speed data processors
2. Computer storage, processing, and information retrieval
3. Time-sharing computers
4. Computers for intellectual and professional assistance
5. General use of automation and cybernation in management and production
6. Inexpensive video recording and playing equipment
7. Computerized and programmed learning for home education via audio and video equipment

Education
8. Educational and propaganda techniques for affecting human behavior
9. New educational techniques for children
10. New techniques for adult education
11. Design and use of controlled environments for recreational, educational, and vocational purposes

Environmental design
12. Architectural engineering (geodesic domes, thinshells, pressurized skins, etc.)
13. Permanent manned satellite, lunar, and undersea installations
14. Practical use of direct communication and stimulation of the brain

Health
15. Increased life expectancy
16. Reliable use of drugs in control of fatigue, relaxation, alertness, mood, personality, perceptions, and fantasies
17. Effective appetite and weight control
18. Controlled relaxation and sleep
19. Improved preventive and rehabilitative medicine
20. Innovative and improved techniques in maintaining physical fitness
21. Innovative and improved techniques in acquiring motor skills

Research tools
22. Three-dimensional photography, illustration, and film
23. Lasers for sensing and measuring

*Modified from Kahn and Wiener, 1967.

---

habilitation of physical and emotional well-being. Both the general quality of life and individual sense of well-being through exercise and motor skill development will be of ever greater importance. These forecasts have a direct relationship to specific concerns in the study of human movement.

When compared with all technological developments in the past 20 years, the computer and the integrated circuit have made the single most important and far-reaching impact on the development of science (Vacroux, 1975). From all accounts, this area of technological development is not expected to slow down in the next 30 years. In fact, it will no doubt continue to burgeon and to influence the conduct of science in many ways (Gregg, 1975). By 1990, we expect to see in science alone 100 times the degree of automation that exists today (Etzioni, 1975).

The increased capacity for data collection and analysis resulting from the integrated circuit and microcomputer technology does not come without inherent dangers. There is the explicit danger of assuming a "shotgun" approach to answering research questions—taking a shot in the dark and expecting that eventually a "hit" will be realized. In other words, with the capability and accessibility of the microcomputer, the scientist can complete a far greater number of studies, and eventually one will produce the desired results and significance level. This rapid turn-around time resulting from the availability and capability of the small, laboratory-based computer can prevent or discourage slow thoughtful construction of hypotheses, examination of data, and reflection on findings and their implications. In effect, we must guard against what Etzioni (1975) has called a "trial-and-error search, rather than a focused effort" (1975, p. 189). Scientific research should lead to confirmation of hypotheses or theorems rather than collections or aggregates of data. It is knowledge we are ultimately in search of, not simply information (Lorenz, 1969).

With this potential hazard in mind, let us continue to enumerate technological innovations that will influence the conduct of the science of human movement and the profession of physical education. The spin-off from the computer technology and the integrated circuit will be tremendous. The researcher will be able to automate the experimental environment in order to maintain exact controls of the experimental setting; events can be carefully timed, data collected, reduced, stored for later analysis by the investigator, and all without experimenter error or intervention. Measuring devices will be increasingly sophisticated, more accurate, and more sensitive and will be directly connected to data reduction and storage centers for later analysis. Prepackaged statistical procedures are now available in a variety of forms ranging from big computer systems such as the Biomedical Statistical Package to preprogrammed magnetic card files for minicomputers. It is conceivable that packages similar to these will be available for research designs within certain types of experimental settings. Packages will be contingency programmed or oriented and, given specific subject responses, will generate either random or specifically detailed experimental conditions during the course of an experimental session.

The development of biotelemetry (Sandler et al., 1975) will allow the human movement scientist to monitor not only critical environmental factors but also an enormous range of physiological parameters. The advent of miniaturized electronic components affords easy access to the continual monitoring of such parameters as temperature, blood chemistry, eye movements, and muscle activity during performance, learning, and exercise. Personal telemetry units will be developed for performers in sports events, for students, and for disabled individuals. These units might be used to monitor performance during sports events to gather research information, during the process of learning, and in the not too distant future to provide immediate feedback for the teacher, performer, student, or researcher.

A final word should be said regarding measuring devices. The study of human movement has long employed cinematography as an important tool for data collection. Measurement has always been difficult, laborious, and time consuming. We shall see the development of a whole range of sensing and measurement devices that will provide a picture very similar to the cinematographic one, but the new images will be much more sensitive and accurate and have the desired automatic measurement capability. This may be accomplished through the use of laser and film or videotape or may involve some laser and optic sensor linking movement parameters directly to the computer or other suitable recording device (Leibowitz and Hennessy, 1975; Kahn and Wiener, 1969). Similarly, we will see an array of our now laborious physiological, neurophysiological, and muscular activity measurements handled in laboratory micro- and minicomputer systems. Although it has been available for the past 10 years, this capability has been limited to large, heavily funded research institutions. Scientists in human movement studies will have a special problem in gathering the resources necessary to provide technological support for their work.

Education, and specifically physical education, also will be affected by technological innovations. The primary difference is the need for educationally sound applications of the technology. Much of this application must await sound theories of learning, skill acquisition, and teaching developed in some conceptual framework. Specific types of learning environments in physical education programs might be controlled from a central panel, which would ensure individualized instruction for students of a specific age or skill level and which would structure the environment so as to maximize the facilitation of the student's skill. There will be the potential for creating moving environments with exact control of objects so as to match the movement capacity of students while at the same time shaping their motor behavior. The student or group of students might choose to practice within carefully structured settings that would be individualized to account for skill level, physiological fitness, sensory function, and perhaps even ongoing physiological responses to exercise.

Feedback, identified as one of the more important learning variables, could be provided in a variety of ways. Already we see most significant gains in the area of biofeedback. Before long, researchers will begin investigating ways of using biofeedback technology and theory in settings designed to improve motor performance (Paskewitz, 1975) as well as in clinical settings. For example, telemetered electromyographic and goniometric data may be fed back to a student learning a new skill. The nature and type of information needed for facilitation of skill acquisition has still to be determined, but we do have some preliminary evidence. It is imperative that research be carefully directed toward the phenomena related to biofeedback and conditions of learning. In so doing, the necessary knowledge about student and performer responses under differing environmental and learning conditions will be closer at hand.

We also need to work diligently on basic questions related to the effects of videotape and other modes of visual display on the acquisition of motor skills. The literature reveals that the use of videotape as a tool for improving performance and learning has produced conflicting results. One explanation of this conflicting information may well be that the relationship between the nature of environment, type and level of skill, and the type of feedback that is appropriate is not clearly understood. Here is an example of the need for fundamental understanding before applications can be adequately made. We know that the future is going to bring specific social conditions or forces that will demand special educational considerations—mass vs. individualized context-specific instruction, meaningful and productive use of time through satisfying motor activity, bombardment of information from the media, from educational institutions, and from daily jobs. What impact does the media have on the acquisition of motor skills? The ever-increasing availability and range of sports events on television are viewed by children and adults alike. How is their learning, their performance, their movement repertoire affected; how does this type of television affect the process of learning and hence the nature of teaching programs. How will we meet these forces? What can the science of human movement do, knowing that there are at least 23 innovations that will affect the teaching of physical education in some way?

Large-scale instruction, continued education, motor skill learning, etc. (regardless of age, level of skill, activity, or interest) will be accomplished in large part through computer linkage and videotape. Packaged teaching programs for learning specific motor skills, for developing physical fitness, or for rehabilitation of a specific physical or emotional difficulty is not a far-fetched projection into the future. It may also be that before too long people can dial their telephone to request a specific instructional or physical fitness training package to be placed on their home television set via cable. At periodic intervals or with some ongoing direct linkage, performance information might be fed back to a primary data center. Given certain performance parameters such as heart rate, a score, the amount of force production, limb velocities, etc., the performer would receive direct instructional feedback to alter or maintain some given parameter of performance.

There is little doubt that human movement studies will play a vital role in the development of techniques, tools, and equipment for highly skilled competitive sport performance on the amateur, collegiate, Olympic, and professional levels. To varying degrees, each level of competition will need researchers to answer questions leading to better training programs, improved movement efficiency and performance strategies, more effective protective equipment, and improved performance (including training) environments. Given the economic status and stability of professional sports, much basic competitive sport research may indeed be financed by professional sports teams or organizations. We may even begin to see a closer working relationship between scientists in human movement with dance choreographers and producers.

It seems likely that tremendous advances in learning theory and methods of facilitating the learning process will ensue over the next 25 years. The education (and physical education) of the individual will not be restricted to the school setting. We will see industry, the family, the community, and technological devices playing increasingly stronger roles in education.

Together with advances in teaching techniques, we will have identified the factors (both innate and acquired) that govern perception and action. We will have identified the factors in the environment that determine the structure of movement, the factors in the organism that influence the structure of movement, and the interactive nature of organism, action, and environment. We will have revealed the logicomathematical structure of movement—in short, the alphabet of movement itself or the syntax of action (similar to recent advances in the identification of basic structures and their transformations in linguistics). It is Bruner's contention that "skilled behavior has much in common with language production . . . and problem solving" (1973, p. 241). It seems likely that we will have a new conceptual framework that will help to explain the many phenomena involved in our interactions with the environment.

Study in skill development will allow us to better understand (1) control of voluntary movement behavior, (2) how children develop control over their own attention, (3) progressive development of coordinated movement, (4) the underlying mechanisms responsible for motor skill (Bruner,

1968), and (5) the anatomical basis for developing skill (Elliott and Connolly, 1974).

The information gathered in human movement studies will create a need for translators or interpreters specially trained in applying human movement research in many related fields. Thus it seems likely that people using this knowledge will in general learn how to structure the environment to maximize learning, to skillfully observe and analyze movement and performance environments, to move efficiently within that environment, and to maintain the "machinery" that subserves movement, namely, the skeletomuscular system. In general, people will understand the factors that influence their perceptions and actions within their environment. This will directly result from the application of multidimensional experimentation in the science of human movement study to a public interested and informed in the nature of their movement potential.

The scope of physical education will be redefined. Physical education will become one of the applied branches of human movement studies. The physical educator will be only one of many to physically educate the people, and all will employ masterful techniques. Assuming that people will be educated in the nature of the human as mover, they will seek technicians to develop particular movement skills within specific environments.

CONCLUDING STATEMENT

Human movement study is a serious but not as yet a mature science. It is in the process of formulation and growth. Its paradigms are immature and insecure. We will no doubt experience and be involved in what Kuhn (1970) and others call scientific revolutions, in which old paradigms are challenged and replaced as a result of new evidence, new ideas, and new ways of solving problems, and in which expansion of information will be great and gains in knowledge and understanding will occur more slowly. Yet as any science matures and becomes increasingly secure, breakthroughs in understanding and insight come more slowly. During this period of slow growth we can expect change. This change is an outgrowth of the process of consolidation and formulation of meaningful generalizations. It is a period when technology can be applied with greater certainty and consistency. The application of the knowledge derived from human movement studies to physical education will be evident in programs, methods, structured environments, tools, and equipment.

During the next 25 years a community of human movement scientists should emerge—scientists from a number of disciplines coming together in shared unbiased and unrestricted endeavors to understand our nature through a more thorough understanding of our movements. This community of scientists will be characterized by a shared set of values cast in humanistic terms and including what Franklin Long characterized in an address to the American Chemistry Society as "honest work, open publication, and openness to criticism" (Hammond, 1974, p. 874). Cooperation in science will be exceedingly important during the next 25 years, cooperation unimpeded by national, local, and institutional boundaries.

It is our task to act now to provide means for the systematic review of what has been researched, to carefully analyze and integrate questions and results from diversified fields of interest, and to identify pertinent questions in the areas of future concern leading to research that will enhance the transition to a future that is consistent with our philosophy. Scientists must be mindful of the trap of intellectual dogma and the temptation to remain close minded and tradition bound to one conceptual framework. These pitfalls are stifling to the open reception of new ideas and are antithetical to science itself. We need to push hard for a general conceptual framework that transcends traditional science (von Bertalanfly, 1969). We need a framework that deals with problems of organized complexity, employing essentially systems laws and pursuing answers at all levels of the hierarchical structure that composes our movement organization, or for that matter, the universe (von Bertalanfly, 1969).

Scientists must see that their work reaches toward some application—knowledge used in practical humanistic ways—and must establish and maintain communication with those who interpret and apply this knowledge. Perhaps somewhere between the scientist and the technician, we will need individuals interested in and capable of actively translating and integrating science and technology into forms useful for consumption by the relevant educational institutions within our society. These individuals will need a broad overview and understanding of all dimensions of human movement studies. They must be able to translate into practice scientific knowledge and technological innovations in ways that affect the teaching and learning of motor skills in the schools. These individuals should possess a special sensitivity to the questions of humanism, biological diversity, educational theory, and scientific knowledge. Whatever is developed and applied must be done with sensitivity for the specific context.

By the year 2000, human understanding of technology should be much improved; we will have a more realistic view of its capabilities and no doubt we will expect less from it. Hopefully we will select more wisely and knowledgeably that which technology offers for improving the human condition. For humanity to survive, science and technology must be increasingly concerned with what Schumacher (1973) calls intermediate technology. Our science must continue to help answer basic questions, and both science and technology will need to strive toward reducing "bigness," to place value on smaller gains and smaller machines. Science may be a slower, less grandiose and as a consequence a more thorough endeavor. The sciences and humanities, all institutions concerned with improving the quality of human existence, will need to work toward a change in attitude, which according to Schumacher (1973) involves a change from a life-style of consumption to one of permanence. Violence against nature produces violence among people, and certainly science and technology have led us to the brink of irreparable violence against nature. Let us then not hide our heads in the sand. Let us instead recognize that scientific knowledge and technological innovation and achievement are going to continue. This will demand new ways of asking and investigating questions, new ways of applying our knowledge and our technology so as not to do violence to nature and ourselves.

We will see a shift in paradigms guiding scientific study (Kuhn, 1970; Gentile and Nacson, 1976), what Kuhn (1970) refers to as revolutions in science. There must be very radical shifts to new approaches for solving movement problems, identification of rules for governing movement organization and behavior, and the identification of the basic elements and strategies that make up our emerging movement repertoires.

No elitist, overspecialized position can work against the formidable background of the social changes looming on the horizon. Problems growing out of population density, leisure, and expansion of knowledge will provide the challenge for science and for technology. The most effective scientist and technologist today will be those whose vision is directed toward the future, whose vision has the breadth and depth of wisdom born out of a specialization within the context of the concern of humankind.

And we close, as we began, with the words of the late Professor Bronowski, "The essence of science: ask an impertinent question, and you are on the way to the pertinent answer" (1973, p. 153).

REFERENCES

Bell, D. 1967. Toward the year 2000: work in progress, Daedalus 96:639.

Bronowski, J. 1973. The ascent of man, Boston, Little, Brown & Co.

Bruner, J. S. 1968. Processes of cognitive growth: infancy, Worcester, Mass., Clark University Press.

Cassier, E. 1944. An essay on man, New Haven, Conn., Yale University Press.

Curl, G. F. 1973. An attempt to justify human movement as a field of study. In Brooke, J. D., and Whiting, H. T. A., editors: Human movement—a field of study, London, Henry Kimpton Publishers.

Elliott, J., and Connolly, K. 1974. Hierarchical structure in skill development. In Connolly, K., and Bruner, J. S., editors: The growth of competence, New York, Academic Press, Inc.

Etzioni, A. 1975. Effect of small computers on scientists, Science 189:152.

Gentile, A. M., and Nacson, J. 1976. Organizational processes in motor skill. In Wilmore, J., and Keough, T., editors: Exercise and sports science reviews, Santa Barbara, Calif., Journal Publications Associates, vol. 4.

Gregg, L. W. 1975. Computers: large-scale usage in the balance, American Psychologist 301:199.

Hammond, A. L. 1974. Chemistry and science: the next 100 years, Science 185:847.

Hebb, D. O. 1974. What psychology is about, American Psychologist 29:71.

Kahn, H., and Wiener, A. J. 1967. A framework for speculation, Daedalus 96:710.

Kuhn, T. S. 1970. The structure of scientific revolutions, Chicago, The University of Chicago Press.

Langer, S. 1948. Philosophy in a new key, New York, The New American Library, Inc.

Leibowitz, H. W., and Hennessy, R. T. 1975. The laser optometer and some implications for behavioral research, American Psychologist 30:349.

Lorenz, K. 1969. Innate bases of learning. In Pribram, K., editor: On the biology of learning, New York, Harcourt Brace Jovanovich, Inc.

Mayr, E. 1967. Biological man and the year 2000, Daedalus 96:832.

Nixon, T. W., and Locke, L. F. 1973. Research on teaching physical education. In Travers, R. M. W., editor: Second handbook of research on teaching, Chicago, Rand McNally & Co.

Paskewitz, D. A. 1975. Biofeedback instrumentation: soldering closed the loop, American Psychologist 30:371.

Piaget, T. 1970. The place of the sciences of man in the system of sciences, New York, Harper & Row, Publishers.

Sandler, H., McCrutcheon, E. P., Fryer, T. B., Rositano, S., Westbrook, R., and Haro, P. 1975. Recent NASA contributions to biomedical telemetry, American Psychologist 30:257.

Schon, D. A. 1967. Forecasting and technological forecasting, Daedalus 96:639.

Schumacher, E. F. 1973. Small is beautiful: economics as if people mattered, New York, Harper & Row, Publishers.

Sidowski, T. B. 1975. Instrumentation and computer technology: applications and influences in modern psychology, American Psychologist 30:191.

Thompson, P. 1969. Traces: basic research links to technology appraised, Science 163:374.

Toffler, A. 1974. The psychology of the future. In Toffler, A., editor: Learning for tomorrow: the role of the future in education, New York, Random House, Inc.

Toulman, S. 1967. Neuroscience and human understanding. In Quarton, G. C., Nielnechuk, T., and Schmidt, F. O., editors: The neurosciences: a study program, New York, Rockefeller University Press.

Vacroux, A. G. 1975. Microcomputers, Scientific American 232:32.

von Bertalanfly, L. 1969. Chance or law. In Koestler, A., and Smytheis, J. R., editors: Beyond reductionism, Boston, Beacon Press.

Wren-Lewis, J. 1974. Educating scientists for tomorrow. In Toffler, A., editor: Learning for tomorrow: the role of the future in education, New York, Random House, Inc.

CHAPTER SIX

POSTSCRIPT: PLANNING FOR THE FUTURE

Raymond Welsh

The future does not simply happen. It is influenced by numerous forces, not the least of which are human actions. The interconnectedness between people and the future is immutable and leads logically to the conclusion that human behavior helps to shape the future. Earl Hubbard states, "The meaning of a man's acts lies in their effects upon the future. Every man is an evolutionary force—a co-author of creation. . . . All [men] serve the future, either well or badly" (1967, p. 91). In this context future's creation represents one of our most important and ennobling activities. To create the future, however, we must do more than delineate the probable from an array of possible futures. We must also define preferable futures and work toward their attainment.

Despite the unusual dynamics of change evident in contemporary society, new ways of probing the future (e.g., futuristics) are making it possible for physical educators to assess the impact change may have on the profession's future. For example, demographics clearly show that the lower birth rate of the last decade will continue into the future. From demographic data we also know that we are in the midst of a significant migration of people from the northern tier of the country to the southern tier or so-called sunbelt (Reinhold and Nordheimer, 1967, p. 1). Demography also tells us that the percentage of older Americans will increase during the remainder of this century. Similarly, certain economic and social indicators tell us that the supply of money and therefore the availability of social services will decrease during the next several years. Similar information supplied by future-oriented scientists is becoming increasingly available. It is precisely on the basis of such information gleaned from a variety of sources, together with an awareness of the internal dynamics occurring within the profession, e.g., Title IX, CBTE, the growing disenchantment between the scientific and physical education wings of the profession, the proliferation of special interest groups and allied associations, that enables today's physical educators to make better estimates about the future.

Unfortunately physical educators, for a host of reasons, have not always been sufficiently attentive to such information in the past. Witness, for example, the scandalous oversupply of physical education specialists who today cannot find jobs, and consider the thousands who are currently pursuing undergraduate and graduate degrees in our teacher training programs.* Clearly, in order to create a desirable future for the profession (and thereby serve the future well), physical educators will have to become more attentive to the interplay of forces both within and external to the profession that will serve in part to shape its future.

THE NEED TO PLAN

Just as the current state of physical education has evolved from a context of sociohistorical events, so too its future will emerge from an amalgam of social and historical forces—some past, others present, and some that are yet to take place. In order that these forces do not overwhelm us, the profession out of necessity will have to invest in new ways of responding to the future that heretofore were deemed inappropriate or inapplicable. Specifically, the nature of change facing the profession today is of such magnitude and intensity and flows from so many different sources that some form of noncoercive planning must be considered.

Instinctively some individuals and groups have eschewed the need to systematically plan for the future. Perhaps because of a belief that systematic planning is somehow antidemocratic and carries with it the seeds of an Orwellian nightmare, planning has gotten a bad reputation. In fact, in some quarters planlessness has become lionized and valued in its own right. Interestingly enough, systematic planning can be highly humane and has been practiced in some form for centuries. For example, the planning that went into constructing the cities of Rome underscores the functional usefulness and humaneness that systematic planning can produce. Unfortunately myth, "ignorance, inflexibility [Groupthink], irresolution, custom, self-interest, politics, socio-economic conditions [and forms of planning that violated human rights] have acted to slow progress in planning for the general welfare" (Branch, 1966, p. 5). Clearly, the nature of change facing us today, and incidently, the raison d'être for the emergence of futuristics, makes it necessary for us to invest more energy, not less, in planning for the future.

Branch states, "Casual decisions or simply trying to counter events as they occur are no longer feasible responses. . . . Well-thought out, longer range objectives, policies, and strategies must underlie short-range actions,

---

*For a more complete discussion of the current employment crisis in physical education see Welsh, 1975.

unless society's course is to be the random product of successive circumstances of the moment" (1966, p. 9). Toffler puts it another way by arguing that the future is so tenuous that "we cannot permit decisions of earth-jolting importance to be taken heedlessly, witlessly, planlessly." He further argues that "to hang loose [i.e., not to plan or as he says, "to grow organically"] is to commit collective suicide" (1970, p. 452). In short, the future requires that fewer actions be left to fate, unthinking reactions (post facto), or pure chance. In the same context and for basically the same reasons, physical educators will have to plan for their future in ways that we never have before.

A PLANNING EFFORT

Planning, as it is increasingly practiced by business, government, and military agencies is of three general types—comprehensive, functional, and project planning. Comprehensive planning is the more inclusive type, including functional and project planning, and it serves to actualize "man's endeavors to perform a major achievement, shape his environment, or affect the future" (Branch, 1966, p. 11). While comprehensive planning seems to offer certain advantages for those who desire to create the future, the complexity of its methods and their basis in the rule of "law" or some other coercive force make it inappropriate for such a diverse and democratically conceived professional group as physical education. For similar reasons the functional and project planning approaches are also inappropriate. Nevertheless, there are adequate practical devices in the planning process in general to enable the profession of physical education to piece together an appropriate noncoercive planning effort that would prove "functional" for its own needs. The remainder of this chapter will be devoted to suggesting ways a noncoercive planning effort might be implemented, for it is only through such an effort that the profession's preferable future can be identified and eventually realized.

Any effort at planning requires the establishment of competent planning groups. For the profession of physical education, the national, regional, and state structures that already exist suggest that planning councils should be established at these three levels. Since the future belongs to everyone, these councils should be elected democratically on regional and state-wide bases by the professional membership. The planning councils would be concerned with the near (1 to 5 years), intermediate (5 to 10 years), and distant (10 to 20 years) future of the profession, attempting where possible to identify significant trends, future potentials, and priorities and communicating this information to the membership so that appropriate action can be taken. While the formulation of specific plans and contingencies might flow from these councils, it would seem more logical for these groups, since they would lack any coercive force, to place their primary em-

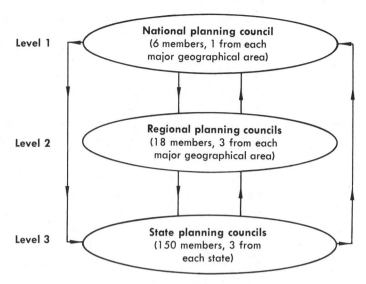

Fig. 8. Planning schema.

phasis on gathering and disseminating information to the membership, thereby leaving the actual planning to the various constituent groups (e.g., professional preparation programs, and local professional associations).

While there are many specific services that the planning councils could eventually provide, at the very least such groups could be expected to accomplish the following:

1. Gather, collate, and transmit data concerning the larger issues affecting future professional capabilities and constraints (e.g., future manpower needs)
2. Provide an early warning service regarding emerging problems within the profession
3. Trace through the implications of current professional practice and where necessary recommend appropriate remedial action
4. Identify long-range professional and societal needs that are not being met by current professional programs
5. Propose short-, intermediate-, and long-range goals for the profession's future based on previous identification of preferable futures
6. Monitor and report, where appropriate, the profession's progress toward goal attainment

Fig. 8 depicts the makeup of the proposed planning councils, but more important, it indicates the reciprocal relationship necessary for the proper functioning of these groups. The planning scheme suggested here is not meant to convey a hierarchical planning approach. Such top-down planning would be counterproductive. What is implied is that the planning effort would be broadly based, with all groups equally involved in the planning process. Thus through the free exchange of information and specifically designed feedback mechanisms, the products of the planning effort would be relevant to all participating groups.*

Since the success of any planning effort depends ultimately on the quality or accuracy of the information on which the plans, recommendations, etc. are based, the planning effort never ends. (This is particularly important in a world marked by accelerated change.) As new information becomes available, it must of necessity be analyzed and incorporated into the planning groups' deliberations. In other words, plans need to be constantly updated. This is not meant to imply that nothing remains constant. Clearly, there will be enduring trends and therefore plans that will retain a certain degree of longevity, but unless the planning effort is ongoing, the entire planning process would eventually prove to be more of a liability than an asset to the profession. As Lawson points out in Chapter 3 of this text, if plans and goals are not periodically readjusted in light of the changing reality, the planning process itself becomes "instrumentally irrational," and it therefore cripples progress toward the future rather than enhancing it. For this reason it is suggested that the planning councils meet regularly (at least once a year) in order to function in an efficient and rational manner. It would also seem logical to arrange for the various councils to convene at different times of the year so that each could consider the information generated by the other. Finally, an annual report reflecting the joint efforts of the entire planning team would have to be prepared and distributed to the membership. In this way the products of the joint planning effort would be made readily available to the individuals and constituent groups that have historically served as the profession's decision makers. Under the planning council scheme, they would have better and more comprehensive information on which to base their decisions. This in turn should serve to lead the profession toward a better if not its most preferable future.

CONCLUDING STATEMENT

"We must cease to be mere spectators in our ongoing history and participate with renewed determination in moulding the future" (Helmer, 1967). This statement by Olaf Helmer, one of the world's foremost futur-

---

*It might also be appropriate to consider the advantages of having a fourth planning level, a planning council composed of the lay public we serve. Toffler argues strongly for the need to democratize the planning process by obtaining input from the public. He states, "We need quite literally to 'go to the people' with a question that is almost never asked of them: what kind of a world do you want ten, twenty, or thirty years from now?" (1972, p. 478).

ists, and co-founder of the Institute of the Future, provides an appropriate ending to this concluding chapter while also concisely summarizing the major theme of this book—a view toward the future of physical education.

To state that we have been mere spectators in our ongoing history is not accurate. We have and will no doubt continue to assert our control over our own destinies. Nevertheless, in the context in which Helmer spoke (contemporary time), we appear, in contrast with our past efforts, to have become more spectators than participants in the events and changes cascading around us. Clearly, the constraints and imperatives of the changing times require that we renew our commitment to the future so that we can once again become the architects of our own destinies. To accomplish this, we must struggle with new ways of gaining anticipatory information about the possibilities and probabilities of tomorrow's world. In addition, we will have to make value judgments with respect to preferable futures, and we will have to design and implement programs of action. In short, choosing the best road into the future (i.e., actualizing the preferable futures) requires gathering extensive data about the future and then incorporating this information into appropriate planning efforts.

Thus for the profession of physical education, a group that desires to prosper in the world of tomorrow, planning represents the final logical step towards ensuring prosperity—it completes the circle; it enables the physical educator to *create* the future.

REFERENCES

Branch, M. C. 1966. Planning: aspects and applications, New York, John Wiley & Sons, Inc.

Helmer, O. 1967. Prospectus for an Institute for the Future, Santa Monica, Calif., The Rand Corp.

Hubbard, E. 1967. Mankind in the universe, The Futurist 1:90.

Reinhold, R., and Nordheimer, J. 1976. Sunbelt region leads nation in growth of population. The New York Times, February 8, p. 1.

Toffler, A. 1970. Future shock, New York, Random House, Inc.

Welsh, R. 1975. Employment prospects for the physical educator. In Gedvilas L. L., editor: Proceedings of the seventy-eighth annual meeting of the National College Physical Education Association for Men, Chicago, The Association.

INDEX

Index

Index